Alison Sandy (*second-left*) is an award-winning print and broadcast journalist who specialises in crime and Freedom of Information. Her passion is ensuring government is held to account and criminals are brought to justice.

Bryan Seymour (*second-right*) is an investigative journalist with three decades of experience in newspapers, television and online reporting.

Sally Eeles (*right*) has 30 years' experience as a broadcast journalist, producer and writer at all of Australia's major networks. She now works in International Development, helping to build the skills and careers of women journalists across the Indo-Pacific.

Marc Wright (*left*) is a veteran of the media industry with over 40 years' experience spanning news and current affairs, children's and lifestyle television, music videos, documentaries, corporate videos and advertisements. He's won awards for his work as both a video editor and podcast producer.

THE LADY VANISHES

ALISON SANDY   BRYAN SEYMOUR
SALLY EELES   MARC WRIGHT

HarperCollins*Publishers*

HarperCollins*Publishers*
Australia • Brazil • Canada • France • Germany • Holland • India
Italy • Japan • Mexico • New Zealand • Poland • Spain • Sweden
Switzerland • United Kingdom • United States of America

HarperCollins acknowledges the Traditional Custodians
of the lands upon which we live and work, and pays respect
to Elders past and present.

First published on Gadigal Country in Australia in 2024
This edition published in 2025
by HarperCollins*Publishers* Australia Pty Limited
ABN 36 009 913 517
harpercollins.com.au

A catalogue record for this book is available from the National Library of Australia

ISBN 978 1 4607 6730 6 (paperback)
ISBN 978 1 4607 1703 5 (ebook)
ISBN 978 1 4607 3575 6 (audiobook)

Cover design by Jason Blandford
Author photograph by Alex Wright Media
Typeset in Bembo Std by Kirby Jones

Printed and Bound in the United States

This book is dedicated to Marion
and to all the missing and their loved ones

Contents

PREFACE

Before we embarked on the massive project of a podcast devoted to finding out what happened to a woman who had been missing for more than 20 years, I hadn't even listened to a podcast, let alone created one. I had the good fortune of working with some of the most talented people I've ever known, namely Bryan Seymour, Sally Eeles and Marc Wright. The last two had already finished one podcast and were about to start another.

Since then, I've listened to many podcasts, not only true crime. My all-time favourite is *The Best Pick* movie podcast, but recently I've been enjoying *Film Stories*, which details the drama, workload and good fortune behind how films are made. These stories always describe how laborious and expensive they are, and how creators never tread a smooth path where everything goes to plan.

Our story is no different. I'm not saying making a podcast is anywhere near as hectic or expensive as making a movie, but when it's something as unknown, unexpected and unprecedented as ours, there was a lot of ground to break. And we were just four people determined to make a difference, along with Sally Leydon, the daughter of the missing woman, Marion Barter. There was no backup, no dozens of talented content makers sharing the workload. And you know what they say: 'If you're on the cutting edge, you bleed.'

For me, *The Lady Vanishes* experience has involved tears of frustration, hand-wringing, anger, fear and sometimes even feelings of helplessness. We were starting from scratch, based on Sally's certainty that her mother would never have cut all ties with her family. It wasn't a story given to us to chase, but one we took on as a labour of love, in addition to our demanding full-time jobs, in the hope that we could use our roles in the mass media to achieve some good. Many people contact journalists with a story. Often it's not a 'news' story; they just need help, which I try to provide even if it's just by making a media enquiry that means their problem is noticed and, sometimes, acted upon.

When I first heard about Marion Barter, she wasn't officially missing and, at the time, the authorities were adamant that she had chosen to leave her family and start a new life. There was no inquest, court trial or previous media coverage to draw upon, but thanks to Sally we had something to start with – a list of family and friends to contact. We hoped that talking about Marion's disappearance on a podcast would jog some memories and generate some leads we could chase down, and that we could put pressure on authorities to do the job that should have been done in the first place. Media is in a unique position to do this.

We had to prove she was really missing, but that was just the first hurdle. From then on, there were many, many challenges, in a journey that was often very stressful and heartbreaking.

Undoubtedly, podcasts have changed the landscape of investigative journalism, but as we discovered, success has its challenges. Not just because it has many fathers as the saying goes, but because of the level of commitment required. Media is often praised when shining a light in dark corners but if a network or newspaper appears to benefit in any way, they're suddenly seen as exploitative. For the record, at the time of writing this, the Seven Network spent far more money on this investigation than it made. Their support was helped by the podcast's popularity and other media picking up on the story, but the momentum wasn't constant and at times I was required to justify the cost.

It's been a roller-coaster of emotions quite separate from what we were trying to achieve, which was justice for a woman who had been missing for more than two decades and whom the authorities continued to ignore, despite the desperate pleas of her daughter.

This book tells the story of Marion and others who fell victim to a man who preys on human vulnerability for his own gain without remorse. It's also about what it takes to chase the truth and how much it costs. And it's about the virtue of going into battle to fight for what's right even though you may not win.

There were times I thought I'd lose my job or be told we could not continue. We ploughed on regardless, knowing that what we were doing was bigger than us. That persistence and perseverance paid off in ways none of us could have imagined.

Alison Sandy
Executive producer and co-creator of
the podcast *The Lady Vanishes*

Willy

It isn't his size or his reputation. The thing that makes your blood run cold is his smile.

Ric Blum shuffles past the open doorway to the small meeting room where Alison Sandy and Bryan Seymour are working feverishly to transcribe the testimony he has just given in the Coroner's Court. As Seymour looks up, Blum cannot resist breaking into a broad grin, fixing him with an intense stare.

After nearly three full days on the witness stand, Blum has revealed himself to be a mass of contradictions. He uses a wheelie walker to move slowly to and from the courthouse, his shoulders slumped and head down, yet on the stand he's often energetic, animated and highly attentive. He gives detailed accounts when justifying his actions but then appears confused and lost for words when confronted with an incongruity he can't explain. And he lies, over and over again.

By the time he became an octogenarian, Blum must have thought he would live out his life in anonymity, remembered only by the fractured members of his family and the women whose lives he has ruined. He is tall, about six feet two inches, with a mop of white hair and a matching beard cut fairly short. He looks strong, with a hulking frame.

He was born Willy Coppenolle in Tournai, an ancient and picturesque riverside town in Belgium, in 1939. He would tell people that his family was wiped out in Nazi death camps, which is untrue. His talents as a confidence trickster emerged in early adulthood and he spent a lifetime honing his skills, hardened by periods of incarceration and tested across multiple countries and jurisdictions.

He claims he studied pre-Columbian civilisation as a young man at the 'Academy of Arts' in Belgium, and that he earned money drafting and decorating. He then enlisted in the Belgian Gendarmerie in 1958.

He suffered a debilitating injury in 1960, or thereabouts, when he was assigned to the Gendarmerie's mounted brigade. While purportedly attending a street procession for the wedding of the Belgian King, he claims he was thrown and dragged by a horse. 'I was crushed and pulverised ... I had multiple fractures, compound fractures in my leg ... I had some broken ribs,' Blum claims, adding that he was in hospital for two years. He was discharged from the Gendarmerie in 1964 and was paid compensation: 'I received money, big money, from the invalid commission.'

After that, he worked sporadically; repairing sewing machines, as a security guard and as a photographer in Belgium, then Australia. Between 1965 and 1973, he was convicted of various fraud offences, which resulted in him being jailed for several years.

By the time police in Australia catch up with him in 2021, Blum is living a seemingly simple life as an old-age disability pensioner in the small town of Ballina near Byron Bay, the latter a seaside playground for the rich and famous. He and his wife Diane De Hedervary live alone, their son and daughter having long since left the nest, and they largely keep to themselves. It's worth noting that there seems to be various spellings of how De Hedervary, and indeed most of his pseudonyms, are spelled. That is because he often spelled them differently depending on where he was. This is typical of someone who engages in illegal activity and doesn't want to be found.

There were clues to something being not quite right.

A neighbour noticed Blum trying to make his own coins with a metal press. He boasted of being an expert in rare and expensive currency. Another time, the neighbour spotted a stack of what looked like bearer bonds sitting in Blum's shed, though how he could have come into possession of them is a mystery. He told a local shopkeeper that his wife was the heiress to a supermarket empire, which might explain how he could travel overseas extensively on a pensioner's income.

Mostly, though, no one notices anything peculiar, let alone dangerous, about the man living a small life in a quiet street. The locals in Ballina have no idea that Blum has allegedly boasted about killing with his own hands.

The first time the world hears the name Ric Blum is during the coronial inquest into the disappearance of Marion Barter in February 2022. Counsel assisting the Coroner, Adam Casselden SC, a tall man with a serious face and a commanding voice, announces to the stunned courtroom that police have received a witness statement and interview from a Mr Ric Blum, a Belgian national who moved to Australia in the late 1960s and has lived in a number of states. 'He informed investigating police that in the 1960s when he was in Switzerland, he met a woman by the name of Marion Warren in a hotel lobby,' Casselden says. 'Mr Blum says that they had a fleeting relationship at that time.'

This revelation astonishes everyone except Marion's daughter, Sally Leydon, who as Marion's next of kin has been kept informed by police. It is immediately apparent that her 25-year quest for answers is about to pay off, vindicating her staunch refusal to give up on her mother.

The claim that Blum had met Marion in the 1960s seems bizarre and unlikely, even more so during Blum's official recorded interview with police, which is played for the Coroner. As Blum faces the video camera, flanked by two female detectives who are clearly sceptical of him, he details what supposedly happened:

DETECTIVE: Do you remember when that horse-riding accident was?
BLUM: Happened in 1961, I think.
DETECTIVE: And what brought you to Lucerne?
BLUM: Oh, because, um, there, um, in that, ah, part of Switzerland, there is a, um, a, what used to be a, a sanatorium, ah, but was now a, ah, um, a place where they

look after people with injuries like I had and rehabilitation and that sort of thing …

DETECTIVE: Now … I'm going to take you to when you first met Marion Barter.

BLUM: Yep.

DETECTIVE: … you recalled that her name was Marion Warren.

BLUM: I didn't, ah, I didn't know her name. Ah, she just told me that, ah, she was, ah, married to a, um, Australian, ah, footballer.

DETECTIVE: And you divorced in 1966?

BLUM: Yes.

DETECTIVE: Now, can you tell me whether this incident here with Marion was before or after your divorce?

BLUM: Oh, I'd say it was before, I'd say, yeah … I was separate from her, but I was, ah, I wasn't divorced, yeah.

DETECTIVE: In any case, it was before you married your second wife?

BLUM: Yep.

DETECTIVE: Okay, now … Marion approached you?

BLUM: Yep.

DETECTIVE: Yep. And you engaged in a fleeting relationship?

BLUM: Yep.

DETECTIVE: Umm, you said that was two nights only?

BLUM: Yep.

DETECTIVE: And I don't mean to be intrusive, but what was the nature of the relationship between you two?

BLUM: Well, she's a sex maniac and, ah, and she just, she just, well after, within ten minutes she said she, she wanted sex.[*]

Blum frequently belittles women, calling them sluts and liars, so his trashing of Marion's reputation is no surprise. He gives further details at the inquest about his supposed two-day sex fest with Marion, claiming that she was there with her husband, Australian soccer great Johnny Warren, who was attending a training camp

---

[*] NSW Police interview with Ric Blum, 14 September 2021.

in Switzerland. Routine checks confirm that no such training camp happened.

Johnny and Marion wed in 1967, so she could not have been in Lucerne with her husband in 1966. Furthermore, Blum claims he was recuperating at a mountain resort after his accident, which he says happened in 1960 or 1961. It makes no sense.

His tryst with Marion clearly never happened, so why would he invent such a salacious story? Perhaps to paint her as an insatiable and irresponsible woman with no sense of morality or respect for the feelings of others. Or perhaps to present himself as the victim of a sexual predator who used men and discarded them without another thought. Regardless, his concocted story reveals a telling aspect of his own character. He is a man who invents outlandish lies and delivers them in a disarmingly earnest fashion.

Some monsters lurk in the shadows, preying on those who share their lust for power and wealth. They live in secure apartment complexes, fortified lairs, surrounded by loyal guards, beyond the reach of justice. But the worst monsters hide in plain sight. They target the vulnerable and live everyday lives to camouflage their true nature. They are your friends, your neighbours. And sometimes they are your mother or father.

Blum seems to enjoy his 'ordeal' on the witness stand before the Coroner. He is literally holding court, frustrating the hopes of Marion's family, toying with the lawyers and placing on the record his brilliantly curated tales and torments.

When he breaks character to leer at the journalists who have hauled him into the public spotlight, he seems happy, patronising and gleeful that they cannot force him to say the words that will bring closure to this tragedy.

He thinks he's had the last laugh.

CHAPTER 1

I've Got a Story

May 1997

'Sprung!'

Sally mouths the word as she animatedly waves her arms to attract the attention of her mother, Marion, who is standing between the petrol bowser and her red Honda Civic Breeze at the service station on Ferry Road in Southport on the Gold Coast in the state of Queensland. It's dark, perhaps close to 9 pm, but the area is well lit and there are no more than 20 metres between them.

Sally and her fiancé, Chris Leydon, are up against the window of the adjoining McDonald's restaurant. The young couple have a weekly fast-food dinner date after Sally's TAFE* class on Tuesday night. Sally's mirth is triggered by the sight of a tall, shadowy figure in the passenger seat of Marion's car, clearly a man, although she can't make out his features because of the reflected light on the windscreen. Sally didn't know her mother was seeing someone again.

There have never been any secrets before. She knows of, or has met, her mother's previous partners. Besides, Marion has just sold her Southport home and is about to embark on a year-long trip to Europe. It's not exactly the best time to begin a new romance.

Sally is sure Marion has seen them, but instead of waving back, she looks startled and stares blankly through them. She quickly abandons any plan to fuel up, climbs back into the driver's seat and takes off. But in her panic she takes a wrong turn and ends

---

* TAFE (Technical and Further Education) is a government-owned vocational training institution in Australia.

up going through the McDonald's drive-thru. The 24-year-old Sally takes delight in the mistake, but even though she playfully smirks and points at Marion as she drives past, her mother gives no sign of acknowledgement. The person in the passenger seat is still obscured from view.

Marion does not even look Sally's way.

October 2018

It's almost summer and Alison Sandy is preparing for a holiday with her family. It's been a tough year. Her mother has been in a coma for several weeks, narrowly surviving septicaemia. Coupled with that, her marriage is recovering from a rocky patch. So, her young family is embarking upon a three-week holiday to Orlando, Florida. The kids are just the right age: the older two 12 and 14, still young enough to enjoy it, and the youngest, at five, is old enough to be able to remember it.

Sandy has recently been contacted by friend and fellow journalist Madonna King about a woman named Sally Leydon who is trying to find her mother, Marion Barter. She doesn't recall all the details of Madonna's message, just that it's a cold case about a missing mum who was once married to Australian soccer legend Johnny Warren. King is adamant it's a story she'd be pursuing were she in Sandy's position.

As always, Sandy has bitten off more than she can chew. This year, she has lodged at least 500 freedom of information (FOI) applications nationwide in her role as FOI editor for Seven News. But, like many full-time working mums, she lives with constant guilt – worried that when she is working she should be spending more time with her kids, and when at home worrying she isn't doing enough work. King thinks Sandy can help Sally with her FOI application, or GIPA as it's known in NSW. Sandy knows better than to promise anything to Sally before meeting her.

Both Sandy and Sally live in Brisbane, the capital city of Queensland. When they meet at a coffee shop in a plant nursery on a sweltering day, Sandy spots Sally sitting patiently with a big blue folder on the table in front of her. Sally is not much older than

Sandy, with long, straight, platinum hair pulled into ponytail. She is fresh-faced and confident, but also anxious. They spend the first half-hour discussing their children before Sally tells the story of her missing mum.

She explains how Marion, a teacher at one of Queensland's most prestigious private boys' schools, The Southport School, quit her job mid-term in 1997 to go overseas. According to Sally, this was highly unusual for a woman who loved her work and had devoted her life to being the best teacher she could be. What made it even stranger was, in November of the previous year, she had been named Queensland's 'Teacher of the Year'. Marion also made the sudden decision to sell her Gold Coast home, which she did very quickly, at a substantial loss. She told Sally and her fiancé, Chris, that after an overseas adventure she was planning to downsize to an apartment on the Gold Coast.

Sally admits that she didn't always see eye to eye with her mum, but they were close, which is why she can't understand her mother leaving without explanation. At the time she didn't suspect anything sinister. 'No, the only weird thing is she wouldn't let us drive her to the airport to see her off because she didn't want to get too emotional.'

Very little has been written publicly about Marion in the 20 years since she disappeared, only a couple of magazine articles – one in *Woman's Day* in 2003, and one in the *Women's Weekly* in 2010. Despite Sally's efforts to attract more attention, including emailing TV programs such as *60 Minutes*, she can't get anyone interested in the story.

Marion was 51 years old when she was last seen before boarding an overseas flight at Brisbane airport on 22 June 1997. She told family and friends that she was heading to the UK and Europe for the trip of a lifetime and could be gone for a year. She said she wanted to ride the *Orient Express* and might even consider getting a teaching job in England.

Unbeknown to Sally at the time, Marion secretly returned to Australia at the beginning of August under a strange new name. Her incoming travel card listed her as 'Florabella Natalia Marion

Remakel', and her handwritten answers showed her occupation as 'Home Duties' in Luxembourg.

In October 1997, when Marion failed to contact her son, Owen, for his birthday, Sally became suspicious and did a check on her mother's bank account. This led to the discovery that her account had been drained of tens of thousands of dollars over a number of weeks, primarily from a branch in Byron Bay in northern New South Wales.

As Byron is only an hour or so's drive south of the Gold Coast, Sally and Chris hit the road to conduct a street search in Byron Bay. After trying shops, banks and eateries, they reported Marion missing at the local police station. Soon after, a police officer called Sally to say that they had spoken with Marion and she had indicated that she wanted to start a new life without her family and friends.

That information has never rested easy with Sally. For more than two decades she has tried, on numerous occasions, to initiate ultimately futile attempts to locate her mum. The one positive is that every time she tries, she gleans snippets of new information.

For instance, she learns that Marion changed her name by deed poll shortly before her trip and her passport was never used or renewed after secretly returning to Australia only weeks after she left. She also learns Marion's bank accounts and superannuation fund remain untouched and that there are no updates to her medical records after 1997.

Marion did not attend Sally and Chris's wedding the following year, even though she had arranged the venue, the chapel at The Southport School, not long before departing on her trip. She has never met her three grandchildren. She didn't attend the funerals of either of her parents, even though she knew her father was unwell when she went overseas. Sadly, she would never say goodbye to her son, Owen, who took his own life in 2002 at the age of 27.

In 2007, Sally was chosen by the Australian Federal Police (AFP) to be the face of Missing Persons Week, but was unexpectedly dropped at the last minute. No one explained why, but she later discovered that it was because NSW Police had listed Marion as 'found' even though no one had seen or spoken to her. Had police failed to follow their own policy and procedures, or were they guilty of oversight, negligence or indifference?

Sally's blue folder contains all the correspondence she has ever had with NSW Police, along with the postcards and letters Marion sent to family and friends while overseas, Marion's bank account details and her medical history – anything that might offer a clue as to what happened. It's clear she doesn't hold out much hope her mum is still alive. Sally reveals the most recent document she managed to acquire under Freedom of Information legislation: a heavily redacted file from NSW Police.

Sandy knows straight away she can use her expertise to help Sally write an external review application, challenging the extent of the redactions. This is her bread and butter.

Marion was married three times. Her first husband was Australian soccer legend Johnny Warren who, many friends believe, was the love of her life. Her second spouse was Stuart Brown, the father of Sally, born 12 May 1973, and Owen, born 18 October 1974. Marion and Stuart's relationship was volatile to say the least. Marion then married Ray Barter, a younger man who didn't seem to have ever truly loved her.

Despite her success as a teacher, in early 1997 she became unhappy in her work at The Southport School. There was a cloud over her employment there, and Sally recalls her mother seeming anxious and sad before she ultimately handed in her resignation.

That's one of many things that has niggled at Sally's consciousness over the years. There are other things too. She remembers a number of times when her mother behaved in an odd way leading up to her trip overseas. The night she and Chris spotted Marion at the Gold Coast petrol station was just hours after Marion had abruptly told Chris to leave while he was helping to pack up her belongings in her recently sold home. When Sally later quizzed her mother about the identity of the person in her car, Marion brushed the question away with a vague response.

Another inexplicable aspect of Marion's behaviour is the numerous postcards and letters she sent to family and friends while she was away. Sally can't fathom why her mother would go to such lengths to keep in touch and meticulously detail her trip if she wanted to disappear. Marion had even made sure a gift arrived in time for her sister's birthday in July.

Then there was the phone call to Sally on 1 August 1997 – the last known time anyone ever heard from Marion Barter. Marion used up all her loose change on a payphone to chat to her daughter before telling her she might not be in touch for a while. A day later Marion, or someone using her passport, returned to Australia.

And yet, after all this time, and despite Sally frequently telling police that something is wrong, Marion is still not on the Missing Persons Register. The seeming injustice of it all, combined with an apparent lack of interest or care, sticks with Sandy after that initial meeting. It's why she got into journalism in the first place: to right wrongs and give people a voice when no one else will listen. How can NSW Police still think Marion Barter, a devoted mother, daughter, sister and friend, went missing of her own volition? Not only has she failed to reach out to anyone in all those years, but there's no trace of her being alive. All activity on her bank accounts and other records abruptly ceased in late 1997.

Some people do elect to go completely off the grid and start a new life without any contact with anyone from their previous lives. But it's highly unusual for someone like Marion, who was very connected to her circle of family and friends and had no known reason to completely disappear. There was no major falling-out with anyone close to her, she was highly regarded professionally and she was financially secure. She also had a collection of antiquities and fine china that had taken her decades to curate and was very dear to her.

Sandy realises there is much more to this story. Before joining the Seven Network five years earlier, Sandy had been the Police and Courts Editor at *The Courier Mail* newspaper. It was a high-pressure role with frequent bursts of insane demands depending on whatever big crime story was breaking; not really conducive to caring for a newborn, which she was trying to do at the same time. Police shootings, missing children and murders were the primary fare and could dominate months, sometimes years, of a crime journalist's life. Even cadets starting out – who do much of the grunt work, like turning up to press conferences and going out with search crews – learn quickly that not every life or death is equal.

As newspapers became increasingly digital, so too did the ability to gauge public interest in stories in real time. Since then, data has had a significant role in determining the news agenda. Sandy can see immediately that readers, especially women, will relate to Sally Leydon's story and admire her tenacity. Sally's story, which highlights the powerful, unbreakable bond between mother and daughter, will resonate. She's also what could be considered the average Aussie mum, working hard to try to give her three children the best start while dealing with life's various challenges.

Marion was in the prime of her life when she inexplicably disappeared. While she had moved house a lot and her children were now grown up, it was a shock to her family when she abruptly quit her job, sold her home and decided to travel to the other side of the world. It's even more surprising that, despite keeping in touch for weeks, she would choose to disappear forever. And more intriguing still is Marion's bizarre new name, which none of her friends knew about or can explain. Yes, Marion changed her name before disappearing.

Sandy has a gut feeling that something has happened to Marion, but also that it's going to require a lot of digging. There are a couple of other problems too. How to tell such a complicated story? How to do it justice? And how to overcome the not-so-small task of convincing her bosses at the Seven Network it's a worthwhile story to chase?

A 'yarn' needs to tick plenty of boxes before news editors give it the green light. It needs to be current, or at least relevant to the issues of the day, to attract a large audience. If it's a cold case, then it must have a new lead or a fresh angle. For TV, there has to be pictures, a variety of interesting and engaging visuals, and people who are willing to talk on camera. For news, it must also be explainable in a short space of time. The average TV news story runs for just 80–90 seconds but takes an entire day of chasing interviews, shooting vision, creating graphics, writing, voicing and editing to pull it all together. Newspapers can produce copious amounts of written copy day after day, teasing out details to engage audiences while mounting pressure on authorities to actually do something. But TV news stories rely on the immediacy of powerful imagery and punchy sound bites to command attention.

It's clear the Marion Barter case is not a great fit for TV news. This isn't a story that can be collected in a day and told in 90 seconds. It's also document-heavy and picture-poor. It will require a lot of time and effort to corroborate facts, chase up documents and investigate details. It will rack up hundreds, maybe thousands, of hours of labour and require significant resources to record, produce and edit the stories. Such resources are sparse and, understandably, prioritised for the major stories of the day.

Television's halcyon days of excess and abundance ended in the 1990s. Since then, there's been a significant rise in workloads and a commensurate decline in spending. These days, every single person in a TV newsroom juggles multiple jobs every day. There's no downtime. Therefore, a story that sucks up resources, with no real promise of a result, is not seen as a great investment.

After all, for all anyone really knows, Marion may be happily living a new life under an assumed identity. A major investigation may ultimately lead nowhere.

Still, Sandy believes it is worth a try.

Sandy first approaches the makers of *Sunday Night*, the Seven Network's flagship current-affairs show, excitedly pitching the story as a long-form exposé into Marion's disappearance and the refusal of police to believe she's missing. While they are politely interested and helpful, they make no commitment. Instead, they ask Sandy to let them know when she's found Marion.

Often, media bosses in southern states consider Brisbane to be something of a news outpost. In fact, there's a general vibe in journalism that most places outside Sydney and Melbourne are less important. That perception is slowly changing thanks to the journalists and producers who are decentralising news to capture the best stories wherever they may be. But if you work in what's regarded as an outpost, your opinions and news judgement are not always taken as seriously. Only the 'big boys' of journalism work in the epicentre of news, and if you're not one of them, then you're not enough.

Sandy is not one to accept rejection easily. The only option she can now imagine is a podcast. There's just one problem. She's never done one.

The popularity of podcasts is growing in Australia. A 2018 investigative podcast called *The Teacher's Pet*, presented by Hedley Thomas of *The Australian* newspaper, achieved staggering success with its examination of missing, presumed murdered, Sydney mother Lynette Simms. Paula Doneman, a Brisbane crime reporter with more than 30 years' experience, enjoyed some success with Seven's first ever investigative crime podcast, *Little Girl Lost*, in 2017.

When Sandy asks Doneman how to produce a podcast, Doneman refers her to Seven News executive producer Sally Eeles and senior video editor Marc Wright, the Brisbane-based duo who introduced podcast investigations to the Seven Network. Eeles is the first woman to hold the position of Queensland executive producer of news at the Seven Network. She prepares rundowns, subs scripts and ensures bulletins time to the second. Her day starts with a conference call at 7.10 am and ends 12 hours later when the bulletin goes to air. She is regarded as unflappable and fair. Sandy thinks of her as an unsung hero of the newsroom.

Eeles is always on the lookout for a new challenge. Sandy sends her a story summary of about eight sentences highlighting the main points of the Marion Barter case, and when they meet, she's relieved to see Eeles grinning broadly. Eeles agrees that this story, with its many layers, mystery and drama, is something else.

'We need to do a list of episodes with summaries for each, and tease out the story,' she says. Eeles is all about structuring the story, and offers to write the episodes. Sandy can't believe it. As a newspaper journo who has dabbled in TV news reporting, the thought of writing a podcast is incredibly daunting. The script for a single episode can be 40 pages long, the more complex ones taking days to write and just as long to edit.

Eeles then leads Sandy to the news editing suites and introduces her to Marc (Wrighty) Wright. He will take care of the sound production and the enormous task of designing and editing the audio for every episode.

Sandy will just need to do the interviews and compile the material.

Wrighty is the kind of person you need in a crisis: reliable and thoughtful, with a can-do attitude. He has spent four decades in the TV industry, in countless roles at every network, but neither Sandy nor Eeles has heard anyone say a cross word about him. He has no sign of the cynicism that can stain the perspective of many seasoned news veterans.

In 2017, when Eeles and Paula Doneman were starting work on *Little Girl Lost*, Eeles pinned a 25-page script she had written on the editors' workboard. Alongside it, she stuck a Post-it Note with a scrawled request asking – no, pleading – for an editor to consider taking on the project, or at least an episode. The incentives were not great: there would be no extra pay, a lot of extra work and no guarantee that the podcast would ever see the light of day.

But Wrighty unpinned the script and took ownership of the entire project, even when Eeles gave him plenty of opportunities to walk away.

'It's going to be a huge job,' Eeles told him. 'I've never created a podcast before and there's no one to support me. I'm making it up as I go along.'

'Well I'll be making it up too,' he replied.

Wrighty was keen to be a part of the process, but it soon became clear that it was more than the newsroom video editing software could handle, and required much more time than he could find in a routine shift. So he set himself up at home with the necessary equipment and software, and worked on it in his own time.

By no stretch of the imagination was Wrighty an audio expert. His career had been in video editing, with occasional dabbling in audio. He had never delved into the depths of sound design and audio production. But when the *Little Girl Lost* project landed in his lap, he learnt as he went. When Eeles takes Sandy into Wrighty's editing suite in late 2018 and he hears Sally's story, he doesn't hesitate to commit. In fact, within days he's come up with a selection of potential music themes.

As the FOI editor, Sandy researches and requests documents from government agencies about topics in the public interest. These documents are then sent to the relevant newsrooms, where journalists turn the information they receive into stories. If the documents are pertinent to Queensland, Sandy will sometimes write the stories herself. She has been in the role for about five years. There are a couple of others in similar positions at media organisations around the country, but their numbers are dwindling due to federal and state governments making it increasingly difficult and expensive to access information under FOI legislation. This has resulted in a federal backlog of more than 580 cases.*

The departments and the watchdogs appointed to oversee FOI requests are underfunded and under-resourced. It can take bureaucrats months to assess and process documents. FOI is a foundational element of democratic societies, but it's rarely a platform a government will get elected on.

Despite her senior role, Sandy feels she's not high-profile enough to present the podcast, so she now has to consider who might host. She sends Sydney journalist Bryan Seymour an email to brief him about the story.

The problem is that Seymour is often so busy he is hard to pin down. The Marion Barter case is just one of a dozen other stories he's immersed in. Sandy likes working with Seymour

---

* Christopher Knaus, 'Australia's FOI backlog: 587 cases remain unresolved more than three years on', *The Guardian*, 21 March 2023, <www.theguardian.com/australia-news/2023/mar/21/australia-foi-freedom-of-information-backlog-587-cases-unresolved-more-than-three-years>.

because he's dedicated, loyal in the sense of never trying to steal credit when it isn't due, and passionate about telling good stories. She also knows that this one will have a special, personal appeal. Seymour successfully tracked down his own father about 15 years earlier and he's pretty open about his past. Sandy has heard him tell several people, some within minutes of meeting him, that he was raised a ward of the state. For the first few years of his life he barely spoke; he was diagnosed as 'special' and placed in an orphanage for intellectually challenged children.

Seymour is intrigued by the facts of Marion's case. 'People who walk out on their lives don't return a few weeks later and stroll around where they can be recognised,' he says.

Seymour is not a schmoozer, yet he has risen through the ranks to become a recognisable face on the network. He also has a good relationship with their boss, Craig McPherson, the director of news and current affairs at the Seven Network. Sandy needs to convince McPherson, along with Neil (Rabbit) Warren, the news director in Brisbane, that a podcast about the search for Marion is a good idea and that the *Lady Vanishes* team can do this while also delivering quality work in their day jobs.

Warren, who is well liked and respected, is a Seven Network career veteran whose incarnations have included gun reporter, foreign correspondent and lauded producer. His current role consumes him. He pours his being into his work and can appear on edge and stressed.

He's open to the idea of another podcast after the moderate success of *Little Girl Lost*. He's also aware that Sandy, Eeles and Wrighty are passionate about the case. He's supportive, but adamant that pulling together the daily TV news bulletins has to remain their priority.

A missing person case, no matter how interesting, is not Watergate, especially when there is very little to go on. Just a bunch of people to call, documents to read and a massive story to tell in the hope of being able to shake something loose. Getting results in these stories takes time, persistence and dedication. The ever-changing media environment doesn't encourage any of that.

Investigations are also expensive, not just in terms of money, but resources. As newsrooms continue to shrink, long-form storytelling is becoming an endangered species. Worse, often it doesn't rate, even if it does drive credibility and respect. A network has to make money, and advertising on podcasts has a much smaller rate of return than ads that air on TV.

'You're not doing a podcast!' Craig McPherson says as he leans back in his office chair, looking up at Seymour with a mixture of indifference and cynicism. Many of the journos, even old hands, are wary of McPherson. He's a man of few words, often punctuated with gruff and abrupt outbursts. He's drawn from a long line of news directors who appear to hate what they do but love it too much to do anything else.

'I don't want to do a podcast!' Seymour says. He's still not sure how they're going to pull this off, but it falls to him to get McPherson over the line. Fortunately, they get on well. McPherson hired Seymour and he has repaid his faith in spades.

'How are you going to find her, the missing mum?' McPherson asks.

'Don't worry about it, it's what I do. We've got a plan and this podcast will give us the best shot. We will find her, I can guarantee it.' Seymour knows that the chances of finding out what happened to Marion, let alone where she is, are extremely remote, which is why there are so many unsolved long-term missing cases. However, he is fully committed to doing whatever it takes.

'You're not getting time off work. How are you going to do that and file for the news?'

'I can walk and chew gum at the same time, we all can. It's not a problem. Look, we'll just go ahead and start, and I'll let you know if there's any problems.'

News directors hate problems and questions. They like solutions. McPherson shrugs. 'Okay.'

It's far from a ringing endorsement. The Brisbane newsroom initially tips in the bulk of resources. The team there believe in their colleagues. Well, most of them. One senior news producer tells Eeles that the podcast is a waste of time. His words are targeted and cutting, enough to make her box up her enthusiasm and store it away from public view. She discreetly shoots an email to Sandy and Wrighty, warning them to avoid the production desk if they want to discuss the podcast.

Months later, when *The Lady Vanishes* bursts onto the podcast scene, that same producer will apologise. He even offers to read excerpts in some episodes.

CHAPTER 2
Sally's Story

November 1996

'What heroes teachers are! And mainly unsung ones at that. I knew teaching was a difficult job, but I had no idea of the enormous stresses and pressures ...'

Media icon Ita Buttrose is giving the keynote speech at the National Excellence in Teaching Awards. She is also the MC, honouring Australia's top educators at the profession's annual night of nights. 'Teachers deserve our nation's heartfelt thanks.'

One of the awards Buttrose presents is to a passionate veteran who's devoted more than 30 years of her life to educating children. Marion Barter, who teaches the youngest students at The Southport School on the Gold Coast, is named Queensland's Teacher of Excellence.

It's the pinnacle of achievement in a career she adores.

Early 1997

It's the start of a new school year, but when Sally drops over to her mother's Southport home she finds Marion in tears. Morale is running low at the school and Marion has been devastated to learn that some of her colleagues have been attacking her behind her back. Unfounded, vicious rumours are circulating.

Sally spends the night with her mum, chatting and watching TV. She has never seen her so deflated about the job she loves. When Marion falls asleep on the couch, she appears ashen-faced, exhausted ... defeated.

November 2018

'Let me ask you first, because you married him after your mum disappeared, what has your husband made of this baffling mystery that's dominated your life?'* Seymour smiles and waits for Sally Leydon to respond.

Sally nods and takes a deep breath. 'Well, I guess I don't know. It's hard for him because he tries to be my even keel and keep me balanced in my busy family with three kids, and he works long hours, and I think he just tries to balance me, because if he gets too involved or we talk about it too much I get stressed, so he's my person, I guess, to look after me. He knew my mum and we'd been together for I think three years probably before Mum went missing, and Mum was quite fond of him and they got on really, really well. It's as baffling for him as it is for the rest of us what happened to her.'

Seymour sometimes begins interviews by having the subject talk about something else, to help take the focus off them as they become used to the very unnatural process. Already Sally is becoming more comfortable in front of the cameras and lights. It's a weekday and Chris is at work while their three children – daughters Ella, 16, and D'Arcy, 13; and son, Caleb, ten – are upstairs in their rooms.

Just a few weeks after Sandy recruited him, Seymour found himself on a plane from Sydney to Brisbane to interview Sally. It's for the podcast, but the interview is being filmed by a camera crew from *Sunday Night*. There's no plan for them to do anything with the story. It's just in case it turns out to be something worthwhile.

No one in the Sydney newsroom believes it will be. When Seymour tells colleagues he's flying to Brisbane for a podcast, he's met with smirks and scepticism. Television journalists think of filing for the network news as the pinnacle of career success; podcasts are considered fringe endeavours.

The Leydon family lives in a modern, two-storey home in a middle-class suburb of Brisbane. The satellite communications company they founded right before the internet boom has

---

* Interview with Sally Leydon by Bryan Seymour, November 2018.

flourished as technology advanced, thanks to their work ethic and drive to provide long-term security for their family.

Seymour tells Sally he will do everything he can to either find her mother or at least allow her to say that she's tried absolutely everything and nothing more can be done. Now he sits facing her, with cameras pointing at them both. The sound assistant holds up a clapper board, closes the gate, then moves out of shot and nods.

'What happened to your mother, Sally?'

'Briefly after the incident where I saw her and she was in tears, she told me that she was going to go on holiday for a year. She had always wanted to go on the *Orient Express* ... She was single, she had no ties here, I told her to do whatever she needed to do. She said she was going to sell the house because it was three bedrooms, had a swimming pool no one was going to swim in. She was going to buy a unit at Main Beach when she got back, so she gave us some of her furniture, and she had a lot of antiques. She said you were going to get it one day so it may as well be now. She put the rest of her things in storage.

'She's very interested in the Steiner School program and she had a passion for being a bit eccentric in her teaching style. If she read a book about the beach, she would take the boys out of class and take them to the beach and play in the sand. If she stayed over there I was going to send her stuff to her. We were happy for her to do that ...'

'You never assumed you would never see her again. Did you have any indication she was leaving forever?'

'Never, no.'

Seymour then reads from Marion's letter sent to The Southport School, in which she advises she will be travelling overseas for an indefinite period.

'That word "indefinite" flags the idea that she's never coming back or wants to be seen again,' he says.

'I think if you read further in the letter it says, "I'm renewing my registration, so when or if I come back my registration will still be valid,"' Sally says.

'All through this, 21 years it's been now, you've been told by authorities and others that some people disappear for no reason and sometimes just don't want to be found, and that your mother is one of these people. Why do you think they're wrong?' asks Seymour.

'There are too many unanswered questions. I don't think the police have dug deep enough … and in the very beginning it seemed easy for them to put her in a box and say this is where you fit so that's what we think. I've had a detective tell me their reasoning is based on assumptions, there's no proof to it, and that upsets me too, because if I knew my mum was sitting on a beach in Venice having a great time, I'd be okay with that. They've told me flat out that they've never found her, never sighted her, yet there's always some contradiction.'

'Is it possible that she's sitting on that beach in Venice but just doesn't want you to know it?' queries Seymour.

'Anything is possible.'

'Is it possible she would leave you in the dark like that?'

'I don't believe so. It's a very hard thing. It's been a 21-year journey for me and it feels like a bit of a life sentence. I have people asking me every day, "What do you think happened? Do you think she doesn't want to be found?" I've tried to keep a very open mind about what could be the case, because sure, she could be living somewhere else and not wanting to be found, but do I think that's what she intended? No. My gut feeling – it's that something has happened to her. For her to leave halfway through a school year and sell her house in three weeks and get on a plane not wanting anyone else to come to the airport to see her off and then to contact us numerous times while she's over there, that says to me, "If I was going to go missing, I would never get on a plane ever again, I wouldn't be bothered to write postcards, I'd be gone."

'The fact she took time to write letters and cards and send her sister birthday presents from over there, that to me is someone who doesn't want to go missing. She also said in her postcards she was terribly concerned about some stuff she had in storage that she needed me to take back to TSS [The Southport School] because she held it at home …'

'She was concerned that the items were returned to the school,' Seymour paraphrases. 'She was managing her affairs. So she hadn't disappeared, she was just away. So you're thinking, "Mum's in regular touch," you wouldn't be seeing her for a while, but this is how we'll be communicating. But then something just stopped?'

'Yes.'

'When did it stop?'

'She rang me. Chris and I had been skiing at Perisher [in the Snowy Mountains of New South Wales] the day before the [Thredbo] disaster happened.* When we got home … back in the days when we had answering machines … the light was flashing and I pressed it and it was Mum. It was the first time she had rung me since she'd been away. It was the 31st of July and she said, "We just had word over here about the Thredbo disaster … I was worried about you and Chris, just making sure you're okay."

'I felt really sad because I wanted to talk to her. I had just bought my wedding dress on the way home, the day before.

'She called back later from a payphone. She told me she was sitting at Tunbridge Wells in the UK and was having a fabulous time. She's having scones and tea with some old ladies that she had just met. We had a big chat and she asked me if I got the things back to The Southport School, which I had. We talked for a bit about what she's doing and she said she postponed her trip on the *Orient Express* because she was having such a lovely time, but the phone kept dropping out then she would ring me back. Back in the day there was that delay when you were speaking to someone internationally, so she was definitely over there. She kept ringing back like five times until her money ran out,' Sally reflects.

'That was the last time you ever heard your mum's voice. Do you ever still hear her voice in that phone call you had?'

'Her voice resonates with me a lot, and I can hear her talking and laughing. She was a big part of my life because my mum and

---

* The disaster near Perisher was a landslide that hit the popular Thredbo ski lodges in New South Wales, killing 18 people on 30 July 1997.

dad separated when I was little, so it was only my brother, mother and me who did everything together.'

'How close were you with your mother?'

'I would say we had a pretty normal relationship. I think if you asked me to compare my relationship with my children, then I'm closer to my children than I was with my mum. I also reflected on that as a child and I wanted my life to be different. I wanted to be a different parent. I wanted to go and watch them at their football games and watch them at gymnastics and be there for them every step of the way, so I would probably go to the opposite end of the tunnel, where I'm probably too motherly.'

Seymour smiles. Sally is clearly a wonderful mother. Her three children are happy, well-adjusted young people – well-cared for by doting parents.

'She [Marion] was all about school and the people at school, not always about Owen and me as such. She just had a different way of parenting,' Sally says.

Seymour asks Sally if she resented having to share her mum.

'I don't think so. I don't think I ever sat back and thought, "Oh my God she gives so much attention to everyone else." There was one time in Year One they put me into her class at school at Springwood in the Blue Mountains. I remember this girl Joanna. I'm friends with her on Facebook now. She used to sit on my mum's lap all the time in class and it really upset me that she always sat on Mum's lap because I couldn't sit on Mum's lap very often because she was too busy with everyone else's kids.

'They made me call her Mrs Brown and for a five-year-old that was pretty tough. So they moved me to a different class eventually because they didn't think I was coping very well. But in saying that, she was a good mum. She fed us well and gave us everything we needed and wanted, and celebrated our birthdays with great love and affection. She was just a busy single mum.'

By 1997, Marion's children Sally and Owen were young adults, living their own lives. But her dream teaching job had started becoming a nightmare.

'She had just won the teacher award for Queensland in 1996. It seemed there was a little bit of talk going around with the new teachers that were coming in that were trying to knock her down, which was what my take on it was from what she told me. She would be in tears telling me these people were saying horrible things about her. She was not in a very happy place.'

'What were they saying about her?' Seymour asks.

'Someone accused her of touching boys and it broke her heart. She'd been a teacher for a very long time, before I was even born. Teaching was her passion and her life. It made me very sad to hear that.

'I remember one particular night I stayed with her because she was very sad. We watched TV together. She fell asleep on the couch and she literally had her palms facing upwards next to her and this exhausted look on her face. It was very droopy, like she had just had the wind taken out of her sails.'

As it turns out, not a single person Sandy or Seymour speak with from the school makes any allegation of that kind of inappropriate behaviour by Marion. While the scuttlebutt might explain, in part, why Marion would want a fresh start, it's a big stretch to conclude that this compelled her to break off all contact with her family indefinitely.

'How would you describe the dedication of the authorities, including the police, in terms of finding out how your mother vanished?' asks Seymour.

'I'm very bewildered and sad because she's a person. She's a human being, she's a mother, she's a grandmother. She's missed out on so many things in life that are really important. It's hard when people don't take it seriously. I don't want to speak badly about anybody, but every time I've reached out and asked for people to help me, they've just slammed the door in my face quite firmly.

'I had so much contradictory information from the police. So the police rang me a week after I listed her missing in 1997 and said, "She doesn't want anyone to know where she is or what she's doing." And I was then told by the Australian Federal Police that they never physically saw her, they only spoke to someone on the phone. I told my grandfather and he said, "That's not good enough!" So he went to the Salvation Army Family Tracing Service. They then started doing a search, but I have documentation from them saying, "We've never found your mother."'

Seymour asks why authorities hadn't put in more effort to find Marion.

'I don't know. We had a conversation on our 20th wedding anniversary when we were in Byron Bay, and I got a missed call from [Detective Senior Constable] Gary Sheehan* [from Byron Bay Police] so I called him back and he was on speakerphone so my husband said, "Gary, if I have all the information you have, would I be able to find her?" and he said "If I spent every day of my working life trying to find her, I would highly unlikely find her."'

'I know that in the conversation you legally recorded with Gary, he constantly apologises. Why is he apologising?' Seymour asks.

'He calls me Sal. I always have a connection with anyone who calls me Sal. He's always called me Sal and he always seems to be sorry. He's said sorry in the past because he just doesn't know how I'm feeling because he's never experienced anything like this. But his hands are tied. They closed the case, he can't do anything.

'I've even gone back to him with a list of things to check, I've said, "Why can't you check the list of passengers on outbound flights and then check the list of people on inbound flights with the passport on it? If you've got a person on the same flight, there's your person of interest." I feel like I'm a bit of a detective with this whole case scenario.'

'Did they do that?' Seymour asks.

'No. I've asked them why they haven't done anything with my DNA. They've asked me to come down, which I did back in 2011 and I said, "Why haven't you sent it to Luxembourg or the UK to run against anything they may have over there?"'

---

* Detective Senior Constable Gary Sheehan worked at Byron Bay police station and took over the Marion Barter investigation in 2007, ten years after she disappeared.

'Have they done that?'

'No. They haven't even gone overseas. They haven't even checked overseas.'

'When did you first realise that they weren't actively searching for her?' Seymour asks.

'Well, I had a lady private message me on Facebook and she said, "I just had a look at the missing persons list and your mum's not on there" ... I went on there, and sure enough, she wasn't there.'

'When was that?'

'That was 2007. I remember that because I was pregnant. It prompted me to ring the Australian Federal Police for Mum's 10th anniversary since she went missing. We still hadn't found her, and everyone had kind of given up and thought we weren't going to find her. I contacted the AFP and created a friendship with Rebecca Kotz. Not a police officer, Kotz was the team leader of the AFP Missing Person's Coordination Centre. So I contacted Rebecca [in 2011] and I said, "Can you check for me?" So she went in and had a look at her file and she came back to me and said, "There's something on the file. I can't tell you what it is because I don't have the authorisation to show it to you but give me a couple of days."

'She came back to me a few days later, and had been authorised, so I got the documentation. It said that my mother had been located in May of 2011, and that they told me in December of 2011 that she had been located, which is all false!'

The one thing police did discover was that Marion had legally changed her name in the months before she vanished. Sally and Chris were left dumbfounded when Detective Sergeant Gary Sheehan paid them a visit in May 2011.

'He came to our house and he brought with him a piece of paper with some information on it which he kind of suggested we have a look at while he went to the bathroom. On that piece of paper it had my mum's passport details and a bank charge on there to some random name – Florabella Natalia Marion Remakel.'

'So who is this Florabella?'

'No idea. I've never heard the name Florabella in my life, I have no idea what that's about.'

'Sally, can you please look at the camera, look right into the lens, and imagine that Marion is watching this story on TV. What would you say to her?' Seymour instructs.

'It's a really hard thing to do,' Sally says nervously, before looking directly into the lens. 'Mum, you need to come home. We want you to come home. Everyone's so sad and you're dearly, dearly missed. There's a lot of confusion as to what has happened to you and we just want to make sure you're okay. We just want to know you're all right.'

Any lingering doubts Seymour may have had about the merits of pursuing this investigation are dispelled as he listens to Sally lay out the story of her mother's disappearance. To him, the answer seems obvious. Marion was taken.

'What's your gut feeling about what's happened to Marion?' he asks Sally.

Sally goes over the behaviours that were out of character for Marion, then adds, 'Something had happened. Something has happened to make her leave.'

As he travels back to Sydney, Seymour is struck by an idea. When he gets home, he goes online and finds an Alfred Hitchcock movie from the 1930s that he saw years ago. It's about a lady who boards a train in Europe and interacts with several passengers before she disappears. Only one of the passengers, a young woman, seems concerned. She searches for the missing woman and asks her fellow travellers about her, but they seem to think she never existed or got on the train.

This is a story about what happens to the people left behind when someone is missing – the nagging doubt, the intense need to know what happened and the emotional roller-coaster that can cause them to question their own sanity.

The title of this movie will be the title of the podcast: *The Lady Vanishes*.

CHAPTER 3

The Hero's Wife

December 1967

The bride smiles shyly as a photographer snaps black-and-white images of the newly married couple in Sydney. Marion Wilson is now Marion Warren, wife of Johnny Warren, a talented soccer player who will eventually captain Australia's national team, the Socceroos.

She wears an elegant white sheath gown with three-quarter sleeves. Her groom, in a black suit and continental bow tie, grins broadly. They make a handsome couple. But the marriage doesn't last. The gruelling schedule Johnny must keep to pursue his dream of one day leading Australia to a World Cup takes its toll on the young lovers.

Two years later, between overseas tours, Johnny announces it's over, breaking Marion's heart.

Late 2018

Getting to know Marion is only possible through the lens of others. The memories of family, friends and colleagues provide an outline of who she was, each person interviewed providing more brushstrokes and colour to a portrait that may never be complete. In photographs, Marion smiles like she's keeping a secret. Her shoulder-length dark curly hair and classic features bear the hallmark of a Jane Austen heroine, and she was, by all accounts, a hopeless romantic.

Marion was born in Marrickville, in Sydney's Inner West, on 3 October 1945, to Colleen and John (Jack) Wilson. She was the eldest of four girls, to be followed by Deirdre, Bronwen and then Lee. The family moved to Queensland when Marion was about five, living in the bayside suburb of Wellington Point near Brisbane in the early 1950s. The Wilsons returned to Sydney eight years later, to the southern suburb of Oyster Bay, where Marion started secondary school at Port Hacking State High School.

Exploring these early years, Sandy speaks to one of Marion's school friends, Kerry Heubel, who says Marion was very smart, popular and pretty. They used to hang out together in the late 1950s and go on double dates at the movies.

'She was never naive as a young person,' Kerry says. 'She was reserved, she was friendly. The boys certainly loved Marion. She was a very attractive girl. I wouldn't have called her intellectual, but I would have called her very smart, very intelligent. I think she told me she got married [to Johnny Warren] and really we then slipped out of the picture. We just didn't see each other any more. I realised once I discovered that Marion was missing that she had moved at some point to Queensland and I didn't know.'

High on Sally's list of key people the TLV team should interview for the podcast are Marion's sisters, but Sandy quickly discovers they don't support the investigation, as they believe Marion chose to start a new life without her family and friends. All three were bridesmaids at Marion's first wedding, so they must have been close at some stage, and may be able to provide crucial information about Marion's early years. They also share another bond: all three sisters, and their mother, were teachers.

Sally tells her aunts about plans for the podcast, and Deirdre, who's still based in Sydney, reluctantly agrees to talk to Sandy as a family representative. Marion's parents are no longer alive, and the two younger sisters don't want any involvement.

'Can we just start off talking about your memories of Marion?' Sandy begins.

'She was two years older than me,' Deirdre says, her manner formal and aloof.

'I gather you were close?'

'Well, reasonably. We lived relatively far apart as we became adults, after she left home.'

'It's been 22 years now … Was it a surprise, Marion going missing?'

'Yes, of course. I knew she was going away in '97. She was looking forward to going overseas. She had a ticket to go onto the *Orient Express* and she was very excited about that. But yes, I didn't know we wouldn't speak forever. I thought she would come home, so I guess it was a surprise.'

'When was the last time you spoke to her?'

'I'm guessing that it would be Christmas of '96. We would have all spent Christmas with Mum and Dad on the Sunshine Coast. So we would have done that as per normal.'

Their father was ill at the time, so it was a stressful affair, but Deirdre recalls Marion being more stressed than usual, particularly on Christmas Day. After retirement, Marion's parents had settled at Moffat Beach on the Sunshine Coast, in 1972, and they remained there until their deaths.

After Sandy's interview, Deirdre was contacted by NSW Police and made a statement on 2 September 2020, where she recalled more of this final Christmas with Marion, particularly an incident when Marion broke down.

'There were a lot of people and not much room [so] Marion was seated with my aunt on a fold-up camping table,' Deirdre says in the statement. 'Somehow it collapsed and Marion ended up on the floor. Some of Mum's good fine china was broken in the process and Mum said something like, "Oh Marion, how could you be so careless?" Marion became hysterical and ran upstairs crying. Apparently Marion ran into the kitchen, where Lee's husband, Raymond, was standing and said, "I can't do this any more, they always treat me like a child." That was the last memory I have of Marion.

'I had seen Marion react like this once before. We had gone down to have New Year's with Marion. My husband at the time, John, who was a large man, sat on one of Marion's antique chairs and it broke. Marion was hysterical and threw herself into the pool. John tried to have the chair repaired and make amends, but Marion wouldn't forgive. I remember another time, when she was living in Lapstone [in the NSW Blue Mountains], when Owen, who was very young, damaged one of her precious plants and Marion became overly upset. Hysterical behaviour was not unusual for Marion.'

Deirdre tells Sandy that Marion went to see her parents again before she left for her trip on 22 June 1997, but by this time Deirdre had already embarked on her own overseas holiday. Upon her arrival home, Deirdre found a birthday present and card from Marion. They'd been posted from overseas. Although she didn't keep the card, Deirdre says she remembers its contents. 'She just wished me a happy birthday and said how excited she was because she was about to get onto the *Orient Express*, so that's really all I know,' Deirdre says.

Sandy comes to learn that Marion could always be relied upon to remember a birthday or mark a special occasion, and was very generous with her family and friends.

'Oh, so she did get onto the *Orient Express*?' Sandy asks.

'Well I don't know,' Deirdre clarifies. 'That was what she told me she was going to do.'

Later, Sandy verifies with the company which runs the Venice Simplon-Orient-Express, as it's known, that there's no record of Marion ever being a passenger on the famous train.

Deirdre says that when Marion was finally considered missing, the family came together to discuss it. This would probably have been towards the end of 1997, after Sally discovered her mum's bank account was being drained. Little did they know that travel records show Marion's passport returned to Australia on 2 August 1997. Yet a postcard from Marion to her sister Lee has the postmark 7 August 1997

'She seemed to have decided to have written all these notes and cards and things and got someone else to post them for her, because the police told Sally that she was actually back in Australia when these things were delivered. So yes, it was quite confusing then when we started to wonder, was she all right?'

'What about your sisters, did they have any more contact with Marion?'

'Not that I know of, no,' Deirdre replies.

Sandy asks if she knows of any other postcards from Marion during this time.

'My postcard came from Tunbridge Wells. My elderly relative's postcard came from Sussex. The card she sent to my elderly relative said she was very excited and had been very brave. "I hired a car and have been touring the streets", "I've been having a lovely time and I'm going to Amsterdam to get the *Orient Express*."'

'When did you hear Marion was missing?' Sandy asks.

'Not for a while after that. I talked to my dad and he said that he was worried about Marion and he was asking for help from the Salvation Army to track her down. I think Sally was about to get married, so she was anxious about Mum being there,' Deirdre explains.

Deirdre defends her apparent indifference to Marion's disappearance. 'I didn't have any contact with Marion and I didn't speak to her for a long time,' she explains. 'I was surprised to hear she had left her job – that stunned me a bit. And also that she had sold the house – that surprised me as well.'

'You mention your father went to the Salvos. Did they get back to him?' asks Sandy.

'Yes, they did. They wrote a letter which I found and read recently, but I decided not to keep it. I went through all of his stuff and decided for some stupid reason to not keep it, but yes, they said they found Marion. They were sure it was Marion because she had actually answered some questions that only Marion would know. They told my father that Marion was angry at Sally because she had an agreement with Sally to sell the car for $15,000 and put the money in her bank account. Marion was angry at Sally because she was expecting that money to go in and it hadn't gone in. My father decided that Marion was the only person who knew about that, it wasn't something a stranger would know,' Deirdre says, indicating that was good enough for her too.

Deirdre's son Simon later finds this letter and sends it to Sally. It's clear Deirdre thinks it's of little consequence anyway, as her father and the rest of the family were 'reasonably satisfied' Marion decided to start a new life without ties to anyone from her old one. 'Hurtful? Yes, very. It was devastating for my mum and dad, but it was what she wanted to do, so what can you do? You have to accept it,' Deirdre replies.

'Is that what you still believe?' asks Sandy.

'It is what I believe. I don't think everyone accepts it. I don't think Sally accepts it and I understand why, but I think the Salvation Army rang my mother and told her, pretty much, the same thing, so I think she accepted it too. Marion just wanted to leave. She wanted to start fresh where no one knew her and where she had a clean slate. I mean it's a weird thing to do, it's a painful thing to do to the family. Marion had been married three times and I think she was embarrassed about that.'

Sandy puts it to Deirdre that it's reasonable a daughter might want to understand how her mother could do this.

'We'd all like to know what happened to her. We'd all like to know that she's okay. It's always a question mark. The police contacted [Sally] and the Salvation Army contacted [Marion's father] and said she drained the bank account and they were sure it was Marion who took the money out,' Deirdre explains patiently.

'I think Sally told me the police told her that Marion wasn't a missing person because she had chosen to go missing; it's her right to do so. They didn't regard her as being a missing person. I'm happy to accept that. I think she's probably met someone and settled down and she's got a new partner, starting life fresh, probably has a new job somewhere. I'm sure she's probably perfectly happy.'

Sandy explains that this belief comes from details that are now considered very dubious and there's a strong possibility no one ever actually spoke to Marion. 'They have reopened the case as of last week,' she says. 'It's a matter of having to track her down again, if they ever tracked her down in the first place and ask the question once again. What do you think will come out of the case this time?'

'Well, I don't know,' Deirdre replies. 'I don't really think anything will come out of it, but maybe it might satisfy Sally a little bit. I hope she finds the answer she's looking for.'

'You seem a little bit disappointed in Sally still pursuing this,' Sandy remarks.

'Yes, probably. It just dredges it all up again. You get on with your life and I just think about it periodically and I think she's in some nice place doing all sorts of interesting things. So yes, it's quite painful to go through it all again. I'm glad my mother isn't around to go through it all again, because it was very upsetting for her.'

'Do you think Marion was wrong? Do you think it was selfish of her to disappear if this is what she's done?' Sandy asks.

'Yes, I think it was a mean thing to do really, because it was so hurtful to so many people. You could always go and live your life somewhere else and change your name and job and not have much to do with your family by just not contacting them, you don't have to openly state, "I don't want to have any contact with anyone in my family again." That's another issue, but yes, I think it was a very selfish thing to do and a mean thing to do.'

'Was she ever mean like that before?' asks Sandy.

'No, it's out of character. I don't know what the answer is. You need to find her and talk to her.'

Sandy decides it's time to change tack and focus on Deirdre's happier memories of her sister growing up.

'I don't really know what to tell you there. She was my big sister and she did more interesting things than me because she was older,' Deirdre begins.

The pair shared a room growing up.

'She had beautiful clothes which I was very envious of. When I was going out somewhere, she would say, "You can borrow this or that." She used to buy really nice clothes. She liked designer-label clothes like celebrated designer Norma Tullo and all of those designers from the 1960s. She had a dressmaker who used to make her things, so she used to design her own clothes and get the dressmaker to make them.

'She was very attractive, Marion. She had a gorgeous figure and she always looked good. She was always immaculately dressed, and she had excellent taste in clothes and décor. She loved old things and used to collect china. She knew a lot about that, what furniture was worth collecting.

'She was very elegant and attractive. She had a very outgoing personality; everyone loved Marion. She used to talk to people and pour her heart out, which may have been a little unwise on her part, so everyone knew what she was thinking and feeling. She wore her heart on her sleeve.'

'That seems to have changed later in life, because no one really knows why she would disappear,' says Sandy before turning to Marion's three known marriages.

Deirdre agrees Marion loved being in a relationship. 'She liked having someone in her life. In fact, she told me once that she couldn't live without having a man in her life. That was important to her.' Deirdre says that Marion had 'a lot of relationships' outside her marriages too. 'It wouldn't surprise me at all if she fell in love with a man overseas and was travelling with him.'

'Would it surprise you if the reason she gave it all up was because of a man?' Sandy asks.

'No, it wouldn't surprise me at all,' Deirdre replies firmly.

Sandy prods again about whether Sally is justified in wanting to know what happened to her mother and where she is now.

'I think she should just leave Marion be and accept that she's gone and that she's got a new life somewhere and just let it go,' Deirdre explains. 'But if she feels the need to track down Marion, just in case something awful has happened to her, then that's what she's got to do.' She pauses briefly. 'I'm not about to judge Sally for what she's doing but it's not something I would do.'

Sandy wants to know if Marion perhaps experienced some sort of childhood trauma. 'Is there anything about Marion that we might not know, like her relationship with her parents. Was it a good relationship?' Sandy asks.

Deirdre replies without hesitation. 'Like all parents' and children's relationships, there were times when it was a bit strained. Generally speaking she adored her parents and they adored her.'

'Did she have any rebellious years as a teenager?'

'No, I don't think so.'

'So a good daughter?'

'We were all good daughters. We were frightened of our father, so if we were told to do something, we did it.'

'So it was a nice, happy household?'

'Yes,' Deirdre says, a little forced.

'I know you weren't as close with Marion as you got older, but were you close with your other sisters?'

'Probably closest to my youngest sister,' Deirdre says, referring to Lee.

'Do they feel the same way as you about Marion?'

'Lee gets distressed. She was very close to Marion. I think she's upset that Sally's dredging it up again. Sally has sent us a couple of texts, implying the three of us, Lee and Bron and I, are trying to hide information from her or not giving information that we had and how she was trying to find out what's happened to her mother and we weren't being very helpful, that we were trying to disrupt it or something, which was untrue.

'I know Lee was very upset about it. I think Bron just ignored it. Sally told me she found out [Marion] changed her name and she even told me what her name was and that [Marion] had a new passport in that name and that she was living in Liechtenstein in Europe,' Deirdre continues. 'When I asked her about that she said there was no real evidence of that, so I think Sally's all over the place.'

'Well that's the whole point, finding out what's true. And it was Luxembourg,' Sandy corrects. 'Speaking of names, does Florabella Natalia Marion Remakel sound like one Marion would adopt?'

'No. That's weird,' replies Deirdre firmly.

Deirdre entertains the possibility Marion may have joined a cult.

'Would that be in character for her?' Sandy presses.

'No, but people get vulnerable at certain stages of their life, don't they? Some of those people can be pretty persuasive, so it's a possibility.'

* * *

Marion loved to be loved. That's abundantly clear.

Her greatest love, according to friends, was her first husband, Johnny Warren. After playing for the Socceroos in the 1960s, by the late 1970s he'd turned to coaching and commentating. He had a huge positive impact on the game's popularity and profile in Australia. Johnny died in 2004 after a battle with lung cancer, but his legend lives on. To this day, the best player each year in the Australian domestic competition is presented with the Johnny Warren medal.

Marion and Johnny married in 1967 in Dulwich Hill, an inner-west suburb of Sydney, with the reception held in more southerly Bexley. The wedding photos show a stylish, good-looking couple. Marion appears shy and demure and is stunning in an elegant white gown. Johnny, with his shock of dark hair, is ruggedly handsome in a black suit. Marion is just 22 years old and Johnny is 24. The couple have a beautiful home in Mortdale, about 20 kilometres south of Sydney's city centre. They look like a perfect pair.

In her statement to NSW Police, Deirdre recalls particularly Marion's marriage breakup with Johnny Warren in 1969. Marion came to visit Deirdre and her then husband, also John, in Lismore, in northern New South Wales. 'She seemed distressed and extremely vulnerable,' Deirdre says in the statement. 'I believe John [Warren] walking out on her was a complete surprise. It was crushing for Marion. I remember my husband saying to me, "She's going to fall in with the next guy she meets."'

That guy was Stuart Brown – 'unfortunately', says Deirdre in the statement. Deirdre also says Marion partially blamed her father for her divorce with Johnny Warren. 'I think Marion thought that if it hadn't been for Dad, she and John might have gotten back together again. When John left Marion, she went home to Mum and Dad's, and Dad immediately went about getting a lawyer friend to organise the divorce papers. Dad essentially forbade Marion from having any more to do with John. There was a history where Marion would involve Dad to help her, particularly with men, and she then went against his advice. I think Dad eventually had enough of trying to help.

'I really miss Marion and I'm sorry that she seems to have got herself into a mess, primarily because of all the men in her life. I do think that there would have been a man involved in Marion's disappearance but I'm not able to assist at all in who that might be.'

Sandy reaches out to Jamie Warren, Johnny's nephew, who runs the Jamberoo Pub a couple of hours' drive south of Sydney. The hotel features a museum dedicated to his late uncle, and Jamie is only too happy to put Sandy in touch with his father, Ross, Johnny's older brother.

Ross is the middle of three brothers and is getting on in years. He's a quiet, gentle man, slightly built and with a bright smile.

'What was your memory of Marion?' Sandy asks him.

'She was just a nice Australian woman with the teaching ahead of her.'*

'When did you meet her?'

'It would have been pretty early, because Mum always wanted to know who you were going out with, my mother did ... John was always out on the go, he was all out socially, you know.'

'I imagine she wasn't Johnny's first girlfriend, but she was his first wife,' Sandy suggests.

'Yeah. John was really flat out playing football. He used to go out with other members of the team and his mate John Economos. Those two went to the same school, Cleveland Street High School.'

Ross says Johnny and Marion were together for at least a couple of years before they married.

'Do you remember the wedding? Obviously you would have gone. I don't know if you were a groomsman.'

'No, I think Geoff, the other brother was,' Ross recalls. 'It was just a nice wedding and a good percentage of people there would have been footballers and their wives. I see here, 4 December was their wedding day,' he says, referring to a newspaper clipping on display in the hotel.

Ross has his own theory on why they broke up. 'He had this bad injury and never thought he'd play again. There was a

---

* Interview with Ross Warren by Alison Sandy, 5 March 2019.

FIFA coaching school for Asian coaches and John was invited to attend that course, and he was away from Marion for around three months. [He] topped the course, of course. Marion had wanted to be with him and John did say, "Look, we're going to have to rent the house and we can't afford the two of us to go." And Marion said, "Well I'm not having strangers coming into the house."'

Ross says she objected because of the 'fancy' furniture she had. 'Everything was the best. It hadn't come from the local tip or something like that, and John said, "Well if you're not prepared to rent the house out for the period of three months, then you can't come with me." When John did come back, Marion had found another friend,' Ross explains delicately, 'and the marriage wound up.'

Sandy will later learn Ross is referring to Sally's father and Marion's second husband, Stuart Brown, but her own research suggests that Marion and Stuart didn't become a couple until 1972.

'Yeah, it was a hell of a shock for the family and I dare say a hell of a shock from John's point of view … and gradually that developed into a bit of a nasty time for both of them, for Marion and for John.'

'What do you mean by that?'

'Just disagreeing with things, being nasty … That's all I really know … just that the marriage blew up.'

Johnny didn't marry again for a long time, and then only briefly. According to Ross, he was consumed by soccer but he was never lonely. One of his many relationships was with a dancer, which led to the birth of his only daughter, Shannon. Ross recalls Johnny was always the last one out of the 'dressing sheds' when he played. The family would always be 'waiting, waiting, waiting'. 'He was too busy talking to everyone,' Ross says.

It seems obvious to Sandy that Marion was often lonely when she was with Johnny. 'So the real love of his life, by the sound of it, was football,' she suggests.

'Yeah, that's true.'

Janis White, who worked with Marion in her twenties and became her friend, remembers her fondly: 'She was a very easy person to talk with, and she was always the person who was warm and you felt you could talk with her and she would take it on board. She would be supportive in what you were saying. She was also a lot of fun as well.'*

Sandy asks Janis how, if at all, Marion's marriage breakdown changed her.

'They had been in a long-term relationship before they had married, but then the marriage didn't last, and I think she was, of all feelings she was probably experiencing at that time, she was lost, she was confused, she was looking for direction. She was wondering where her life was leading.'

It seems that lasting love was something Marion craved.

---

*   Interview with Janis White by Alison Sandy, 12 March 2019.

CHAPTER 4

Marrying Marion

24 October 1998

It's been one year and two days since Sally drove to Byron Bay and searched the tourist town for her mother. Upon learning Marion's bank accounts were being drained, Sally and Chris pushed copies of Marion's photograph in front of blank faces at the bank, in shops and on the street. They reported their concerns at the local police station. Nothing has come of it and the trail has only grown colder since.

But if there's ever a time her mother might make an appearance, it's today. Sally and Chris's wedding is taking place at The Southport School chapel. Before she left on her trip overseas, Marion had used her sway as a former teacher to secure the chapel booking. She knows the time, the date, the location. Surely she won't miss her daughter's big day!

Sally's father, Stuart, is in the bridal car as they drive through the school grounds towards the chapel. His heart breaks as he watches his daughter scan the surroundings in search of Marion's face. 'Sally was looking around every tree to see if her mother was there,' he later recalls.* 'I get upset thinking about that. When she didn't turn up, it must have gutted her.'

2019

Stuart Brown and Marion met through Stuart's sister Robin Creevey, who was deputy principal at Peakhurst South Public School in Sydney, where Marion worked at the time. Sally has a soft spot for her 'Auntie Rob'.

---

* Interview with Stuart Brown by Alison Sandy, 1 March 2019.

Robin straight away gives her unvarnished opinion. 'Regrettably, she married my brother,' she says. 'Marion was such a prized teacher.* I would have to say that she was probably one of the best teachers I have ever encountered. She had great energy. The house they lived in was absolutely beautiful, and she was a great gardener. She spent many, many hours in the garden. Everything she did was perfect. I always found her to be a person of integrity and intelligence. She was very creative, and nobody worked harder with children in the classroom.'

Marion and Stuart bonded because they had both recently emerged from failed marriages, but it would ultimately prove a troubled coupling. Marion quickly fell pregnant. Sally and Owen arrived within 17 months of each other, and things rapidly soured between their parents.

According to Robin, Marion left Stuart and moved to Queensland in 1975. When Stuart's father was diagnosed with leukaemia the couple reunited, moving to Springwood in the NSW Blue Mountains and officially tying the knot in 1977.

But by 1979 it was all over. 'We didn't realise at the time. My mother and father went up to stay the night with … the children, while they went to this big do,' Robin says. 'And when they went there, they saw Marion had a black eye. Mum then said, "Oh, what happened to you?" Marion said, "I slipped in the bathroom and caught it on the washbasin." It wasn't until a long time later, after they separated, we found out what had happened.'

Robin is clearly sorry she ever introduced Marion to her brother. 'She was a very smart lady and I blame my brother. It was because of him that the marriage failed [and] she went off on a bit of a tangent and got involved in different men … Then she finally married this younger fellow,' she says, meaning Ray Barter, Marion's third husband.

In his phone interview with Sandy, Stuart admits hitting Marion but says she also hit him.

Stuart is a solid man, not overly tall, but Sandy understands from photos and hearing others talk about him that he could be

---

* Interview with Robin Creevey by Alison Sandy, 1 March 2019.

intimidating and had a surly demeanour. She is careful how she raises the issue of violence, wary of him shutting her down. So she acknowledges an incident where Marion apparently lashed out at him before asking whether he physically assaulted her.

'Only after she smashed my eye socket,' Stuart says. He discusses their many fights and says Marion once hit him in the face with a saucepan. 'She smashed my glasses and fractured my eye socket. And I just lost it, I got her on the ground and I thought I was gonna kill her, I was so angry with her,' he says.

'Anyway, Jeff from next door heard what was going on and took me up to Katoomba Hospital and the nurse said, "What happened to your eye and [how did you get] the glass in your eye?" and Jeff turned around and said, "His wife hit him with a saucepan and the glass smashed in his face and broke his eye socket." The nurse said, "Do you want me to call the police?" and I said, "Don't call the police … it was my fault as much as hers." Then Jeff said, "Oh no, you have to report it to police," [but] I didn't want to have a criminal record for something domestic which had boiled over from the both of us.'

Stuart reflects they should have called it quits a lot earlier. 'It was a very unhappy marriage, I guess.'

'Why did you get married?' Sandy asks.

'I don't know. The thing is, we lived together for years quite happily. It wasn't until we got married.'

Sandy asks him to help fill in the gaps about Marion as a person.

'Marion had a lot of problems,' he says quickly.

'Yes?'

'I remember when we went to marriage guidance and she didn't want to go. Anyway, I said, "We've got to go and try and sort this out." But she always used to say, "I don't want to be here, it just gives me the shits."'

Stuart thinks surgery made his ex-wife cheat on him. 'She had a hysterectomy. It really, well and truly affected her, she became promiscuous. I used to do a lot of shift work and my neighbour, who was a bit of a busybody, said, "You know what, Stuart, I know why you're not home at night; there's a different bloke there every night.'"

Sandy cuts in. 'Is that what you think, then? That she's just found some bloke and decided to start a new life?'

'I don't know if she found another bloke. She used to say to me, "All I want to do ... is lie in a field of daisies and make beautiful love with somebody," and I would say, "Let's go find a field of daisies!"'

'When we were breaking up, she had a couple of boyfriends and people couldn't work out how I'd put up with it, but I thought maybe she'll get over it.'

Not long after marrying Ray Barter in 1985, Stuart says Marion sent their son Owen to live with him. 'She rang me up and said, "You've got to get this bastard out of my life."' He says Marion was angry with Owen when she dropped him off: 'I can still see now, Owen had a little Qantas Airline bag. He had Stubbies shorts on and a T-shirt. And she said, "Get out of my life, you little bastard, I'm sorry I never reported you." This is from a woman who is a highly qualified kindergarten teacher.' Stuart doesn't explain why Marion would have needed to report Owen, but indicates it was due to behavioural issues.

Sandy struggles to believe Marion could have said that, but she can't discount it.

Stuart continues: 'I said, "He cries himself to sleep and says, 'Why doesn't my mummy love me?'"'

He claims Marion didn't want Owen and it hurt him. He recalls that when Owen was a groomsman at Sally's wedding, he got drunk and very angry when his mother didn't show up. 'He turned around and said, "That bitch has done it to me again."'

Apparently, Marion and Owen had some kind of reconciliation before she left on her trip.

Stuart clearly harbours a lot of animosity towards Marion. Perhaps this bitterness has tainted his memories, given that Marion's other friends and relatives can only recall the deep love she had for both of her children. But Marion did ultimately choose her third husband, Ray Barter, over Owen, and that decision undoubtedly scarred him.

Sally says Ray and Owen never got along, and it ended up causing ructions in the household. 'Owen had an IQ one shy of being a genius, so he was an odd person,' Sally says. 'I was the extrovert, and he was the introvert. We were only 17 months apart, so we did everything together. We had matching BMX bikes and everyone thought we were twins,' she recalls.

'Ray used to get cranky. I remember one day the lawn mower wouldn't start and he couldn't work out how to start it, so Owen walked out, tinkered with the spark plug and got it to start. But Ray got really mad at him. Ray and Owen's relationship involved Ray giving Mum an ultimatum, meaning that one of them had to go. So Mum sent Owen to live with my dad.'

'Was Owen happy then, do you think?' Sandy asks Stuart. 'Was he ever able to recover from his mother's rejection?'

'No, I don't think so. She used to say to me, "I want to talk to Owen." … He would've been around 14 at that stage. So I would have to say, "Marion, I'm trying to get him to talk to you," and she would say, "No, you're telling him to hate me," and I would say, "I do not tell him to hate you" … and he would just say, "Just tell her to piss off."'

It appears that the relationship between mother and son was never fully mended and Marion, in her will, left everything to Sally.

The only nice thing Stuart has to say about Marion is that she was good at her job. 'She was an excellent teacher. She would teach her craft down at the college, down at Wagga which was the big demonstration school.'

'What do you think has happened to her?' Sandy asks.

'I don't think she's dead. I just think she doesn't want to be found. Marion has this strange thing. If she doesn't want to do something, she won't do it.'

'Why wouldn't she want to be found?'

'I have no idea. I don't think she's a bad person. Last time I saw her, she wanted to know what to do with her life. The thing that worries me is that Sally is becoming so intense about it. That's not good for her.'

'Do you think that Sally deserves to know, one way or the other?'

'Yeah, sure. But not at the expense of … I think her husband, Chris, is the most tolerant man I've ever met.'

'Do you think Marion could have killed herself?'

'No.'

'Why not?'

'She's just not that sort of person.'

Before ending the call, Stuart tells Sandy how much bad luck he's had with women. 'I'm not a vicious person,' he says.

A stark contrast to Stuart is Johnny Warren's best mate, John Economos. Before Sandy starts asking questions, he turns the tables and starts interviewing her.

'Briefly, can you recap what you've gathered? Who have you interviewed besides Ross?'[*]

'I've interviewed everyone,' she replies. 'Well, that's probably a little bit of an exaggeration, but with regard to Johnny, it will only be you and Ross. With regard to Marion, as many family and friends and former colleagues as possible.'

'How did you find Stuart?'

'I think Stuart has a few issues.'

'A lot!' Economos agrees. 'I only saw him one night and he became an enemy of mine … sorry, I became an enemy of his,' Economos says, 'because he was highly jealous and very, very cunning, very sharp. He actually thought I was having an affair with his wife. He was violent.'

'I'm aware of that,' Sandy replies.

The questioning continues like this for another couple of minutes before Economos finally allows Sandy to do her job and she asks him how he and Marion met.

He says he first saw her listening to records in the lounge room at a Young Liberal Party meeting at Oyster Bay in Sydney around the mid 1960s. 'So I started talking to her and I said,

---

* Interview with John Economos by Alison Sandy, 4 March 2019.

"I want you ..." Pregnant pause. "For my best friend!" She was a bit embarrassed because I was told she didn't have anyone, no partner, ever! Then I spoke to Johnny about her and ohhhh, it was laborious pushing them together. She was willing, but John was so wrapped up in his soccer. Anyhow, eventually we went out together a couple of times and they got together.'

Economos is clearly a larrikin and likes to chat. He recalls the couple's breakup, saying it was Johnny's decision. 'He just said to her over breakfast he didn't want to be married any more and within three hours he'd packed up and left. I think from memory he went to his mother's home. He felt responsible to answer to me because I'm the one who picked Marion. She was the best girl he'd ever had. He wasn't a womaniser, but because he'd become a star – captain of Australia, and then a TV personality – women were throwing themselves at him and he was going through them. Marion was the only decent female that he had and I handpicked her.'

Economos doesn't believe Marion was 'fooling around' when she was married to Johnny. 'I got that story from Ross too. That's bullshit, I know. But you know people with rumours, they believe anything they're told. She didn't have anyone, but this guy got his claws into her, that Stuart.

'I met him one night out of the blue when Marion rang me years after. She said, "Would you like to come up for dinner and see my children? Please. Besides, Stuart would like to meet you." I'd never seen him in my life, and when I got there. Oh God, he was exactly the opposite to what I had contemplated or envisaged. He was short, more than half bald, he wasn't attractive at all. He was wearing glasses. But very, very sharp, very intelligent. I didn't know he'd built up a hatred for me. Somewhere along the line, his brain was contaminated with a disease of jealousy that I was having an affair. How? We were miles apart?' Economos then admits Marion caught up with him when visited Sydney.

Economos says that after finishing his meal, Stuart slammed down his knife and fork and stalked out. Marion later told Economos that Stuart had gone to the garage because he was part of an international radio club.

'I saw it after, as I was leaving, on his roof. Even though it was night-time, I could see he had 50 or 60 aerials on it. He was a radio fanatic. He used to talk to people in bloody New Zealand, and people overseas on the radio,' Economos says.

Economos says he saw Marion one last time after that and she had two black eyes. 'Her eyes were bloody, blackened and she just snapped at me and I said, "That's it," and I just left.'

Sandy is glad to have spoken to John Economos before he died in October 2021, at the age of 78.

Marion married Ray Barter in the Blue Mountains on 9 June 1985. Sally recalls her mother first bringing Ray home, possibly in late 1983 or early 1984, when Sally was ten: 'He came to live with us very quickly and we barely knew him.' We'd been at Dad's over the weekend, and I remember her picking us up from the train station and she said, "I've got something to tell you kids." ... Then she said, "Oh, we've got a guy who's going to come and live with us," ... I was a bit shocked by that and I didn't really understand it either. I didn't get it.

'But as I grew up, I learnt that he had walked out on his wife and his three kids, so he needed somewhere to go. Mum had been with him for a couple of days, so she, being the person that she is, let him come and live with us. He came with an Adidas bag and that's all he brought with him, one bag. I remember Owen and I walked straight out. We didn't speak to him when he was in the kitchen. We just sat on the trampoline and looked at him through the kitchen window thinking, "This is really bizarre. There's a guy in our house with one bag." Anyway, Mum later married him, and the problem that stemmed from that is that Owen and Ray never got along.'

When Sandy does finally interview Ray, she thinks he comes across as a little narcissistic.

'Yes, so I was a car detailer a long time ago, and once we had divorced, I moved to Canberra and worked in Parliament House and worked there for 20 years, then I remarried a few years after, then from there I worked in India for three years, and now I'm a production manager for a small oil company,' Ray tells Sandy in almost one breath.

Ray says of Marion, 'She was a lovely person, very dedicated. All the students loved her. They adored her.' She was a very soft, obliging type of person. In some respects that may have been why we had our problems. She didn't have room for anything else.'

Sandy surmises that Ray doesn't like to share the spotlight. It seems he wanted to be the focus of his wife's attention. More out of curiosity than any thought it will help with the investigation, she asks him about the 'ultimatum' he gave Marion with regard to Owen.

'He was a funny young kid. He was extremely intelligent,' Ray says.

'[Marion] always said he needed to be in a special school or a special class because he was so intelligent. He was so far ahead of the other kids that he used to be very bored and he was always in trouble at school. Sally was a good kid. I used to get on well with Sally.'

Sandy pushes Ray on his relationship with Owen.

'Oh, how do I say it without sounding awful? He was an odd child. He had funny ways, I don't know. Sally was very normal. She was an everyday Australian kid, but Owen was different.'

'Was it just being the male in the household? Did he feel threatened?' Sandy asks.

'No, it was more than that. It was also that. I remember one time Owen came out and took the mower and said, "I'll do that," and I said "Why?" Then he said, "Because I'm the man of the house," and I said, "Well, you're too young to be pushing a mower, so go inside and I'll finish it." So there was a little bit of tension there with him, but I didn't worry about it, I just ignored it. But [Marion] did have a soft spot for Owen.'

'You didn't get along with Owen and that's why he ended up living with his dad,' Sandy says, more as a statement than a question.

'Yes, that's part of the reason. He did go and live with his father and we didn't see eye to eye, to be honest.'

'He loved his mum?' Sandy asks, trying to make him see the cruelty of the situation he instigated.

'Yes, absolutely, they were pretty much inseparable, the two of them. She appreciated him for what he was.'

Despite choosing Ray over Owen, by 1990, Marion was divorced for a third time. By now they were living in the beautiful beach town of Gerringong on the NSW south coast.

'We had just drifted apart,' Ray explains. 'There was a little bit of friction, I suppose, but it was never bitter. It was never stand-up arguing. It was tense, but not nasty.'

'Did she try to get back with you?'

'Not really, no. She never really approached me to try and resolve any issues.'

Sandy asks about the divorce settlement.

'All I wanted was what I was entitled to. When we married, she had a house, and as far as I was concerned, that was all hers. We went on to build another house and we went on to make a bit of money, but all I wanted was my fair share of that. That's pretty much what I got. She was pretty upset. It's never easy, [but] there was never any anger or abuse or arguments. We were never like that, ever. I'm not that sort of person. I don't like confrontation all that much.'

Sandy understands Marion would have sold the other house to build their new one. She then asks Ray if he thought the breakup possibly caused Marion to make some bad choices that led to her disappearance.

'I don't believe so. She'd been divorced twice before.'

With three ex-husbands, Marion found herself single and on the move again. But before too long, she landed a job at a private boys' school on the Gold Coast.

CHAPTER 5

Walking Away

7 March 2002

A ringing telephone shatters the night-time silence, jolting a bleary-eyed new mum from her slumber and threatening to wake her tiny daughter. Sally has just dozed off after feeding and settling baby Ella. She looks at the clock. 10.21 pm.

It's her father, Stuart. He's panicking, speaking loudly, quickly, frantically. A stream of profanities punctuates his sentences. 'The police are here,' Stuart blurts out. 'He's done it! I've got to identify him at the morgue.'

Sally is wide awake now, sitting up in bed, trying to make sense of what her father is telling her. The abrupt realisation delivers a powerful, devastating blow. Owen is dead. Her little brother has taken his own life at the age of 27.

Sally paces around the house, her robe pulled as tight as possible around her, clutching a photo of Owen to her chest and muttering repeatedly, 'I don't know what to do. I don't know what to do.'

Sally wonders if their mother's disappearance has been playing on Owen's mind. She suddenly, desperately wants to find her, and resolves to ramp up her efforts to track her down.

2019

The Southport School is the richest boys school on the Gold Coast, its sandstone buildings dotting beautifully landscaped lawns and manicured gardens. This bastion of privilege and wealth is renowned as a school for the leaders of the future. For more than 120 years, the institution has thrived on its reputation for excellence and success. Decades later, however, the public becomes aware of allegations that sexual predators have for years infiltrated the school and that the now adult victims have brought compensation claims.

Sandy sets about catching up with as many people as possible who worked with Marion at The Southport School, including her former colleague Carrie Allwood, who was on the interview panel that hired Marion.

'It was probably towards the end of 1993 and she applied for the position to teach the first reception [preparatory] class at TSS,' Carrie recalls on the phone. 'We interviewed her and the references! She had gone to a lot of trouble to get references from former students and also former colleagues and other schools, and look, she interviewed quite well, better than the others. I was a little bit concerned in the interview, but we thought she would do a good job because she was very experienced.'

'What were your concerns?' Sandy asks.

'Well, it's a little bit hard to remember. I really don't like speaking badly about people who have passed away, or in her case we don't know. I thought at the time she was a bit of an actress in the interview. She was highly excited, calling everyone in the room "precious" and "darling". Going by professional experience and references and so on, it seemed okay.'

Carrie was also the director of the Education Centre at The Southport School and oversaw Marion, though she was not her boss. There seemed to have been a bit of a power struggle between the pair.

'She was the most unusual person to work with. Most people are not like her in the teaching profession. Completely unusual,' Carrie recalls.

'What do you mean by that?'

'Some people would call it eccentric. I do remember that term being used to describe her. And some of the staff, they gave her a bit of a wide berth, particularly the other females. I remember one, who is now passed away, she went to her home a couple of times for afternoon tea and described it as being in a Laura Ashley catalogue. That sticks in my mind too. Everything is very florally and it's like a bit of a fantasy.'

Apparently Marion did not get on with her teacher's aide, Jane Kerr, who was friends with Carrie. 'Issues started to arise fairly early on, and they were a range of issues – such as her ability to relate to another person … like the teacher aide. That didn't go so well. And there were some concerns about the treatment of the boys,' Carrie says. 'I never observed any of this, but I remember she was a bit harsh with some of the boys. I remember hearing a story about some boys hiding under a bed, because they had beds to sleep on during the day, that kind of thing.

'Through 1994, the main counselling I had to do was actually with the teacher aide, to help her through managing working with Marion.'

Carrie makes no mention of any sexual assault as was alleged to Sally, so Sandy contacts Jane Kerr, who doesn't know anything about it either.

'I did experience one occasion,' Jane recalls. 'There was one little boy that was challenging her, and I suppose you could term him a naughty boy, but he wasn't. Perhaps his upbringing wasn't the best. He had [a] broken family, a few things that had impacted on his behaviour in school, and one particular incident, I think it happened twice, she just grabbed him by the arm and took him into the boys' toilets and I just thought, I believe she smacked him, and I just thought, "Oh my God, no that's totally inappropriate." To cut it short, I actually thought I should write a little report and document that. It was vague then whether I did ring Family Services or whether I did report her to Peter Rogers, the head, or Mrs Allwood. I just can't remember how I played that out, but I was concerned her actions would impact the classroom.'

Perhaps word got out that Marion did something 'inappropriate' and that's how the sexual assault rumour started.

'Overall, she was a very creative, good teacher, good for the role, but those were the things I was concerned about,' Jane continues. 'But I found out Marion was finding fault in what I was doing.'

Over the time they worked together, Jane says she lost respect for Marion, who seemed insecure about Jane's friendship with Carrie. 'I don't know whether she felt threatened by that friendship or not. She was quite an ambitious lady, and I think she probably felt that perhaps she could become the head of the department, I'm not sure. But that's the feeling I was getting. I had no idea she was a troubled soul as much as she was.'

By the mid-1990s, there was a new addition to the staff at The Southport School, and at first he seemed to have Marion's back. Luke Glover, who has since passed away, was hired as master of the Preparatory School. At the time he lived on site, not far from the building where Marion and Jane worked each day.

According to Carrie Allwood, Glover was not popular from the outset among many of the staff. But he and Marion seemed to hit it off, at least at first. 'As soon as Luke Glover started, January 1995, we had around 17 staff starting to feel a little concerned because he was the most unusual man. It became apparent very early on he was a bully and treated staff, both males and females, dreadfully – openly and behind closed doors in offices. Dreadful bully, you couldn't get away with it today, but I tried my best to work with him.

'Luke palled up very quickly with Marion, probably because he was living nearby, so he would see her in the mornings before he came across to the other campus at the start of the school day. She also babysat for [his] family. When I resigned at the end of 1995, they were still quite close friends.'

Sandy asks if they might have been more than friends.

'No, because by the time I'd finished up it was very apparent that Luke was very interested in his secretary, so I don't think Marion got a look-in in that regard.'

'Can you explain what sort of bullying Luke did? Was it verbal?' Sandy asks.

'It was absolute put-downs, one on one, he would yell. He did that to me. I presented a report ... and felt a child needed some sort of psychological help, and he just sat there quietly for a moment, then leapt out of his chair ... He waved it around and said how inadequate and incompetent I was, stuff I had never ever experienced before. I said, "Luke, I want to call this meeting short." Then he said, "Nobody finishes this meeting but me." He blocked me at the doorway. He was a big, burly man and put his hand out to try and prevent me from leaving the room. So that's the kind of bullying.

'According to some of the men who taught with him and tried to do their job, similar things happened to them. One on one he could be very abusive.'

Carrie says at the end of 1995, 11 staff resigned. Sandy asks if he could have been the reason Marion resigned too.

'Well, I think he could have probably turned on her.'

Sandy and Seymour spoke to several more Southport School staff, Luke Glover's widow Sandra and son James, the headmasters – past and present – and former pupils who were victims of sexual assault while in attendance. None of them could link Marion with child sexual assault allegations. At the time, there was also talk of Marion having possibly gone into witness protection, but that, too, was a red herring.

Around this time, Marion was in a relationship with the school groundskeeper, Greg Edwards. More than 20 years later, he's still working there. Sally and Sandy travel to the school to catch up with him because Sandy is worried he won't take her call.

Now 64, Greg has the look of a man who's spent a lifetime labouring outdoors. He seems wary, but happy enough to talk. He can't remember exactly when he and Marion dated, but knows they ended it about a year before she went overseas.

He says he got sick of Marion complaining about all the school politics. 'I didn't need that. After we broke up I kept away. Not that I was angry, it was just awkward. Then one day she came up and said, "I'm going to England."'

He describes Marion as a bit of a dreamer who once told him she wanted a knight in shining armour to sweep her off her feet. 'And I thought, "Oh come on."'

Her friend Janis White says Marion was 'stressed' and 'short-tempered' when she visited around this time. 'Her generosity of spirit was rather dented. She wasn't as outgoing. She was obviously under pressure, because she was unhappy. She did have a conversation with me about moving to South Australia and working in a school there, but she obviously had things on her mind. She just wasn't the same happy, light-hearted, generous person she had been.'

Janis says Marion was not in a relationship then that she knew of, but acknowledges she may have had her sights on someone. 'She didn't mention any names, but it was someone she had met through her work. It was not a staff member at the school.'

'Another parent or something like that?'

'Yeah.'

Before long, Marion announced that she'd booked a flight to London for an extended holiday. She gave Sally and Chris some of her furniture and put the rest of her things in storage in a shipping container, including her prized collection of fine china, and artworks by acclaimed Australian artists Arthur Boyd, Jamie Boyd and Norman Lindsay. Sally would send these over to the UK if Marion decided to stay. Despite efforts to trace the items through removalists and storage companies, Marion's most valuable possessions have never been found.

Sally and Chris do say, however, that they started noticing some odd behaviour, which probably became more apparent in hindsight. Chris recalls one evening in May, not long before Marion departed on her trip: 'Sally was at TAFE, Marion had sold the house. I was around there helping Marion pack, and I remember I was on the lounge-room floor and I was packing up the TV cabinet.

'She walked out and said, "What's the time?" and I don't remember the specific time but she just told me, "Right, drop everything, I need you to go now." It was a little bit weird, a little bit out of character, but I said, "I'll just finish packing this box." She said, "No, just leave it all there and go – I need you to go right now!" So I packed up and left.'

Marion's friend Janis also noticed a change in Marion's personality around the same time, but it was a positive shift. She was happy again. 'I actually spoke to her the night or two before she left and she was excited,' Janis says. 'It was freedom, really, and it was freedom in a different way than what she had before, because she wasn't thinking about anyone else but herself. She was planning on doing things. She was always very much into Jane Austen and she was going to go to places where Jane Austen had lived and that sort of thing.

'She was very excited, very happy about going overseas. I must admit I was surprised when she told me she sold the house, because when you go overseas, you don't usually sell your property before you go.'

'Was she going to meet anyone over there or was she just going?' Sandy asks.

'It's a while ago now, but I think she said she was going to meet up with an aunt in the UK.' Janis adds that there was no mention of any romantic tryst.

The last known person to see Marion alive was her former neighbour, Lesley Loveday, in whose house Marion stayed in the weeks between selling her home and travelling overseas. Lesley tells Sandy how polite her guest was: 'Marion was beautiful. She would never come over home unless she had a bunch of flowers, and when Mum was sick, she'd sit on the edge of her bed to talk to her.'

Sandy asks how close they were.

'Not best friends but we were very friendly,' Lesley says. 'She was very good to me when my mum passed away, and we got quite close.'

Lesley is the type of person who respects people's privacy. She's reserved, and definitely not one to spread gossip. 'Marion went her own way at home and I went on mine. We only met up at breakfast and dinner.' She does admit, however, that one night she found Marion's behaviour unusual. 'She said she was going over to stay at Sally's, so I said, "Fine, I'll see you when you come back home," but that night Sally called and said, "Can I speak to Mum?" I said, "I'm sorry, Sally, but Marion is staying at your place," and Sally said, "No, she's not here either," so where she went, I don't know.'

Sally remembers that night too, because she had wanted to discuss with her mother an assignment she'd been working on. She was surprised when Lesley said she wasn't there.

'Unless people tell me things I don't ask, because your life is your own private thing,' Lesley says. 'You don't delve in and ask, "Why did you do this?" or "Why did you go there?" She'd tell me if she wanted to, but she mustn't have wanted to.'

While Marion gave most of her possessions to family or put them in storage, she left some items with Lesley. Before leaving, she gave Lesley an ornamental porcelain chicken. 'She actually gave me that because she said, "I want you to have that to remember me by,"' says Lesley.

Lesley recalls that the day she took Marion to the bus station, she had refused Sally's offer of a lift to the airport, and was planning to take a coach. Marion had so much luggage that they struggled to get it all to the bus stop. 'About four ports [suitcases] and a couple of bags,' Lesley laughs. 'I can still see it. We were so early for the bus, and when we put it on the bus the driver looked at us as if to say, "Oh God." We had a laugh about it, just so much luggage. That's what I remember … [and] her face at the window.'

Lesley stops laughing and becomes serious again. Marion's sudden disappearance continues to weigh on her more than two decades on. 'I never stop looking for her, Alison, I never stop. I'm always looking.'

CHAPTER 6

The Lady Vanishes

1 August 1997

Sally watches the news updates with a mix of horror and hope. A landslide at Thredbo, in the New South Wales ski fields, has crushed a ski lodge, killing 18. Sally and Chris have just returned from skiing at Perisher, not far from Thredbo. Marion, concerned about their wellbeing, has left a message on their answering machine, checking to see that they are okay. Sally hasn't spoken to her mum in ages, and wants to tell her all about the wedding dress she just bought. Now the ring of her phone interrupts the live report on TV. She's delighted to hear Marion's voice, who says she is on the line from Tunbridge Wells in the UK. It's doubtful she was actually there at this time.

Early 2019

Only a handful of friends and relatives have kept the postcards and letters they received from Marion while she was overseas. From the correspondence she was sent, Deirdre believes her sister was enjoying the adventure of a lifetime.

Marion's friend Barbara Mathie got a letter too. 'I remember, because I'd told her about the new blinds I'd put in the old farmhouse and she commented on that … but I don't think I kept that letter,' Barb says. 'I'm sure that the letter I got was postmarked from London, I think.'

An elderly relative received the following postcard from the seaside town of Brighton on 7 July 1997:

Dearest Noni, Margie & Dub, hope you are all well.
Thinking of you as I passed this interesting little shop!
Having a wonderful time exploring and am finally
beginning to relax. Because of all my luggage I decided to
hire a little car + have been rather brave motoring carefully
about this gorgeous place.

I'm shortly off to Amsterdam & the Orient Express on
15th July.

Lots of love Marion

please give love to sister D + hope she's home safely after
a wonderful trip x*

A mother of two boys who attended The Southport School told
Sally she remembered the boys getting a postcard from Marion
that was read out in class. 'Sally kept two postcards. The first
is from Alfriston, a scenic village in East Sussex, about 130
kilometres south of London. Marion didn't write the date on the
card and the postmark is too faint to read. It features a photo of
some little shops in the village, one of which is called Sally's Craft
and Gift Centre.

Dear Sal,
Thinking of you as I explored this little shop on my tour
to the historic village of Alfriston. Am feeling much more
relaxed ...

... the strawberries taste divine and so do the raspberries.
Lots of love to you both – Mum xx**

The second postcard, of London's Tower Bridge, has the postmark
July 1997:

Dearest Sal and Chris,
Hope you are well and I guess eagerly looking forward to
your snowy trip – have a great time! I really quite love just

---

* Postcard sent by Marion Barter, 7 July 1997.
** Postcard sent by Marion Barter to Sally, 1997.

being a tourist ... I decided to experience the Tube travel
around London to see the sights and of course drop into
Harrods ... David Jones – move over! What a shop! So
crowded and so much stuff!!

Lots of love,

Mum xx*

In all of the correspondence there's no sign that Marion is unhappy
or about to cut off contact with her family and disappear. She
seems full of life, enjoying the sights, and keen to keep track of
what her loved ones are doing at home.

In a final phone call to Sally, however, Marion explained that
she wouldn't be sending as much correspondence, as she wanted
to have a holiday. 'She had said to me, "Don't expect me to call all
the time," which I was totally fine with, because I wanted her to
have a holiday and have a rest,' Sally explains to Seymour. 'That
was quite rational and okay, and then when my brother's birthday
came around ...'

Owen's birthday was 18 October and Marion never missed it,
always calling her son and making a fuss. Not this time.

'I rang Owen two days after his birthday and asked if he'd heard
from her, but he said no,' Sally says. At this point, she realised
that ten weeks had passed without any word from her mother. 'I
started to get a bit worried. I thought, "I need to know where she
is. I don't know what hotel she's staying at. I don't know where
exactly she's located over there," so I started to get worried.'

She discussed the matter with friends, and then, alarmed,
contacted her mother's bank, hoping that recent transactions
could tell her where she was. 'I had her bank details because she'd
given me her car, and the plan that we had was I was going to sell
my car and give her the money from my car and keep hers,' Sally
says. 'I rang the bank while my friends were over, and I said, "My
mum's travelling overseas by herself. We haven't heard from her
in a while and it was my brother's birthday and we are concerned
for her. Can you check to see if she's using her account?"

---

* Postcard sent by Marion Barter to Sally, July 1997.

'The standard answer was, "I'm really sorry, I can't tell you anything due to privacy," but then she paused and asked, "Did you say your mum's overseas?" which I said yes to, and then she said, "Oh my God, money is coming out of her account in Byron Bay!"

'She then said, "You can't tell anyone I'm telling you this information because I'm not supposed to tell you, but I'm actually concerned." She then told me everything that happened on the account, and she counted it, then said there's around three and a half weeks of every day in Byron Bay, $5000 increments being stripped out of Mum's account." If it was her taking the money out, why wouldn't you take it out as one sum? Why would you do it every day in $5000 increments?'

The bank official also told Sally that on three occasions, money was withdrawn from a branch at Burleigh Heads on the Gold Coast.

'Now, she taught on the Gold Coast. Chris and I were five minutes from Burleigh,' Sally says. 'Why would you come back to the Gold Coast, where you are at absolute risk of being seen, if you wanted to go missing and everyone thinks you're in the UK? Why would you walk the streets of Burleigh?'

The next day, 22 October 1997, Sally and Chris drove to Byron Bay and walked the streets with a school portrait of Marion.

'We went to the pharmacist and we went to the natural shop because she was quite into natural foods and things. We went to Woolworths and the newsagent, so anywhere you went if you lived there,' Sally says.

They also visited Lois Lane shoes, a place that Marion had previously visited, but no one had seen her.

'The last stop was the Commonwealth Bank down there,' Sally recalls. No one there recognised Marion either.

Byron Bay is a beachside town in northern New South Wales about 800 kilometres north of Sydney and 100 kilometres south of the Gold Coast. It's known for its pristine beaches, spectacular scenery and laidback, outdoorsy lifestyle. It's very popular with travellers, from backpackers to high-end tourists. People from all walks of life go there to get off the grid and start anew.

Having drawn a blank trying to find anyone who recognised Marion, Sally headed for the Byron Bay Police Station to report her mother missing. The following report was filed by Senior Constable Graham Childs at Byron Bay on Wednesday, 22 October at 2.37 pm:

> The next of kin is concerned that the POI [person of interest] who is her mother has travelled to England and has returned to Australia on the 2/8/97 and did not contact her upon return. Members of the family have received postcards dated 30/8/97 from England. Enquiries with the POI's bank indicated that she has acted on her account a number of times including several transactions at Byron Bay. The latest transaction was the sum of $80,000 by telegraphic transfer possibly to an overseas account. A stop has been placed on the account with a narrative for the POI to contact her daughter as a matter of urgency. At this stage it is not planned to list the POI as missing as it is believed she is capable of behaviour of this nature. It is not unusual for her to not contact members of the family. She is a three-times divorced woman in her 50's and one possible scenario for her behaviour is that she has returned to Australia with a companion and has transferred the funds to England to purchase a property there with the view to move to England.

Already mistakes are being made. The last postcard from Marion they were aware of at the time was dated August 7, not August 30, and, crucially, Senior Constable Childs entered this report not as a missing person file, but simply as an 'occurrence'. This is police language for a report that needs no follow-up investigation.

After returning from Byron Bay, Sally called each of Marion's friends and loved ones to find out if they'd heard from her. They met the news of her disappearance with disbelief.

'To me she was just going on a holiday. She didn't mention

who she was going to see or whatever. It was just a shock that she disappeared,' says Marion's friend Janet Omedi. 'She was so passionate about her family. She was very close to her mum and dad, she talked about them a lot, and of course Sally.'

Janis White is certain Marion would not have abandoned her family: 'It was a complete shock to me that she'd come back to Australia relatively soon after leaving, and that she'd disappeared. She was restless, but she has been restless before and she had managed to turn her life around and reinvent it, still teaching, but doing it very well. She loved her children, and I can't imagine her leaving them for good, voluntarily. She was a dreamer and she did like to live in different places and meet new people, all that type of thing, but she loved her children and loved her parents. I couldn't see then, and I can't see now, that she would let them go … no.'

Marion's parents were traumatised, her father, Jack Wilson, seeking help from the Salvation Army Family Tracing Service. It doesn't help that there was no police action taken. When the TLV team track down former police officer Graham Childs, who filed the report as an occurrence, he struggles to recall the details from 22 years ago.

'I've got to be really, really honest with you … I have the vaguest recollection, as you can imagine – 26 years in the police force and I've been out for 16 … I vaguely remember you coming into the station and I think we contacted the Federal Police, but really that's about all I've got. I'm really sorry I'm unable to give you any more,' he tells Sally and Sandy.

'I certainly haven't dealt with a lot of missing persons. Normally the general duties fellow would be at the counter, they'd take the report. Back in those days, we would have been logging it onto the computer and usually pass something like that on if there were suspicious circumstances,' he explains. 'The uniform guys didn't have the time, the access to the phone records or bank records and all that. So that would have been passed on and allocated to a case manager or one of the detectives. Anything that happened was just recorded as an occurrence and then determined from there.'

He adds that if Sally's mother had been missing for more than a few days, that should have escalated the case to a senior officer to take action. Marion had been missing for two months when Sally reported her to police, but the report was not flagged as suspicious.

Sally tries to jog Childs' memory by recalling the circumstances that led her to go to police in Byron Bay, and questions how he made the conclusions he did in his report, particularly in relation to money drained from her mother's bank account. 'I'm just trying to work out how you would have got that information,' she says.

'I'm guessing – this is pure speculation – that it would have just been a phone call to the local bank. It would have been a phone call and they would have pulled up the records and that's why I would have been quite vague,' he explains. 'I'm guessing by the fact that it's written off as occurrence only, that would have meant to me no further investigation at this stage. I would love to be able to say I remember talking to your mother and being able to pass that information on. I can't tell you any more.'

Sally asks an important and obvious question. 'So would it be normal practice for you to ring me and tell me that you'd located her. Would you have written that on the file?'

'Ah, I'd like to think I would have, but I may not have,' Childs tells her. 'I'm sorry this is all summation, because, Sally, I can't imagine what you're going through, but ... if I did do that, that sounds like I fell down on the job by not recording that ... If I did ring you, it's pretty lousy of me not to have recorded and gone back and updated the system to say that I made that phone call.'

Sandy asks Childs if he remembers actually speaking with Marion as he claimed.

'No, and that might seem hard that I didn't remember that ... There's no disrespect in this, but if there's one person coming into the station making a report that I recorded as an occurrence only, it's quite low probably on the memory scale.'

It's disheartening to learn how quickly and easily Marion's case was dismissed from the outset.

CHAPTER 7

April Fools

1 April 2019

'The first thing I'd do is introduce her to my kids.'

Sally's voice falters and tears well as she describes how desperately she wants her three children to know their grandmother. Her heartache is clear as her face fills the TV screen.

The story of Marion Barter features on Channel Seven's *Sunrise* program, Australia's top-rating early morning TV show. The program's hosts, David Koch and Samantha Armytage, announce the launch of *The Lady Vanishes*, a Seven News podcast into the disappearance of Marion Barter, and introduce Sally, Seymour and Sandy for a live interview.

'Sally, why did you want to be involved in this project?' Koch asks.

'It's been a very long and lonely journey by myself to find out about my mother, to find out what happened to her. I think it needs the media exposure to get the word out there, because I've had lots of doors closed and not a lot of help, and I feel that this is a great opportunity for our story to be told.' Sally explains she's been searching for her mother for half of her life. 'I'm happy in my life, but I feel like I have an empty hole in my heart that I need to make sure she's okay.'

Armytage asks Sally what her gut feeling is.

'It's a question I get asked a lot,' she says. 'My gut feeling tells me she has met with foul play.'

The *Sunrise* segment lasts seven minutes, an eternity in TV terms, and word quickly begins to spread.

Episode 1 of *The Lady Vanishes* 'drops' to major podcast providers precisely one minute before the clock ticks over to 1 April 2019, instantly available to stream or download by people around the world. April Fool's Day is perhaps not the most auspicious of dates to publicly launch a project you've poured your heart and soul into, but at least no one in the team will ever forget when TLV began.

Episode 1, titled 'Left Behind', runs 51 minutes and 26 seconds. The show notes read: 'In 1997, Marion Barter boarded a plane for England for the trip of a lifetime. Instead, her loved ones never saw her again. What happened? Where is she? Marion's daughter will never give up trying to find her.'

A two-and-a-half-minute preamble delivered by Sandy sets the scene, providing statistics about the number of people who go missing in Australia, before Marion Barter is introduced. The haunting sounds of a piano melody kick in, followed by the introduction that will be used at the start of every episode.

Sandy, Eeles and Wrighty have prepared a video promo that's already running on the Seven News social media channels, enticing listeners and pointing them in the direction of the podcast. Seymour has produced a TV news story to run on the evening bulletins. Sandy has written an online story. Eeles and Wrighty have produced the audio trailer for all of the major podcast platforms. It's also being hosted on the 7News website. The network requests that the team coordinate the launch of the podcast with the rollout of their new online platform, 7plus, to capitalise on interest in the case.

A Facebook page is created in anticipation of listeners wanting to share their theories on the case, or provide real clues. Seymour also creates a webpage that allows tipsters to email anonymously. Who knows, perhaps Marion herself will hear of Sally's search and send an email to let her know everything's okay.

It's all part of a carefully devised plan to maximise exposure of Marion's story, direct listeners to the podcast, and hopefully shake out some real answers.

A few short hours after their appearance on *Sunrise*, the segment is posted to Facebook and Twitter, attracting 1800 hits. Seymour has no idea if that's good or bad, but a producer from the digital team assures him it's good.

Seymour then writes and posts an article outlining the investigation.* He commits to writing regular online articles, checked by Eeles and Sandy, to keep promoting the podcast.

For Eeles and Wrighty, 1 April is a regular workday in the Brisbane newsroom. Eeles's usual deadlines are punctuated by repeated clicks on the refresh button of her browser to check the number of 'listens' Episode 1 is generating. As the day progresses, the numbers rise quickly from the hundreds to the thousands. With each major leap forward, Eeles sends an excited text message to Sandy or drops in to Wrighty's edit suite to keep him informed. All up, there are 5520 listens on day one.

The team is cautiously optimistic. They know it's an incredible story with two strong central 'characters': Marion and Sally. And the timing couldn't be better. Podcasts are coming of age in Australia, and avid listeners are on the lookout for a new bingeworthy title. Just as *The Lady Vanishes* is making its debut, the popular *The Teacher's Pet* podcast is about to take a break. A ready-made audience of true crime fans is looking for its next podcast fix.

While Sandy and Seymour find and collect information and interviews for the podcast, Eeles and Wrighty are the creators, developing stories, scripts and soundscapes to give each episode life.

It's Eeles's job to decipher the information and pull it together into coherent and engaging chapters. It's difficult, because despite the incredible paper trail that Sally has carefully curated, nothing fits together well. With every fresh sliver of information, it becomes more complicated. It's like trying to put together a giant jigsaw puzzle where many of the pieces are missing or misshapen and the picture on the box keeps changing so you have no idea what it should look like when it's finished.

There's an abundance of documents – redacted police files, letters, postcards, emails, photographs, notes about bank accounts and house sales ... Every item has to be meticulously checked,

---

* The first online story about *The Lady Vanishes* was Alison Sandy & Bryan Seymour, 'The Lady Vanishes: The disappearance of Marion Barter', 7News, updated 26 April 2019, <7news.com.au/news/qld/the-lady-vanishes-new-police-investigation-into-22-year-old-mystery-of-missing-teacher-marion-barter-c-31142>.

categorised and cross-referenced. Some information overlaps or contradicts. There are dates that don't correlate. Spelling and details are often inconsistent. Sometimes it's difficult to know which version is correct and what can be put down to human error.

There's also a growing mountain of transcripts for the ever-expanding collection of interviews that Sandy and Seymour are gathering. A single interview takes hours to transcribe and time-code accurately. Time-coding is the process of logging when each question and response is made during an interview. For instance, a question may begin at 5:30 minutes into an interview and run until 5:50, a duration of 20 seconds. The response to that question may start at 6:00 and run until 8:00. It's essential for interviews to be time-coded, because it makes the process of writing and editing faster and smoother. Segments to be included, or excluded, can easily be identified on scripts by their time-codes and associated transcripts.

As a general rule, a 30-minute interview takes more than two hours to listen to, time-code and write out in full. Sandy and Eeles quickly realise they don't have time for this. Sandy begins tasking the university students who sometimes help her with FOI admin with working on transcripts instead. As the years progress, and technology advances, the team ultimately adopts an AI transcription service, which can transcribe and time-code hours of interviews in as little as 15 minutes. It may not be as accurate, but it's efficient.

Sandy has the idea that this podcast will be unique in defying a typical narrative structure and taking listeners on a journey with an unknown destination. Seymour is all for it. That leaves Eeles having to invent a fluid storytelling style to carry each episode. From an introduction that frames what the story is about, Eeles develops an intuitive and workable approach to the podcast format that will soon entrance millions of listeners around the world.

Early in 2019, Seven graphic artist Jason Blandford puts up his hand to create the cover art for the podcast. He's given the professional portrait of Marion taken by a school photographer, the clearest and most recent image of her, and free rein. He comes back with a design that has a foreboding and mysterious feel. The colour has been drained from the image, making Marion's eye the focus as part of her face fades away behind the title.

Eeles starts nutting out a handwritten episode plan after a brainstorming session with Sandy in late 2018. She envisages up to eight episodes, and writes an overarching theme and dot-point topics for each. Everything hinges on what has been collected, what soon might be collected, what will hopefully be collected and any as-yet-unknown information. There's a great need for flexibility.

Because Sally's interview is so engaging and all-encompassing, Episode 1 is dedicated to her story. Episode 2 is all about Marion – her life leading up to her disappearance, as told by those who were central people in her world at different times. Episode 3 focuses on the trouble that was brewing at The Southport School. How could a devoted teacher turn her back on the profession she was passionate about, just months after being lauded as Queensland's best? Episode 4 ends up becoming Episodes 4 and 5 because of the incredible amount of information that has to be checked and made clear. These episodes take a long time to write. They include people's last memories of Marion and the final conversations, the postcards sent home, the bank accounts being drained, and the trail of letters, emails and documents as Sally and her family tried to find out where she was.

While Eeles is writing these episodes, it becomes abundantly clear that voice actors will be needed to distinguish each piece of correspondence from the many others, to make it easier, and more interesting, for listeners to follow. Thus begins a revolving door of Seven News journalists, producers, camera operators and editors entering the voice booth to portray a growing cast of police officers, lawyers, bank staff and administrators.

They're handed a page of script to voice, with a brief description of the context and who they are representing, before being ushered to the microphone to lay down a voice track. Despite everything else they have to do in their workday, no one ever complains or refuses. When the talent pool runs short in Brisbane, the team calls upon a handful of people in the Sydney newsroom too. And later, when COVID lockdowns force team members into isolated bubbles, family members and friends are asked to become characters.

One key voice that must be found is Marion's. Her words on her postcards home, and the message left on Sally's voice machine, have to convey a sense of what she was really like. The actor needs to be someone who is familiar with the whole story, so Eeles is reluctant to hand the script over for a quick voice hit. Excerpts of Marion's actual voice exist in a grainy home video of her reading a book to her class, but trying to copy that seems cartoonish. Ultimately, because Marion has become close to her heart, Eeles volunteers her voice and hopes she does Marion justice.

Episode 6 is the Byron Bay episode, covering Sally's return to the beachside town, with Seymour and a news camera crew, to retrace her footsteps from October 1997, when she searched for any sign of her mother. By the time writing begins on Episode 7, the original episode outline is cast aside.

Since their first foray into podcasts two years earlier, Eeles and Wrighty have refined their skills and learnt from their mistakes. They now know that it's important to have several episodes complete and ready to publish because, especially in the early days, listeners don't want to wait any more than a week for the next instalment. But they're now finding that so many listeners are coming forward with their memories of Marion and theories about what may have happened that team has to be more responsive than prescriptive.

There's frustration when points that were made in early episodes have to be revisited as new pieces of information are unearthed. Sometimes it will feel like walking around and around a slowly expanding circle. What none of the team realises at the time is that the podcast will be groundbreaking not only for the way it tells a story, but for enlisting help from around the world in real time to investigate a case.

While writing, Eeles finds herself having full-scale discussions in her head (and often out loud in character voices). She speaks through the scripts to ensure they flow, make sense and will roll off the tongues of Sandy and Seymour, who present them. She generally enjoys the process, but it can take days of stop–start writing after work to pull together a complex script.

As well as providing information, she's acutely aware she needs to create the right tone. The podcast needs to feel as if the hosts, Sandy and Seymour, are having an intimate, one-on-one chat with every listener. The audience must be able relate to Marion, feel a connection with Sally like she's an old friend, and become invested in what happens to them. The language must be conversational, congenial and assume nothing. Sound effects and music must enhance the storytelling and emotion, not overwhelm it.

Once a script is complete, Eeles alerts the rest of the team. Sandy and Seymour go through it and make alterations if they want to, then the script is sent to the legal team for approval and any necessary edits.

When Wrighty sees the script for the introduction that plays at the start of every episode, he helps to find the best short, sharp snippets of interviews to knit together a compelling hook for the podcast. He isolates the unforgettable grab of the AFP's Rebecca Kotz, one of the first people in authority to truly listen to and believe Sally, which will become an iconic statement: 'I am a hundred per cent sure … a hundred per cent sure … that somebody knows something.'

With each episode, Wrighty's job starts with up to 80 pages of script. He collects all the interviews, sound effects and music in his audio production software, adding Sandy and Seymour's voice recordings. Then, using the script as a guide, Wrighty places, rearranges, moves and modifies the hundreds of pieces of audio to create a soundscape that tells the story with dramatic but appropriately respectful effect. The goal is to carefully position all of the raw material to comfortably, and sometimes uncomfortably, create a rhythm and tempo to the story that helps take the listener on what has to be a factually accurate but fascinating journey. He creates atmosphere by regulating the pace of what is being said, adding pauses at relevant positions, and blending in complementary music and sound effects.

After hours of creating and moulding, the episode is almost done and it comes time for the final run-through. This is when Wrighty discards his 'audio producer' hat and dons his 'everyday listener' hat. It's extremely important that he listen to each episode in its entirety, as would a typical podcast consumer. He goes for a long walk, headphones on, and listens for anything that doesn't quite make sense, or a sound effect that may be a little loud.

Once he's happy with the completed episode, he passes it on to Eeles, Sandy and Seymour, who also listen and suggest changes. There may be a reason to re-record a piece of voice, move part of an interview or discard something altogether. The audio file is sent to the legal team to check for anything that may be contentious. Once approved, the MP3 file is uploaded to the hosting service and scheduled for release.

Music and sound effects are vital for creating the sonic landscape of the episodes. They set the tone, mood and atmosphere for everything that's going on around the listener. Get it wrong, and they scream their presence from the highest rooftop, making everything else less believable and distracting. Get it right, and the sound highlights every twist and turn, underlines moments of tension and high drama, and complements an often complex narrative.

When Wrighty has that initial chat with Sandy and Eeles about *The Lady Vanishes*, the only details he really has to go on in his quest to imagine the audio footprint of the series is that a woman has gone missing and her daughter is searching for her. On top of that, there seemed to be a litany of administrative and investigative failings.

The theme music is the signature of the series, which listeners will automatically recognise from the first few bars. In his mind's ear, Wrighty hears heartfelt, sad but tragically beautiful piano music as the appropriate accompaniment. And from the little he knows about her, he feels that Marion might prefer a classical feel to the music too.

The cost of using any form of commercial music makes dreams of using pieces by well-known artists totally out of the question. So with no budget at all, Wrighty goes on an internet hunt, eventually stumbling upon an artist by the name of Myuu, real name Nicolas Gasparini, at thedarkpiano.com. Wrighty ultimately chooses Myuu's 'Identity Crisis' as the emotive and evocative thematic companion to Marion's story. At the same time, he earmarks many more of Gasparini's tracks for use later in *The Lady Vanishes*. They will become the predominant music throughout the series.

Just as crucial as the music are quality sound effects. Freesound.com is a site where members from across the world upload their own effects and make them available to anyone to download and use. There are sounds for almost anything you could think of. On those occasions Wrighty can't find exactly what he's looking for, his mobile phone comes in handy. When something grabs his attention on his morning walks, he'll whip out his phone to record it – a barking dog, a babbling brook or an ice-cream van.

He also makes planned recordings. A cutlery drawer opening, digging in the backyard and a baby laughing are all sounds he's set up and recorded in his Brisbane home. Occasionally, when it benefits the storyline, he creates his own music, using guitars, keyboards and percussion instruments.

He wants each episode to be sprinkled with moments that compel the listener to inhale deeply, shake their head from side to side and mutter 'wow'. Each 60 minutes of completed episode takes Wrighty a good 20 to 30 hours of audio manipulation to hone the polished auditory experience listeners expect.

Interviews can be pre-planned and conducted face to face, over the phone or with Skype or FaceTime. But many interviews for *The Lady Vanishes* are recorded under 'emergency' circumstances, on the fly, with no chance to arrange studio time or even a quiet spot for a chat. Sometimes the interviewees have no real desire to be interviewed.

Discussions and conversations are therefore often recorded with a small digital recorder or whoever's mobile phone happens to be available at the time. Frequently the interviewee can be very hard to hear because of wind noise, knocks and bumps, or clothing rustle. Wrighty can fix, or at least improve, a lot of that in the edit. He applies a filter to reduce the 'pops' of air hitting the microphone, especially on words starting with 'P', and another that can take a short segment of an interview where no one is talking, listen for any unwanted background noise and remove it from the entire interview.

Listeners aren't shy when it comes to letting the team know they've got it wrong or there's something they don't like. Initially, some listeners blatantly criticise the voices of Sandy and Seymour, accusing them of being too polished and professional, or not polished enough. Later, others hit out at the French accents of native French speakers and repeatedly ask when the story will be resolved. Overwhelmingly, though, the response is positive, and ratings and reviews reflect this. As the team will discover four years after its launch, *The Lady Vanishes* continues to be the most popular of all of Seven's podcasts by a long shot.

From the first day, it's clear *The Lady Vanishes* will be a hit. There are 28,489 listens in week one, 32,024 in week two and 37,738 in week three. By week five, the number of listens in a single week has snowballed to 361,818. By 12 May, the total number of listens since the start of the podcast reaches 930,495.

Then, one million listens clicks over.

The team feels overwhelmed, grateful and empowered. They're the little engine that could. Their hunches are proven correct. The extra work and the cajoling of bosses has been worth it. More than that, though, they have given Sally Leydon a voice, and no one will be able to push Marion's story back into the shadows. They have each shed tears while working on the series. It's heavy going, but they constantly remind themselves of the frustration and heartbreak that Sally has experienced.

By 2024, people in 89 per cent of the world's countries will have tuned in to an episode of *The Lady Vanishes*, and the total number of listens will be fast approaching 20 million.

CHAPTER 8

What's in a Name?

May 2011

It's the week of Mother's Day and Sally's 38th birthday when Detective Senior Constable Gary Sheehan arrives from Byron Bay at her Brisbane home, sits down with her and pulls out a file. He has new information that he doesn't want to share over the telephone.

Detective Sheehan places a document in front of Sally and her husband Chris, wordlessly indicating that they should read it, while he excuses himself to go to the bathroom. They're not sure why he's being so cautious. Is it because he shouldn't be divulging this information? Or does he just want them to absorb the information and come to their own conclusions? Regardless, what the couple learns is as baffling as it is shocking. And it changes everything. Detective Sheehan has uncovered a major clue. After making enquiries of the Department of Foreign Affairs and Trade, he has discovered that Sally's mother never travelled to the UK in 1997 as Marion Barter. Instead, she used the bizarre moniker Florabella Natalia Marion Remakel. It turns out she had changed her name by deed poll on 15 May 1997 and applied for a passport in that name the following day.

The documentation contains Marion's passport details plus a bank account change to the name Florabella Natalia Marion Remakel. There's also information from an incoming passenger card indicating 'Florabella', or at least her passport, returned to Australia on 2 August 1997. In the box on the passenger card marked 'Occupation', handwriting claims she's a married housewife living in Luxembourg and that her visit to Australia is to be temporary, a matter of days. Sally is told the passport never leaves Australia again.

Sally has no idea why her mother would create a new identity with such a fantastical name. She can't even imagine her mother knowing how to change her name via deed poll. This new knowledge prompts more questions than answers. As soon as Detective Sheehan leaves, Sally hits the internet to start searching for any sign of Florabella Remakel.

February–March 2019

Marion Barter's name change is one of the key reasons Sandy, Seymour, Eeles and Wrighty find her story so compelling. In their minds, it's a piece of information that elevates the case from a 'routine' missing person to something more calculated, perhaps even sinister. What if someone else was involved? Someone who swept Marion off her feet, convinced her to change her name, then took off with her money.

Was Florabella really Marion at all? Once she'd changed her name, maybe something happened to her, and then *someone else* assumed her identity as Florabella, flew to Australia and drained her bank account.

Unpicking the complexities surrounding Marion's new identity is a high priority on Sandy and Seymour's ever-growing 'to-do' list. They compile a log with the names of the people they want to quiz, the databases and phone books they intend to check, and the Freedom of Information (FOI) searches that may yield a shred of new information.

One of the first things the TLV team does is search the internet with various combinations and spellings of Florabella Natalia Marion Remakel. Unsurprisingly, in early 2019 there's nothing to link it definitively to Marion, but they explore the origins of the name to try to determine why it might have appealed to her.

The information they discover is hardly earth-shattering. Some of it is glaringly obvious. They confirm that Florabella is a girl's name meaning beautiful (bella), flower (flora), originally derived from Latin. No surprise there. From what they've been told, Marion loved flowers and spoke a bit of French, a language with Latin roots. But whether that would prompt her to change her name to Florabella is a long bow to draw.

Sally is at a loss. 'No idea,' she says. 'I've never heard the name Florabella in my life.' Marion's sister Deirdre calls the name 'weird'. Marion's long-time friend Janis White describes her reaction as 'flabbergasted ... I haven't come to grips with that. It's such an extraordinary name ... I'm still speechless.'

Marion's new second name, 'Natalia', is a Russian or Ukrainian girl's name meaning 'born on Christmas Day'. Again, no one in Marion's circle can explain why she would choose that. Sally does, however, recall a strange incident relating to that name. Just before 10 pm on Tuesday, 7 May 2013, she received two comments on her Facebook page 'Missing Person Marion Barter' from someone using the name 'Clark Hunter'. The first reads: 'Natalia is alive but you never see her again.'* And soon after: 'It was not her intention to disappear. She was forced.'

Sally is well aware of online trolls who target vulnerable people through sheer malice. But these messages raised such a red flag for her that she took a screenshot. At the time, relatively few people knew about Marion's new identity. So why would someone who was following the Marion Barter page use the name Natalia in a cryptic message, unless they knew something? Sally says she questioned this Clark Hunter and heard back a few times before the profile abruptly disappeared.

The third part of Marion's new name is Marion, her birth name. According to Sally and Marion's friend Janis, it's the only name she was ever known by. She never had a middle name or a nickname that they knew of. 'The very fact that she's retained Marion,' Janis says, 'and it could be my wishful thinking, shows that the true Marion is still there, still part of that person.' Perhaps it's a sign that Marion didn't want to eliminate her past entirely and start afresh. Indeed, it seems to suggest the opposite – that she wanted to hang on to a piece of her true self.

---

* Facebook message to Missing Person Marion Barter page (<www.facebook.com/MissingMarionBarter>), May 2013.

The last part is of course the surname, Remakel. The team cannot recall ever hearing this name, and it's so uncommon, they can find no one in Australia who has it. Worldwide, they find only 108 people alive with that surname (including similar spellings, mostly 'Remacle'). A handful are in the United States and the rest in Luxembourg.

This name is so rare that it would be nearly impossible for Marion to have chosen it at random. But if Marion was so desperate to separate from her family and forge a new identity, why adopt a name that stands out rather than one that blends in? Surely, they think, it is easier to disappear with a name like 'Smith' than one as unusual as 'Remakel'.

The writing on Florabella Remakel's outgoing and incoming passenger cards appears to be Marion's own. At least that's what Sally believes. Handwriting experts consulted later on come to no firm conclusion.

Details on the passenger cards add a layer of mystery to what's beginning to feel like a strong lead. The birthdates on both cards ring true: 3 October 1945 is Marion's birthday. Also, as noted on the outgoing card, she did leave Brisbane on 22 June 1997. Family and friends can verify that. The mention of Luxembourg on both cards is intriguing. The outgoing passenger card indicates that Florabella Remakel is an Australian resident who is leaving the country permanently to take up residence in 'Europe', a word that has been crossed out and replaced with 'Luxembourg'.

None of Marion's family or friends recall her ever mentioning any plan or desire to travel to Luxembourg. But the fact that she changed her surname to Remakel, a name with Luxembourgian roots, is telling. Was she planning to meet up with someone there, or was she perhaps travelling with someone no one knew about? Obtaining a passenger list for Marion's flights is added to the to-do list.

The incoming passenger card indicates that Florabella, or someone using her passport, returned to Brisbane on 2 August 1997, the day after Sally last spoke to her mother on the telephone, when she claimed to be at Tunbridge Wells in England. It shows that Florabella is making a temporary visit to Australia and will stay at the Brisbane Novotel hotel for a number of days, with the intention of catching up with friends and relatives. The passport in Florabella Natalia Marion Remakel's name expires in 2007.

An extra snippet of information that hints at another Luxembourg link comes to light in the weeks after the podcast is officially released. A journalist colleague in Luxembourg, Sarah Cames, emails about an expensive but discontinued line of Villeroy & Boch crockery called 'Flora Bella'. Featuring a white background with a distinctive floral design, it was produced in the early 1990s in Luxembourg and distributed worldwide.

It's possible that Marion came across it in Australia, and Sally agrees it's precisely the kind of dinnerware her mother would have purchased and kept.

The discovery of the name Florabella Natalia Marion Remakel and the incoming passenger card convinced Detective Gary Sheehan that Marion had purposely estranged herself from her family: 'It appeared to me that it was something premeditated by Marion for whatever reason, and she kept it away from her family so they were none the wiser.' Even though Sheehan has never seen her in person, he believes Marion is alive, with a new identity.

When the Marion Barter case landed on Sheehan's desk in 2009, Sally believed her mother was regarded as a missing person. Two years earlier, in 2007, on the tenth anniversary of her mother's disappearance, she'd been shocked to learn otherwise from the AFP.

Sandy contacts Rebecca Kotz, who was then the team leader of the AFP Missing Persons Unit.

'I was working back late one night and I took a phone call on our 1800 line, the free-call line into the Missing Persons Centre,' Kotz recalls. 'Sally introduced herself and wanted to tell me a story about her mother who was missing. We spoke for quite a few hours that night. We struck up an immediate rapport. She was very poignant, had a lot of detail around what had happened, but was adamant she didn't think enough was being done around where her mother was.

'From the detail that Sally was able to present, it seemed very obvious to me that this was an adult going missing of their own volition. It's not illegal in Australia to go missing as an adult. I definitely reiterated to her that if her mother Marion had decided that she wanted to walk away from her life, that was her legal right and all she needed to do was let authorities know that she was okay and they would then pass it on to the family. But no personal details of her whereabouts or where she was going or whatever she was doing would be passed on.'

Marion's outgoing passenger card.
(Courtesy NAA, A8140, 36677 5818 F)

It was Rebecca who suggested that Marion's case be profiled for Missing Persons Week in 2007, and Sally agreed to front the media campaign. Sally felt it was the first time anyone in authority had taken her seriously. But when she was dropped from the project, it seemed to be because someone from NSW Police reported that Marion had been located.

Sally received an email from the AFP in July 2007:

Dear Sally
I would like to confirm the details of the discussion you and I had yesterday regarding the decision to withdraw the use of your mother's story for this year's launch.

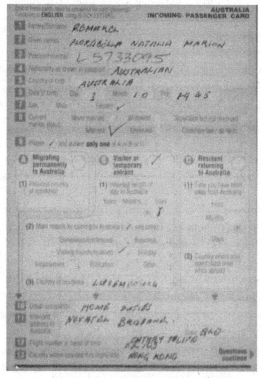

Marion's incoming passenger card.
(Courtesy NAA, A8140, R36916/F2800)

We cannot utilise the story for National Missing Persons Week 2007 due to the current sensitivity of the case. I explained yesterday that we need to respect the privacy of both yourself and your mother given that it appears that your mum has been located by NSW Police and that at those times your mum had decided not to resume contact with your family.

I also wanted to acknowledge the hard work and amazing dedication you've made in trying to locate your mother over the last ten years. I hope that the current investigation gives you the results you've been waiting for so long to achieve. I am also hoping in the future that other media opportunities may arise that would be more suitable to your story, please let me know if you think this is an option for you.

If you require any further information of the details surrounding your mother's case you can contact the NSW Police officer currently responsible for the investigation.

As always, both myself and the staff of the unit are available to you for whatever enquiries or advice you may need.

Sally, extremely disappointed, sent an email back to the AFP on 23 July 2007, where she expressed sadness at the AFP's response:

My family, myself and my mum's many friends saw this opportunity of hope – a great chance to locate my mum and hope to have her come home safely.

I was very surprised by a phone call from one Senior Constable from Missing Persons NSW (11/7) to hear that it is their opinion that my mother is not a missing person just because she 'apparently' said she didn't want to be found 10 years ago!

I say 'apparently' as the questions I was asked by the Senior Constable have led me to believe that the NSW Police have no records of who it was that took my report at Byron Bay 10 years ago or who called to advise me my mum didn't wish to be found.

Sally then requested full documentation from NSW Police to prove they handled her report correctly 10 years ago. Her email to the AFP was forwarded to NSW Police, which led to a prolonged email exchange between the two agencies. Sandy later acquires the correspondence through an FOI application, but it's heavily redacted. It can, however, be gleaned that in 2007, a NSW inspector of police believed Sally was 'seeking a scapegoat' and claimed that 'her mother was spoken with' recently and again 'refused to make contact with her daughter'. The AFP's response on 10 August 1997 was terse, saying, 'Sally's mother had not been located recently and that maybe the information he had received around this was incorrect.'

What does it all mean? Was the AFP at odds with the NSW Police on this case? Why? And has anyone ever located Marion? If so, who? When? And how?

Kotz believes it entirely possible that Marion was never on the Missing Persons Register: 'No, so she wasn't on our register to start with, so Sally was asking for her mother to be both uploaded to our national database but also then be promoted and to seek media attention to raise awareness of her missingness. As part of our protocol, I then contacted NSW Police to seek permission to be able to do that like we would with any missing person's case. The AFP doesn't own those investigations nor the rights to promote them, they have to seek permission from the only investigative team. With that, NSW Police came back and said no, we couldn't promote the case, we couldn't add her to the database, for reasons best known to the investigators.

'I was obviously very hamstrung by the fact our team were not investigators. I just would have loved to have been part of finding those answers for Sally, because at the very least, that's what she deserved.'

Kotz became a supporter and friend to Sally over many years. When she passed away from cancer in April 2022, Sally felt the loss profoundly.

In 2007, Sally specifically had the police file changed from an occurrence, as it was listed in 1997, to a missing persons case. An

email Sandy acquires via FOI proves this. Dated 11 July 2007, it's
from an officer in the NSW Missing Persons Unit:

> On 22/10/1997, Sally BARTER the daughter of ████
> ███████ attended Byron Bay Police Station in regards to her
> mother. Police at the time created an event as an occurrence
> only and not as a missing person. From 6/7/2007 █████
> ███████ has been recorded as a missing person and is being
> investigated as such.

So, after a long battle, Sally got Marion on the missing persons
database. But following the discovery of Marion's new identity,
the case status was changed to 'located' on 17 October 2011. The
manager of the NSW Missing Persons Unit determined, after
a lengthy investigation, that the missing person had changed
her name and left her home by choice, and noted that Sally was
notified of the status of the case by Detective Senior Constable
Gary Sheehan on 7 December 2011. What led them to make this
determination is unclear.

Most people would accept at this point that nothing more
could be done. But not Sally.

The team does not have access to the full police files so they
are forced to generate and track down leads as they do in any
complex investigation. They have numerous avenues of inquiry
at once, divided between them to speed things up.

Sally and Sandy are chasing the banks and information on
Marion's name change and her immigration records. They need
to confirm the date she changed her name by deed poll and find
out how long she would have needed to wait for a new passport
in that name. And they want to know what happened to her
old identification documents. Did she surrender her passport in
the name of Marion Barter? What about her driver's licence?
The team enlists journalist Paula Doneman to help track down
Marion's missing artwork. Doneman has a contact in the art
world. Seymour chases down tips that Marion may have joined
a cult. His long-time reporting on religious groups makes him

something of a cult expert and there is fertile ground here to examine. There are some groups in and around Byron Bay, some of which require new members to adopt a new identity and hand over their worldly possessions. Hare Krishnas, Osho, (aka Orange People, Rajneeshees), and Raelians are just a few of the groups that have communes in the area. One tip is about a group called Hermes Far Eastern Shining, or the 'Water People', in Tyalgum, a small town near Byron Bay. The tipster claims a woman who served them at the group's local cafe looks like Marion.

Seymour travels to the village and is met with hostility and suspicion from members of the group. He's dubious about them too, especially after learning they sell glass and crystal fountains they call 'bubblers' for up to $10,000 each. Byron locals, too, are suspicious, and a federal Senator, Nick Xenophon, has previously called for the group to be investigated for allegedly exploiting members.[*] After meeting with several current and former members, Seymour is satisfied Marion is not among them. It's possible that she joined a group like this, but it seems the least likely explanation for her disappearance. He is also following up with the Salvation Army in the hope he might be able to access records from their now defunct Missing Persons Service. If they, or any of their former staff, kept records, Seymour is determined to find them.

Sandy is keen to identify the father of a student at Marion's school, a pilot, whom friends and colleagues say she was interested in romantically. Using a list of children in Marion's 1997 class, she begins working through the names and making calls.

Sally surprises everyone with the news that, for the first time in a long time, she thinks she may have spotted her mother on the street. The sighting happened outside her workplace, where a woman in a car gave her the fleeting impression that it could be her mum. She snapped a quick photo of the woman. While the face was obscured the number plate is clear and Sally gives it to Sheehan to check. It turns out not to be Marion.

---

[*] Danielle Gusmaroli, 'Calls for probe into secret society Hermes Far Eastern Shining', *Daily Telegraph*, 24 October 2016, www.dailytelegraph.com.au/news/nsw/calls-for-probe-into-secret-society-hermes-far-eastern-shining/news-story/93aa6554401a0feba1d7e7c4c4e59ca.

The entire team is charged with reaching out to the politicians, state and federal, who may be able to assist in the search for Marion. Di Farmer, the Queensland Minister for Child Safety, Youth and Women and the Minister for the Prevention of Domestic and Family Violence, wants to meet Sally. Sandy also reaches out to former homicide detective Ron Iddles, known as the 'Good Cop' by millions of Australians. Iddles joined the Victoria Police in 1972 and by 1980 was a detective in one of the most bruising and challenging criminal environments in Australian history. By 2012, Ron was heading up the Cold Case Homicide Division. Over 25 years, he investigated more than 300 murder cases, with a homicide conviction rate of 99 per cent.

Since retiring, Ron has dedicated himself to helping people solve cold cases. His streaming series *Ron Iddles: The Good Cop* and *Homicide with Ron Iddles* are favourites with true crime fans. After reviewing the case, Ron's response is categorical: 'Somebody in the community, either here in Australia or overseas knows exactly what's happened,' he says. 'The answer is always in the file.'

Those words will prove prophetic.

CHAPTER 9

'Punishment Swiftly Follows Crime'*

March 2019

'I can't believe he's doing this.'

Seymour shakes hands with the hulking police detective towering over him as the camera crew sets up under a canopy of vines and flowers. Detective Senior Constable Gary Sheehan is an old-school police officer who has worked his way through the ranks to carve out a career in the middle. He works at the Byron Bay Police Station handling assaults, homicides and the occasional missing person.

Police often speak at press conferences, but they rarely do one-on-one media interviews. Following months of persistent approaches from Sandy, NSW Police has agreed to let Sheehan sit down with Seymour to talk about Marion Barter on camera.

As they wait, Seymour makes small talk with Sheehan, who visibly relaxes. When he was handed the case to review ten years ago, Sheehan checked with the Department of Foreign Affairs and Trade and found Marion had obtained a new passport in the name Florabella Natalia Marion Remakel. He also chased up a tip, made some years earlier, that Marion was buried on a rural property near Armidale in northern New South Wales. He arranged a small search team with a cadaver dog, but they didn't find anything. After that small flurry of activity, Sheehan did what his colleagues before him had done. He closed the file.

'We never closed the case, that's not true. It's an ongoing investigation,' Sheehan says.

---

* The NSW Police motto, adopted in 1959, is 'Culpam poena premit comes', which translates to 'Punishment swiftly follows crime'.

The splendid gardens of the holiday home they are standing in will be the scene of Sally and Sheehan's first meeting in several years. The other purpose of the trip is to film Sally retracing the steps she took in Byron Bay in the days after realising her mother was missing.

Seymour has wasted no time since his arrival, filming with Sally on Byron Bay streets as bemused locals look on. He asks Sally if she thinks her mother was physically in Byron Bay 22 years ago.

'I actually don't know. I really, honestly, don't know. Yes, she could have been, but at the same time it seems very odd to me, and it's always what resonated with me – if it was her doing it [withdrawing cash], why wouldn't you just do it in one lump sum? So I question whether someone was forcing her to remove her money, and that's the problem for me.'

It's the first time Sandy, Seymour and Sally have worked together so closely and Sandy notices they're all alpha personalities, all like being in control.

Sandy finds herself holding back more than usual, letting Seymour take the lead as TV is his expertise. Sandy is primarily a print journalist but Seymour had been doing TV for most of his 30-year long career.

Sally is running a little late the next morning, which gives Seymour more time to talk with Sheehan before filming gets underway. At one point, the detective leans in close to Seymour to confide in him: 'You're wasting your time on this, mate. Sal's great, I love Sal, but her mother's not missing. She's decided to start a new life and that's her choice. There's nothing more anyone can do.'

Seymour nods calmly, even though his mind is spinning. It feels like the police have dropped the ball and don't care what really happened to Marion.

Finally, the camera crew is ready and Seymour invites Sheehan to talk about the case.

'How difficult has this investigation been?'*

---

* Interview with Detective Senior Constable Gary Sheehan by Bryan Seymour, March 2019.

'It's been an unusual one in that we haven't had … normally jobs that I do, we normally have offenders, crime scenes, things like that. This one is unique in its nature in that it's gone on for such a long time and it's been very, very hard to work out what has happened. I know that Sally has put her heart and soul into finding her mother, but it's been very difficult because of the passage of time. But also it's a different sort of investigation to the one I normally do. So it certainly has had its challenges.'

'And when did you first come into this investigation, Gary?'

'It was first given to me back in 2009, so I've had it for about 10 years, 11 years?'

'How would you compare it to other investigations you're involved in?'

'Again, very, very unique, very, very different. Again, it's been hard because you want to do the best for Sally and her family, but there have been a lot of restrictions based on the information I've found. And again, time has been a big issue for me.'

After a nervous start, the tension lifts. Seymour eases Sheehan in, keeping it conversational as he tries to make the detective forget about the cameras and lights before digging in with some more unsettling questions.

'Unlike other missing persons cases, the thing that strikes me with this one is just how much potential information there is around bank accounts, passports, identity, movement, postcards, travel, people, behaviour, rumours. It really does seem to be the most complex jigsaw around a missing person that I've encountered. What's your experience?' Seymour asks.

'Yeah, look, it has been more work than most of the jobs I do. I have to reiterate, too, that when I first got this job, there wasn't a great deal that was known. I came across a great deal of what you just mentioned over the period of time I've looked at it and it's certainly painted a different picture to what I first thought it was. When I spoke to Sally, she gave me a rundown of her life and her mother's life and the relationship she had with her mother, and also relationships her mother had with other people. And it wasn't until I started delving in and looking at a few things that it made this job very, very different to a lot of the others I've ever done.'

'You had one impression, and then when you started looking into it, it changed?'

'It did … I'll just give you an example. When I started looking at her movements from Australia, I found that prior to leaving, Marion had applied for a new passport in a different name … And it appeared to me, it was something premeditated by Marion … As I looked a little bit deeper, she had actually come back to Australia on the same passport, that is, the passport in the new name … So it became more complex and it went away from the traditional missing person to a position that I believed Marion had deliberately done these things and decided for whatever reason she no longer wanted to be associated with her former life, and possibly setting up a new life for herself. So, it took on a completely different type of job once I got into it.'

And there it is. Marion had deliberately abandoned her family. Case closed.

Over many years and hundreds of investigations, Seymour has learnt that the more a politician, corporate PR flack or police detective tries to convince you that it's a waste of your time to pursue a story, the more likely it is that you're onto something.

'Has she touched her superannuation?'

'No she hasn't, but that's not unusual. We have to remember the age Marion was when she went missing.* And as it is with most people, unless there are extenuating circumstances, people can't touch their superannuation, it has to sit there for a period of time until you retire or become a preservation age. So it wasn't unusual for Marion in this instance not to touch her superannuation. The super is still there, it has been unclaimed. But there could be a number of reasons for that.'

This has always bothered Sally and the team. Australia introduced compulsory superannuation in 1992. Employers have to contribute to their employees' retirement funds by paying a mandated percentage of their wage into their superannuation accounts (currently 11 per

---

* Marion was 51 years old when she went missing in 1997.

cent). At the time Marion disappeared, people aged 55 or over could access their superannuation money. Today, people can access superannuation as early as 60. If Marion was voluntarily starting a new life, why wouldn't she take her own money?

'Sally reckons someone might be acting in a coercive manner. Do any of Marion's actions, as you've just described, indicate a motive either for her or for someone she knows who possibly could have been coercing her?'

'No, there's nothing that I've found during the period I've had the investigation that would suggest there's been any coercion, other than perhaps her becoming involved with somebody who has impressed upon her that this might be a good idea – that is, to move away from her family and start a new life. There's been nothing to suggest she's in any danger whatsoever. There's been nothing like that at all. Everything I've found, factually and circumstantially, indicates to me that Marion has decided to start a new life for herself.'

Why would Sheehan think that if a third party was involved in Marion's disappearance, it must have been someone she trusted, such as a lover or new spouse? And if so, why would he assume that this other person did not mistreat, even harm, Marion? Because the original investigators claimed Marion told them she had left of her own volition?

'Sally told me,' Seymour says, 'when she first reported her mother missing just down the road from here at Byron Bay Police Station in 1997, about a week later, the sergeant, or someone at the station, contacted her and said, "We've spoken to her, she doesn't want to be found, she says she's okay," and essentially closed the case. But in the case file, there's no record of that. Did you find any record of that conversation or indication that had happened?'

'No, I haven't been able to find anything like that. And again, it's very hard for me to comment on something that happened back in 1997 when I had no involvement yet whatsoever.'

'But it's not in the file currently? You haven't seen a note or an address, or a record of a conversation with Marion?' Seymour persists.

'The first time that I realised, understood, that Marion had come back was when I discovered it myself back in 2009 or 2010, whenever that was.'

'Gary, pointedly, Sally would like to know, just in case it is the case Marion has decided to go missing. Gary, do you know where Marion is?'

'Unfortunately I don't. It would be great if I did know. I'd like to give Sally some closure. One thing I would like to say in regards to that, in situations like this when people go missing and set up new lives for themselves, and it's not unknown for that to happen, I think we have to be mindful of the privacy of that person too. There are two sides to that story. In this particular case, I haven't been able to speak to Marion, nor has anybody, so we don't know what her circumstances are in regards to her deciding to do this.'

'If she has done it,' Seymour speculates.

'If she has done it. Yeah, it's my belief that she has. We have to be careful we don't impinge upon her privacy too. People are entitled to explain themselves. It would be very, very nice if they did, especially for the families. I can't imagine how traumatic it would be. But we've got to be mindful we need to afford them a level of privacy as well if that's what they've chosen to do.'

This seems a telling point. Sheehan's position is essentially that Marion chose to vanish, and therefore there is nothing more for police to do. However, our investigation had revealed evidence that suggested Marion may not have been the master of her own fate. And for Sally, her right as a daughter to know what had happened to her mother was just as valid and important to her as the right of her mother to abandon her. Seymour's father had done exactly that to him, but it didn't stop him from looking for, and finding, him. At that moment, Seymour locks in the commitment to see this through to the very end, wherever that might lead, however long it might take.

Sheehan continues to answer questions about Marion's trip overseas and her claim to be living in Luxembourg. Seymour thinks he's trying to suggest that Marion lied about coming back to Australia to throw her family off her scent, or at least muddy the waters for anyone looking for her.

'And that would indicate a Machiavellian level of scheming to throw you off, to throw any inquiry off,' Seymour says. 'It seems at odds with the sweet teacher who loved her job and was close to her family. Again the contradiction. I know people are contradictory in nature and can surprise us. Does this seem at the extreme end of that?'

'Look, I don't know what goes through people's minds when they make decisions such as these ... If she didn't want to be located, I think it'd be a reasonable thing for someone in that mind-frame to do, but to the average punter it would seem unusual. I mean, you have to remember, prior to going to England, again, she applied for a passport with a complete name change, didn't tell anybody, travelled overseas as if nothing had happened in regard to that. So, if you look at it from the perspective of a person who had gone to that length of trouble to do that before she left, it just seems to be a step in the same direction.'

'... Have police to your knowledge ever sighted or located Marion, spoken to her?'

'Not that I'm aware of. Certainly not since I've been involved in the investigation. I don't know what occurred prior to me getting the investigation, but there's been nothing I've read that would suggest that.'

According to the NSW Police, no one has ever made a proof-of-life check on Marion. Legally, that means she must be presumed missing. That fact that she's not even on the Missing Persons Register confirms the TLV team's worst suspicion. There was, and is, no real investigation into what happened to Marion.

'If I had all the information you have Gary, would I be able to find Marion?'

'No, I don't think so. I believe Marion doesn't want to be found. I've done searches throughout Australia in every state and every territory, for things like driver's licences, births deaths and marriages, Medicare, Centrelink, a whole gamut of things we normally look for when people are missing, and I can't find a trace of Marion or Florabella, which she probably goes by now, anywhere in Australia. That's not to say she's not here. I just can't find her.'

'There is the lingering doubt that some misadventure may have befallen Marion,' Seymour says, 'in that Sally saw her with a mysterious man in the days leading up to her disappearance. This was totally out of character. And we know people are often coerced, often by an abusive partner, or another party, into doing things which we are now describing – changing their identity, emptying their accounts. Marion was a collector of antiques and artworks; we don't know where they've gone. Does anything lead you to the conclusion that possibly she may have been a victim of foul play?'

'I haven't been able to come up with anything in my investigation that would suggest she was a victim of foul play.'

'What would you need to go down that avenue of inquiry? What sorts of evidence, what sorts of things would you need to come across?'

'It's hard to say because everything is different. But if there was something there, it certainly would be something I would follow up. But there's nothing to suggest that at all.'

Sheehan mentions the trip to Armidale to check whether Marion was buried in a paddock there after a tip came through to Crime Stoppers:* '... it's been the only information so far that would lead me to suggest there was something wrong with Marion. And it proved to be false.'

'And, I guess, to your relief?'

'Oh, absolutely. Yeah, nobody wants to find out someone comes to an end.'

'A grisly end, a murder?'

'Absolutely, yeah.'

Seymour marvels at Sheehan's certainty. There are 1600 long-term missing persons in Australia, and just a tiny percentage of them, maybe a dozen, fit the profile of fleeing their families to live under a new name. Even Sheehan says that in his 33 years as a police officer, this case is 'probably the first or second one I've worked on, so they are unusual'.

---

*   Crime Stoppers is a national police initiative in Australia that allows anyone to provide anonymous tips on crime by phone or email.

'Hopefully what we're doing now will generate something,' Seymour suggests.

'Yeah, look, Sally has been passionate about this especially getting involved with the media and I think it can only be a good thing. We have to be careful about Marion's privacy but if we got to a point we could talk to her … at least we'd know without pulling her back into a life she doesn't want to be in.'

'And also, to play devil's advocate, to find out whether she did come under someone's spell or fall victim to some sort of misadventure.'

'You spoke before about how Sally said she had seen her mother with that gentleman,' Sheehan says. 'To my mind … it tends to sit on the timeline of her being involved with a male person and quite potentially setting up a new life for herself that didn't involve her old one …'

'I know Sally is grateful for your enduring interest in the case. She was a bit mystified that she wasn't notified when her mother was declassified as missing. Was that a conscious decision not to tell her, or was that a bureaucratic thing. How did that play out?'

'No, once I found out all the information and I was satisfied with my interpretation of the evidence I had found, I actually went up to Sally's house and spoke to her and I thought I'd made it clear her mother didn't fit the criteria of a missing person and I was going to take some steps to remove her from the database. If Sally thinks otherwise then perhaps I didn't make myself clear enough and I apologise. But it was my understanding I had explained that to Sally.'

Sally remains adamant she was not told, by Sheehan or anyone else, that her mother was removed from the Missing Persons Register.

'What chance is there that you, Sally, we, will find out where Marion is, or what happened to her?'

'Tough one to answer, Bryan. I really don't know. Given the fact it's been 22 years now, I don't know what the future holds. As I said before, I'd like to think if she was around, that we did get the chance to talk to her, to find out her circumstances at this point in time. And for Sally's sake that would be fantastic. I would get a kick out of it as well because I would love to see this through to finality … For Sally's sake, I hope we get a result.'

After the cameras stop rolling, Sheehan leans in again but the microphone is still live. 'I think if you really put your mind to the fact that you didn't want to be found, you'd do it. I mean, we don't know that this gentleman she was found with is in fact involved,' he says, referring to the mystery man in the car. 'If he was someone who was extremely wealthy, she wouldn't have a need to go to the government to get a lot of the things the normal punter gets.'

Seymour is startled. 'In terms of welfare?' he asks. Is Sheehan suggesting that Marion hasn't touched her money because she found a 'sugar daddy' to take care of her?

'Yeah, superannuation, because it's only a very moderate amount. I think it would be possible. I don't know I'd be able to do it, but if you found yourself in the right circumstances, I don't think it would be impossible.'

'It seems extraordinary. Even if that's what happened, it seems extraordinary.'

'… I think extraordinary is the right word for it.'

Sally arrives and the camera crew scurries to attach a microphone to her shirt so they can film her meeting Sheehan.

'Hello!'

'Hey Sal.'

'How are you?'

'Good, how are you?'

'My God, you do look different to when I saw you last. Did you have a beard or something?'

'I did, I had a beard yeah. How's the family?'

'Good.'

They're both smiling as they exchange pleasantries. Sheehan's easygoing closeness with Sally seems at odds with the way he just referred to her as 'obsessed'.

Seymour steps in and says to Sally, 'Twenty-two years since Marion went missing. If she did want to disappear, she's performed an amazing magic act, hasn't she? You don't think she did any of that stuff, do you?'

'I'm just thinking, I don't know. Gary and I have had plenty of conversations about this, haven't we. We've tossed over every possible scenario. I think she's met with foul play. I think something has happened which sparked her to go into a frenzy, changing her name, going overseas and coming back. But why the money was stripped out of her bank account in such a unique fashion … And to change her name to such a random name like Florabella Remakel. If you want to go missing, you'd be Jane Brown … it's not the character of my mother. I don't think she would be that person.

'So … I think something definitely went wrong. Not to say she didn't meet somebody and then it went pear-shaped. Or if something happened, I'm still questioning who the guy was in the car … If she's happily married and living a great life, if someone can show me that, and I know she's okay, I'm at peace with that.

'I haven't had my mum in my life. I'm 45, she's been missing for 22 years – it's half of my life she's been missing. And pretty much my whole adult life. So as much as it saddens me, I'm pretty much used to not having a mum. Chris's mum's passed away, so I don't have that female figure in my life. All my grandmothers have passed away too. So I've had to be that person, be all those roles for my children, so I can cope with lots of things …

'But I also need to know she's okay. And for people just to say we can't find her, we don't know where she is, that isn't enough for me. I need to know she's okay. And whether she wants to come back if she is alive and well or whether the worst has happened, I have to give this a go.'

'Yes, not knowing is the hardest part,' Sheehan agrees.

'I really need to be able to sleep at night and know I've done the best that I can … If she turns up buried in bushland somewhere, that'll be the most horrendous thing for me, but I'll be happy that I kept looking.'

'Take it from me,' Sheehan replies, 'as long as I'm in the police force, I will always be looking at this one. I've got a vested interest in it now because I've had it for so long. And I'm intrigued by it too. I'll try and help you to work out what occurred. It may not happen, but it won't be through lack of trying.'

CHAPTER 10

Supersleuths

It's one thing to build and engage an audience for a TV news bulletin. It's quite another to have that audience actively want to engage with you.

After just a few podcast episodes are published, *The Lady Vanishes*' audience is fast becoming a global online community. Hundreds of people, mostly women, are following the TLV Facebook page, and that number will balloon to more than 31,000. These dedicated podcast fans love a real-life mystery and want as much information as possible. But it's more than that.

Those flocking to the TLV Facebook page are invested in Sally and Marion's story. Sally has opened herself up to the world, made herself vulnerable, exposed her biggest fears and anxieties, and listeners have responded. There's rarely a day when a post on the TLV Facebook page does not attract scores of comments from supporters across the world:

> 'Sal, when all of this is over I'm coming to Queensland to give you the biggest hug!'
> 'You are a beautiful daughter and your mum loves you so incredibly much. She's with you always.'
> 'Your mum would be so proud of you. We all are.'

There's also a stream of support for the podcast team, especially the hosts, Sandy and Seymour. The TLV online community is an example of what social media can achieve for good. That said, Seymour and Sandy also cop a constant stream of personal abuse, another staple of social media. But neither is bothered by barbs thrown by strangers.

Other social media threads, often on Reddit, explore the full gamut of opinions and theories on the case. While no one is immune from online trolls and negativity, to build an online community as safe and supportive as that surrounding *The Lady Vanishes* is quite extraordinary.

A number of TLV listeners who will become known as the supersleuths are making themselves known and offering to lend a hand.

Kristina Panter is one of the original supersleuths. She lives in West Sussex in the UK, not far from the places where Marion sent postcards home. She first learnt about Marion through Sally's Missing Person Marion Barter Facebook page and is also an avid listener of *The Lady Vanishes*. With Sandy's efforts to reach authorities and organisations in the UK by phone and email often thwarted by time-zone differences, Kristina offers to take up the case, investigating what she can in her part of the world.

To start with, she finds out the flight numbers for airlines arriving in London from Japan on 27, 28 and 29 June 1997. Marion left Australia on 26 June, but the fact that she wrote a letter on paper with a Japanese hotel logo, which she posted in the UK, indicates she may have had a stopover in Japan. The envelope is postmarked 30 June 1997. Kristina then embarks on a mission to find passenger lists for the flights she has identified.

Kristina also learns that Sally's Craft Centre, mentioned in Marion's postcard to Sally from Alfriston, East Sussex, no longer exists and hasn't done for years, but Kristina's planning to make contact with the current shop's owner.

She has also reached out to local Facebook groups around Alfriston, and a local woman has offered to put up a poster on the noticeboard in the village store. Kristina's husband, who works with the railways, has a contact with the company that does the bookings for the *Orient Express*. He's checking to see if there are any booking records that go back to 1997.

Kristina emails hotels in Tunbridge Wells to see whether any have guest records from 1997, but many of them have changed ownership since then. She also tries car rental businesses, without success. No one has kept documents from 22 years ago.

She reaches out to British Telecom Archives manager James Elder, asking whether records still exist for a payphone in Tunbridge Wells that Marion may have used to call Sally. He confirms that there are definitely no payphone records from 1997.

Kristina is tracking the path of Marion's travels through her postcards. 'Marion was in Tonbridge, which is actually very close to Tunbridge Wells,' she tells Sandy over the phone. 'It looks like Marion visited a castle in Tonbridge, and the letter that she sent to Sally and the postage stamp had the town Tonbridge on the stamp – that was dated the 30th of June ... then she's made her way further south, travelling around the south-east of England down towards the coast, which leads to another postcard she sent from Brighton. She visited a shop there ... but ... the owner of that shop retired and moved to France around 2002, so it may be a bit of a challenge to track her down.'

Kristina thinks Marion bought a postcard in this shop in Brighton, then posted it in the town of Hastings, a little further east. She firmly believes Marion bought and wrote the postcards of her own volition. 'I think if anyone was to try to make it look like she had written those postcards, they would have had to go to great lengths to obtain those postcards from the obscure little shop tucked out of the way. I believe she was here and having a good time, but after that, I really don't know.

Kristina is also trying to track down Susie Cooper – a teacher from England who, on an exchange trip to Australia, worked with Marion at The Southport School. Marion told friends that she might contact her, should she decide to stay and work in the UK.

'I've always had that investigative mind.'

'I'll just keep digging and I'll keep notes of everything that I'm finding and everything that I'm guessing,' Kristina says. 'Whatever I can do.'

Jennifer 'Jenn' Marsh is another of Sally's faithful supporters who does whatever she can to help. Jenn first came across Marion's story through the Aussie and UK Angels Facebook page, which aims to reunite lost family and friends. There are more than 50,000 members, and Jenn is a volunteer who tries to help people reconnect.

When Sally posted on the site about her quest to find her mother, Jenn got in touch, as did a number of other women. Since then, not only have people in the group become firm friends and advocates of Sally, but they've also become staunch listeners and contributors to *The Lady Vanishes* and the Facebook page.

When a petition is started to get Marion on the National Missing Persons Register, Jenn takes it upon herself to urge anyone who comments on the TLV and Missing Person Marion Barter accounts to sign it.

Jenn and June Clydesdale, another devoted fan of the podcast, are also instrumental in dealing with the overwhelming number of public posts and queries on the TLV Facebook site. They regularly monitor the page and, because they're so familiar with Marion's story and are able to confirm information quickly with both Sally and the TLV team, they will often clarify misconceptions, provide accurate details and even issue warnings if people posting may be at risk of breaching the law.

A retired mental health nurse who goes by the pseudonym Rose also keeps across the public comments on both the TLV and Missing Person Marion Barter Facebook pages. She'll politely let people know when they're out of line with their opinions and statements, and will clear up any confusion over details of the case.

Rose wonders briefly if a mental breakdown may have caused Marion to disconnect from her life, but says, 'I just couldn't, honestly couldn't, feasibly come up with one single attribute or trait that I could think would make Marion actually walk away. She's a woman with a high conscience, a caring person. There's only one psychiatric condition that I think could happen to Marion. It's very, very rare, and I personally, in 40-odd years of nursing, have not come across it myself, but that's a condition called disassociation.'

Dissociative identity disorder, once known as multiple personality disorder, is a very rare psychological condition in which a person's identity splits into two or more distinct personality states.* It's a coping mechanism that enables the person to disconnect from something stressful or traumatic, or helps them separate traumatic memories from everyday reality. It can be triggered by reminders of past events, stress, illness or even relatively small incidents. Sufferers may not be aware of the other personalities, yet they can generally still function at a high level.

But, Rose tells Sandy, such episodes would not go on for more than 20 years. As people age and memories return, they often want to rebuild bridges with those with whom they have lost touch. 'I think with Marion, as a caring and loving person, she just wouldn't be able to live with her conscience. Only the sociopathic type personality that has no feelings can just walk away and wipe their hands of it. And Marion is certainly not like that. My gut feeling is that she's met with foul play.'

Her biggest concern is for Sally when she does start getting answers: 'Given the traction that this has now that it's on the world stage, there's a very high chance Sally will get the answers she wants. Sally's obviously prepared for it, but does that have some sort of psychological impact as well?' Rose says that, despite the growing level of interest in Marion's case, if Sally finds out something she can't, or doesn't want to share, her supporters will be understanding. 'As long as Sally is happy with what comes along, nobody needs to know the answer. I think the majority of people would respect that.'

Over the coming months, countless listeners reach out to offer their support and tips to Sally and TLV. Some of the interactions lead to major breakthroughs, others are fleeting.

The core group of supersleuths, however, proves staunch and unyielding for as long as it takes. One of them, a woman from Victoria named Joni Condos, will become Sally's good friend and confidante. And she will discover a vital clue.

---

* 'Dissociative identity disorder (DID)', factsheet, SANE, <www.sane. org/information-and-resources/facts-and-guides/dissociative-identity-disorder>.

CHAPTER 11

Getting Personal

10 December 1994

Le Courrier Australien

MONSIEUR, 47 ans, célibataire, grand, brun, sobre, non-fumeur, universitaire, multi-proprio, intello, polyglote, chaleureux, motivé et jusqu'au-boutiste avec qualités morales et avoir important, cherche dame de coeur libre, B.C.B.G, vue relation permanente et ou mariage:
M[onsieur] F Remakel, Box L51,
LENNOX-HEAD, NSW 2478.
Tél. (066) 864788.

May 2019

Contact from listeners is becoming more frequent.

Some are missives from those who just want to reach out. Others contain photographs snapped in stealth of women who resemble Marion. Almost every email contains an idea or a nugget of information. One day in early May, something lands in the TLV email inbox from Joni Condos. It more than piques Sandy's interest, so she sends it to the rest of the team.

A personal advertisement posted by a man looking for love, it was published in French on 10 December 1994 in the French–English newspaper *Le Courrier Australien*. Eeles's memory of high-school French is operational enough to decipher the bulk of what it says, then realisation rolls in like a wave and random pieces of information start clicking into place. 'This is the missing link,' she states excitedly, without waiting for Sandy to look up.

A flurry of research begins in earnest.

The ad describes a tall, 47-year-old single man with brown hair. He's a non-smoker, who is cultured, intelligent and can speak multiple languages. He owns multiple properties or businesses and is highly motivated. He's warm and welcoming, but also quite serious. And he's looking for an unattached lady with a view to a permanent relationship or marriage. The letters B.C.B.G stand for *bon chic bon genre* – which translates as 'good style, good class'. It's an expression used in France to describe members of the upper class, who are typically well educated, well connected and descended from 'old money'.

Sally confirms the qualities and characteristics listed in the ad are ones that Marion would find very attractive in a man. If his age in 1994 was 47, then by 1997, when Marion went missing, he would have been around 50. The really fascinating bit is of course his name: Monsieur F Remakel. This is the key to unlocking everything. Remakel. It's the precisely same spelling of the extremely rare surname Marion chose in May 1997 and starts the process of finding him.

The ad provides two ways to respond: a phone number and a post-office box for Lennox Head, in northern New South Wales, barely a 20-minute drive from Byron Bay and less than 90 minutes' drive from Marion's home at Southport.

Sandy dials the number listed and it rings, before diverting to a private message bank. She leaves a friendly request to call back, but no one ever does. Over the coming weeks and months, she calls the number repeatedly, but there's never an answer. When she changes the digits slightly, just to see what happens, she connects with people living in Ballina, just ten minutes down the road. A cursory examination of decades-old phone books from the area, and an electoral roll search, yield nothing. Any Monsieur F Remakel who may have lived in the Northern Rivers region of New South Wales in the 1990s appears to have long since moved on.

Sandy calls Joni, the listener who discovered the ad, and learns she had become an avid amateur detective when finding out what happened to a member of her own extended family a decade earlier. The process equipped her with excellent research skills and knowledge of where to find information.

'As far as getting involved in a podcast, it was simply another one that I listened to … as I'm doing my housework or whatever I'm doing, and it just struck a chord and I was very interested right from the word go,' Joni says. 'And especially because there was a bit of a play for the public to help, that's very unusual. Normally, it's very much a closed shop. So I … thought, because of the age and cold case nature of it, that I might be able to help in some way.'*

Joni is unwell and awake at midnight when she decides to run the name 'Remakel' through Trove, a searchable digital database of printed material published in Australia, compiled by hundreds of partners, including libraries, museums, galleries, the media, government and community organisations.** Set up in 2009, it now has billions of pieces of information stretching back more than a century, including full editions of newspapers, magazines and periodicals.

'After putting [Marion Barter], through the newspapers, there was nothing. But then I ran [Florabella Natalia Marion Remakel] through the newspapers,' Joni says. 'Then suddenly, from December 1994, this ad popped up in a French-speaking newspaper coming out of Sydney.'

She adds, 'I've been a social worker for 21 years, and family violence is one of my specialities … Purely looking at [Marion's] actions and how quickly things change, I can just see coercive control over a lot of her actions.' She gives a list of red-flag instances: 'Looking at the letter Sally posted online – "Don't worry about me, I'm okay" – that sort of thing. Also, putting her name in a string of names so the fact she's retaining a small little piece of herself. The money coming out of the bank – $5000 coming out every day.

---

* Phone interview with Joni Condos by Alison Sandy, April 2022; Interview with Joni Condos, *The Lady Vanishes*, Episode 10, May 2019.

** The name Trove is based on the French word trouver, which means 'to discover'.

'It just really frustrates me, as a general Joe Blow on the street, that the police would just take the fact that she took the money as a tick against her ... that she didn't disappear ... as the years have progressed, we're a bit more aware of how predominantly men can control women, and can do it very quickly.'

'How do they go about it, in your experience?' Sandy asks.

'Well, certainly it can start off with love-bombing all the way, meaning it's just the most overwhelming feeling of safety, security, love, passion, romance – you're their world, you're everything to them ... then that turns into, "I want to see you all the time, I want to know where you are all the time, I want to phone you five or six times a day."

'Things can progress quite quickly, especially for someone like Marion who has been looking for love. I would certainly count her as an absolute prime candidate for someone who could quite possibly repeat this behaviour time and time again with women, and that was how he operated. I could see certain aspects of it: putting all her things into storage, keeping all these things out, but then not telling her daughter where these things were, throwing her son-in-law out of the house so there was no meeting of the minds.'

'Isn't that a part of the control thing as well? Keeping them a secret from everyone else?' Sandy adds.

'Yep, definitely,' Joni responds. 'My gut feeling ... I think she's no longer with us. I just think she was quite possibly a prime candidate for an exotic man ... the exotic man came and something happened from there. Financially she had a lot of money on her, she was quite vulnerable.

'I can most definitely see, even from a week or a few weeks in, Marion was potentially a prime candidate for getting swept up, you know. "Sell your house, sell everything, let's go live in Luxembourg with all of the lavender bushes and the music and the art and the French-speaking" ... I just think it's something well worth pursuing for sure.'

Trove is maintained by the National Library of Australia, and Seymour checks with their staff to find out what he can about the ad.

It was uploaded in 2015 and no altercations or corrections have been made to the text since then. NLA staff explain this means that anyone who typed in the name 'Remakel' without any modifications would immediately see the ad in the handful of results.

If police had checked, they would have discovered this clue years ago!

Fortunately, Joni had the initiative to check it out shortly after she started listening to the podcast, and her discovery is transforming the investigation.

TLV includes the ad in the script for the next episode of the podcast. Creating an audio version proves a challenge for Wrighty. He needs to find the voice of a sophisticated, cultured, intelligent, multilingual, French-speaking, 47-year-old eligible bachelor, or at the very least, a male with a French accent. No one in his or the team's combined circles of acquaintances comes close to fitting the bill. So he starts playing around on various language translation websites. Many of these have multiple translation capabilities. Not only can they convert the text of one language into the text of another, but they can also read text aloud.

He cuts and pastes the French text of Remakel's advertisement into a text-to-speech window, then selects 'French male' as the reader. The first result sounds very young and almost flippant. Wrighty repeats the process with a second website, and soon the computer-generated voice of a sophisticated but slightly creepy, middle-aged, French-speaking male emanates from the speakers. It's convincing, if a bit mechanical, and slightly off-putting – sort of how you'd expect a personal ad from the 1990s to sound. It seems to suit the context perfectly. He adds the voice to the audio palette and saves it.

No one is aware then just how often it will be required in future episodes.

CHAPTER 12

Monsieur Remakel

The TLV team drills down on the name M(onsieur) F Remakel. They already know there's no one in Australia with the surname Remakel, apart perhaps from Florabella, so they start looking around the world.

From what they know of the name, they of course focus their attention primarily on Luxembourg. The fact that the personal ad is in French and that the writer claims to be multilingual is one more reason to do so. Luxembourg is bordered by France, Germany and Belgium, and its residents are generally multilingual. There are three official languages: Luxembourgish, French and German. This seems like far too many coincidences for Monsieur F Remakel not to be in Luxembourg.

If the age in the personal ad is correct, then Monsieur Remakel would now be in his early 70s. Is he still alive and well? A quarter of a century has passed since the ad was published. Would he remember it? Would he even *want* to? There's always the possibility that he was looking for an illicit love affair, or perhaps using a fake name to discreetly cover his tracks.

Social media is a good place to start, although people aged 70 and older are far less likely to splash their daily lives across social media, and many people use abbreviations or nicknames on their personal social media accounts. The name Remakel pops up numerous times, particularly on Facebook, but there's no 'F' Remakel in sight, and no photograph resembling a man in the right age group. It doesn't help that so many people use images of their pet or a pretty sunset as their profile picture. If one of the Remakel profiles is linked to the man from the 1994 ad, finding it will require an exhaustive process of elimination. At best, it's an unreliable game of chance, so that line of inquiry is shelved as a last resort.

Eeles follows the name Remakel down a rabbit hole of internet searches. In 2019, at least ten years of the lives of most people under the age of 50 can be traced quite easily thanks to the digitisation of the modern world. Been snapped by a photographer for the social pages? Won an award? Written a review for a business? Chances are it's recorded somewhere online. The digital footprints of people over the age of 70 are generally harder to find, but over time, paper documentation of significance has been scanned and uploaded by government agencies, private companies, professional archive services, sports organisations and amateur history buffs. And so Eeles finds herself scrolling through documents about Luxembourg's national football team in the 1960s. There are a handful of black-and-white photos of various team members from different matches. An F Remakel seems to have played for the team before suffering a career-ending injury.

Not only is this footballer around the same age as the man from the 1994 personal ad, but he was playing soccer at the same time as Johnny Warren. Eeles excitedly shares her discovery with Sandy, only to learn that Sandy's own searches have led her to the same place.

In Sydney, it takes Seymour just a few hours to find F Remakel is listed as a director with two companies in Luxembourg, established in 1991 and 1997. His birthdate, 2 December 1947, means he's also the same age as the man in the personal ad.

The TLV team now considers this man a person of interest. As it stands, there's no real evidence he's connected to the ad or that Marion ever knew him, but it's a possibility they need to explore thoroughly.

The team considers its options. Once they find out this man's contact details, one of them can try to call, email or send a letter, but if he does happen to know something about Marion's whereabouts, then a phone call or a message might be enough to send him into hiding. The best option is to go to Luxembourg with Sally and meet him face to face, but first they need to convince the boss. It's a huge, expensive ask to send a crew to Europe on a hunch, especially during increasingly lean financial times for Australia's free-to-air networks. It's even more of an ask when it's for a podcast, but by now the public's interest in what happened to Marion is apparent.

Sandy emails the head of Seven's news and current affairs, Craig McPherson, adding that Seymour and Marion's daughter Sally could also retrace Marion's movements while they're on the other side of the world. To her surprise, rather than kill the idea, McPherson makes it clear he still needs to be convinced, so Seymour goes to his office.

'You're not going to Luxembourg!' McPherson thunders.

Seymour, nonplussed, flops down in the seat opposite. 'I don't want to go to Luxembourg, believe me,' he says truthfully. He's busy working on two major investigations on top of his daily news duties. This trip will take at least two weeks he doesn't have, but he's certain it's the only way to advance the story.

'How do you even know this guy in Luxembourg is related to the missing woman?' McPherson asks, clearly sceptical.

'Well, he is, I'm certain. There are just over 100 people on the planet with his surname and there's only one person with his initial and his age. That phone number and address for that ad are just 20 minutes from where Marion lived and that name, Remakel, is the name she chose for herself right before she disappeared, claiming she was a housewife in Luxembourg. It will be more incredible if he *isn't* linked to this case somehow and, either way, we'll get material for a dozen stories, all of which you can promote across the network.'

A smile creeps across McPherson's face. Soon after he started at Seven, Seymour realised that, in TV, promos are more important than the stories, and he quickly made it his priority to become proficient in developing them. In his years working with McPherson, he has focused on drawing in big audiences with good teasers.

'You'd better find her,' McPherson says.

Seymour leaves his office before McPherson can change his mind.

Arrangements are made for Seymour, Sally and a camera operator to travel to Luxembourg and England to retrace Marion's last known footsteps, using the postcards she sent home as a guide. The trip will form the basis of several podcast episodes, online articles, videos and TV news reports.

In the meantime, Seymour puts in a call to *Le Courrier Australien*, the newspaper which published the ad in 1994. Sandy now believes the podcast is raising enough questions and concerns to warrant an investigation by the Coroner, even though a coronial inquest being triggered by a podcast would be unprecedented in Australia.

Coroners are a type of judge, independent judicial officeholders who investigate unsolved crimes to determine if someone is alive or dead, how they died and if anyone else was involved in their death. They hold hearings and have the power to compel witnesses to give evidence. At the end of an inquest, the Coroner releases their findings, which may include recommendations to charge a person with a crime. Coroners are a legacy from the United Kingdom, where the office was established in 1194. In the United States, the role is often filled by a medical examiner, a physician who specialises in pathology and forensics.[*]

Any request for an inquest will have to come from Sally, so Sandy sends her a template.

Hi Sal,
So I've found out what we need to do in the application process for a Coronial Inquest, which will force NSW Police to provide reasons why one shouldn't take place.
Sally, in the first instance, would have to email the Coroner.
I've drafted up an email you could send when you have a chance, the sooner the better, (if we aim for Monday

---

[*] 'How is a medical examiner different to a Coroner?', City and County of San Francisco, <sf.gov/information/how-medical-examiner-different-Coroner>.

morning to send), but have also included our lawyer Richard
in this email in case he has any advice.

Your emails are always great Sal, so write it the way you
would normally. My draft is just a guide. But we will get
you to read it for the podcast and we can discuss it in our
next Conversations.

The next day, Sally emails the Coroner of New South Wales,
outlining her mother's case in detail. Sandy follows up with the
Coroner's office almost every week as the investigation continues.

Meanwhile, Seymour and Sandy reach François Vantomme,
the editor of *Le Courrier Australien*, who agrees to join them for
the seventh 'Conversations' episode. François reveals that he and
his business partner bought the brand in 2016, three years earlier,
relaunching the title as an online publication. The newspaper,
based in Sydney, has a long history.

'It was launched in 1892 and is the longest-running foreign-
language newspaper in Australia,' François says. 'It was very
fundamental in uniting the French-speaking community in
Australia and exposing Australians to the best of French culture.'*

Seymour explains why he and Sandy are getting in touch,
recounting the details of the personal ad. 'It might be the only
mention ever, anywhere in Australia, of this name – before our
podcast.'

François has already heard of the podcast and about Sally's
search. 'I have two copies of the edition of 10 December 1994,' he
reveals, 'so if you want to receive one, you can have it, an original
one as well.' François suggests that the names of the people who
worked on each edition were printed in the paper, which may be
helpful for the investigation.

'Can you tell us, the previous owner, are they still alive and did
they keep paper records of who may have placed ads with the old
print version of the newspaper?' Seymour asks.

'We bought it from the widow of the former owner.'

---

* Interview with François Vantomme, *The Lady Vanishes: Conversations*,
no. 7, June 2019.

Seymour seems disappointed. 'Right, so the former owner has passed away?'

'Yes, unfortunately, 2012. The widow is still alive. We still have the details of this lady and we will try to contact her to see if we can do something.'

Sandy then chimes in: 'Back in the '90s, do you have an idea of what the distribution was? Was it just in Sydney?'

'The distribution was in Sydney mainly, but all over Australia and overseas, even Europe.'

Sandy's hopes of perhaps isolating the search to a small geographical zone are dashed. 'Was it a subscription-only back then?'

'There was a subscription. You could pay for a yearly subscription quite cheap, and there was distribution through different libraries. Some big libraries in Australia had it every week or every month in their shop where you could buy it. I think, but I'm not sure, it was between two and five thousand copies.'

That doesn't narrow the search either. Whoever placed the ad may have had a subscription or may have read copies at any of Australia's major public libraries.

Seymour wants to know whether personal ads, for people looking for love, were often published by the newspaper in the past.

'That was quite common. We had a lot of classified ads like that.' François refers to the 10 December 1994 edition of the newspaper: 'I see on the same page you have a lady, 50 years old, who is looking for a partner.'

Seymour had hoped that if such ads were uncommon, then whoever requested it would be more memorable. No such luck.

The conversation ends with François offering to publish an article on Sally's search for Marion, so it can be exposed to a French-speaking audience. And he assures them he will catch up with the widow of the former owner to see whether a paper trail still exists for people who placed classified ads in *Le Courrier Australien* in the 1990s.

It turns out there's a physical archive of *Le Courrier Australien* papers held in the State Library of New South Wales. In the ornate, cavernous reading room, Seymour slowly trawls 17 boxes of paper records: receipts for paper and printing costs, letters to and from subscribers, missives between French Embassy staff and the proprietor, and so on. But he finds precious little paperwork relating to the purchase and placement of personal ads, and nothing linked to the 1994 ad.

The one thread of the investigation that now needs immediate attention is the one tied to Monsieur F Remakel in Luxembourg. He's the only person they have found in the entire world who shares the same rare surname, the same initial, and the same age. Additional research has confirmed he's a perfect match for the suave, educated, high-class man described in the ad. Seymour has also learnt his first name.

Fernand.

CHAPTER 13

England

Undated postcard, 1997

Dear Sal,

Thinking of you as I explored this little shop on my tour
to the historic village of Alfriston. Am feeling much more
relaxed ... The strawberries taste divine and so do the
raspberries.

Lots of love to you both – Mum xx

22 May 2019

It's late at night at Changi airport.

The permanent twilight of the terminal is filled with dim
lighting, disembodied voices and sterile indifference. Sally and
Seymour are waiting at the gate to board their connecting flight
to London. 'This is kind of is weird for me,' Sally says, 'because
I always think to myself if somebody is going to vanish and
never see me ever again that's a lot of effort to pick out a card
that has "Sally's Craft" on it, stick the little sticker on the back
and say, "Oh, thinking of you." So if you were going to vanish,
wouldn't you just go to the local newsagents and pick out a few
touristy postcards and send them? Instead of actually going that
specific?'

It's a simple yet profound point. If the police are to be believed,
Marion had already abandoned her family when she was shopping
for those postcards for her aunts and Sally. Why would she be
browsing for personalised gifts for people she never wanted to see
again?

Soon they're back aboard Qantas Flight 1. Nearly 22 hours after leaving Sydney, Sally and the Seven crew land at Heathrow. They've travelled 17,000 kilometres to retrace the steps Marion took 8000 days ago.

The drive to Royal Tunbridge Wells takes just over an hour. A spa town in the 1600–1700s, it's now a quaint holiday destination with small hotels, cafes and historic sites. At one of these, the Pantiles, a public colonnade through the town centre, Sally meets the original supersleuth, Kristina Panter. They have been corresponding on Facebook for years and hug like old friends.

Kristina, her husband Gavin and their two children lived in Sydney for a few years, but it wasn't until they returned home that Kristina came across the story of Marion Barter. 'I live in the county of Sussex which is in the south of England. I was born here and I grew up here. I saw Sally appear on a Facebook group and that got my attention, firstly because it's a really unusual and intriguing case. And then I saw the Sussex postcard mentioned and I started to look into it a bit more. And of course that has led on to listening to the podcast. And I thought if there was something I could do to look into some things here in the UK, even if it was just making inquiries into the area where Marion visited, I was willing to do that.'

It's less than two months since the podcast launched. Sally, Seymour and the sleuths have been trying, without success, to find out where Marion might have stayed. The Tunbridge Wells Hotel has a lovely outdoor area, perfect for taking tea, inviting the assumption that Marion sat here chatting with the old ladies she mentioned to Sally. The payphones are long gone.

A quick check with the manager reveals there are no records of guests from 1997. So far, everywhere they know that Marion visited has yielded the same result: their records were either not kept or destroyed accidentally; in many cases the establishments have changed hands or closed down.

As they explore the rest of the hotels and alleys, Sally receives an email from a listener, a makeup artist, who has created a new age-progression photo of Marion showing what she might look like now, in her early 70s.

'Oh, that's a great photo, that's much better!' The team has never liked the age-progression image they commissioned from a forensics laboratory in Sydney, which appeared cartoonish.

Cheered, they head to Tonbridge Castle, which they hope might keep visitors' books stretching back to the 1990s. Built in the 13th century, the castle is tiny, its grounds ringed by a wall in various stages of ruin. Sally is excited to hear that several staff members were working there in 1997, but not unexpectedly, none can recall the face in the photograph Sally shows them. There are no visitors' books from the time of Marion's visit either. They offer to post the photo on their Facebook page in the hope of triggering someone's memory.

Sally, Seymour, Kristina and Seven cameraman Paul Walker are soon driving south towards the tiny town of Alfriston. Rain clouds cast a grey pall over Sally and Kristina as they walk around the town centre, and Walker films them, leaving Seymour to park the car. Huge mistake! After failing to find an empty spot on the cobblestone streets, he decides he can reverse into a narrow laneway and confidently backs in. The screech of rock tearing metal probably isn't that bad, he thinks. The long scratch in the Volvo SUV ends up costing several thousand pounds to repair!

The iconic English postbox featured in Marion's postcard is still here. Kristina is yet to hear back from the original owner of Sally's Crafts, a woman named Carol. The current store is closed, but in a happy twist of fate the new owner, Diana, arrives minutes after Sally and lets everyone in.

Sally is overcome as she walks in the steps her mother took 22 years ago. Afterwards, she tells Seymour what she's feeling: 'This is actually Sally's Craft, which is the postcard that mum sent me back in 1997. Diana is an interior designer and that's now become an interior design shop, lots of trinkets and cute, gorgeous things that my mother would love.

'It's actually a nice, comforting feeling for me. I felt very much like Mum was around … like everything in there was her taste, and she loved fabrics ... so it was kinda nice to be in there and know that she's stepped there and it could have been her last steps for all we know – sounds a bit morbid, we don't know ... but I know for a fact she was there and it was nice in there ... I had a good feeling about it.'

A gloomy feature of this trip is the increasing speculation among podcast listeners that Marion took her own life. It's a theory Sally rejects outright. 'She always bounced back ... quite strong, she was always ... I never saw her in a corner crying or even upset for that matter. I never really even remember her being a sad person, except in those last few months when I was going over there and she was telling me about all this crap that was going on at The Southport School.'

At a nearly empty car park at one end of the town, Seymour unpacks his drone to collect video for feature stories. The drone's bird's eye view reveals how relatively remote and isolated this town is. It's hard to imagine Marion driving randomly through the English countryside and landing here without someone guiding her or suggesting it.

Their final stop on this road trip is Brighton, but as they've been going since dawn, they stop for lunch. Sally, Kristina and Seymour then take a short stroll to the Police Station, where Sally is expected. Sally and Kristina go inside and emerge 20 minutes later.

'I just met a ... I'm not sure what his status is, maybe he's a sergeant, his name is Luke, really nice young guy ...' Sally says. 'They've been discussing [the case] this morning and talking about what they can and cannot do. No surprise, they cannot do anything unless Australian police contact them directly and ask for their help ....

'I couldn't leave my DNA and he couldn't take a report or anything unless it's a directive from Australian police. Back to square one, I guess. I said, "At least you know that I'm here to give my DNA and leave it. I find it really difficult that it's such a big deal here, because I literally just walked into Byron Bay Police and they stuck a thing in my mouth and put it in a bag and that was my DNA test. It literally took two minutes ... I'm sitting in your office. Can't you take it? If you need it you can keep it; if you can't use it you can throw it in the bin." But obviously, they have different rules and regulations here, so there's not much to tell. I told him the story about our lead in Luxembourg and he said that's very odd as well.

'When I left, I said my goal would be to get my DNA here so we could run it against any Jane Does and put her on the missing persons list, because there are a lot of elderly people living in these areas who potentially may have sat down and had tea with her. There's every chance someone could recollect seeing her, or speaking to her.'

'But without that inquiry from our police, they're not gonna look, are they?' Seymour asks.

'I, 100 per cent, need the police to step up here, Sally replies.

'Time's up isn't it?'

'What am I supposed to do? She's 73. She could die naturally as well, of old age.' Police in the United Kingdom have long collected DNA samples voluntarily given. Since 2003, they have had the power to collect and keep DNA samples from anyone they arrest even if they are not subsequently charged with a crime.* They have a database of 6.1 million profiles, including half a million from children under the age of 16.** There's no facility under UK law granting police the power to take DNA samples from law-abiding foreign nationals.

When *The Lady Vanishes* podcast launched, the police investigation had been languishing in obscurity for nearly a decade. Officially, the case was still open, but nothing had been done. It was like a farmer leaving the barn door open in the absurd hope that a sheep lost 20 years ago would somehow wander back in.

---

* 'DNA retention by police', Justice, <justice.org.uk/dna-retention-police>.
** *National DNA Database Strategy Board Biennial Report, 2018–2020*, UK Home Office & NPCC, London, 2020, <assets.publishing.service.gov.uk/government/uploads/system/uploads/attachment_data/file/913015/NDNAD_Strategy_Board_AR_2018-2020_print.pdf>.

'You know what, the fact is Gary said it's not even closed, just suspended. Surely it's not hard to unsuspend something, particularly when we have so much evidence that there could be something.'

'Well, we have given them fresh leads,' Seymour says. 'The ball is back in the court of the New South Wales Police. Let's go.' As they jostle along the narrow roads, Seymour checks his emails and shares updates with Sandy back in Brisbane. She has news of her own. They've previously confirmed that the $20,000 Marion transferred to Barclays Bank in London before she went overseas has never been accessed. NSW Police told them that when they checked, the balance had fallen to $14,000.

An officer from Barclays' Personal and Corporate Banking office had just emailed Sandy to say they have no current record of an account in the name Marion Barter or Florabella Remakel. A little more digging reveals that when UK accounts have been inactive for 15 years, the funds may be distributed for the benefit of the wider community, although the right of the customer to reclaim their money is preserved. The TLV team can only assume the money from Marion's dormant account has been transferred to the reclaim fund.

Sandy also plays a voicemail she's received from an officer of the court in New South Wales that ends: 'The Coroner's Court say they will respond directly to Sally and they have that request and they've been talking to Byron Bay Police so the response has been received.'

Seymour is floored. As he listens he feels a sense of inevitability creep over him and he thinks, 'There will be an inquest, there has to be!' They crest a hill and the Atlantic Ocean appears, as does Brighton, England's seaside playground. This once fashionable resort, which has become a party town with a large LGBTIQA+ community, is informally dubbed the 'gay capital of the UK'.*

---

*   Robert Booth & Michael Goodier, 'Why is Rochford England's straightest place and Brighton its gay capital?', *The Guardian*, 7 January 2023, <www.theguardian.com/society/2023/jan/07/why-is-rochford-england-straightest-place-and-brighton-its-gay-capital>.

It was here Marion found the Cat Shop, which has long since been replaced with a small liquor store.

'I wonder what the Cat Shop was exactly,' Sally says. 'Whether it was things for your cat.'

'The lady who ran the shop sold basically everything cats: cushions, ornaments, gifts, trinkets,' says Kristina. 'It was "cat world", basically. She sold these weird cat dolls, basically these cats dressed up wearing clothes and spectacles. It was a strange, bizarre concept for cat lovers. That would've been where Marion [bought] the postcard.'

The shop is closed. Sally peers in the window. 'I'm not sure how long she was here for. Given the trip we just did, it's definitely not all in a day. Alfriston you could do in a short time. You certainly wouldn't do this and then go back to Tunbridge Wells.'

Kristina nods. The trip they've taken today has been a lightning-fast race between known points. Any tourist visiting these same sites would take at least two days, likely several more, to work through the same journey to Brighton. Sally indicates she feels like a tourist on speed and can't imagine her mother covering this territory so quickly.

'It's a big city and there's a lot to see … I would imagine these lanes that are quite popular for tourists, she would have spent some time around these looking at the little shops …'

Kristina alludes to the personal touches Marion applied to messages to people she had, supposedly, put firmly in her past.

'I think in her postcard she literally said "there was this shop and it reminded me of you",' Sally agrees. 'I have a funny feeling it was the postcard she sent to her aunties – they loved their cats. It's fitting that if she would stumble across it, that was a nice thing to send them. Once again, putting a real personal touch and keeping in contact with the family.'

'With that postcard to your aunties and to you from Sally's Crafts centre, it shows that her family was in her thoughts,' Kristina says.

Sally nods. 'And she would send Deirdre a birthday present. You don't do that, in my opinion, if you were planning to disappear. Some people have said that was to buy some time, but why would she have to buy some time? It was in an era where we didn't have computers, we didn't have social media. It wasn't as easy to be found as it is today.'

'Imagine if she hadn't sent the postcards. We wouldn't have very much to go on at all,' Kristina says.

The Cat Shop postcard is postmarked Hastings, another seaside town and fishing port about an hour's drive east of Brighton, and a drawcard for tourists due to the pivotal battle fought nearby in 1066. There are no leads as to what attractions Marion might have visited there.

Her trail turns cold here in Brighton.

Walker films Sally and Kristina walking along the path overlooking the pebble beach as the sun slides towards the sea. Then Sally takes the steps down to the flat round rocks that cover every inch of beach along this coast. She stands alone, the wind whipping her hair, as Walker films her looking across the sea at possibly the same coastline Marion last saw.

She rejoins Kristina near the car as Walker begins packing up his gear. Sally talks about her children.

'D'Arcy is ... 14 so she's not particularly interested in this, and Ella, she's only just becoming invested, because I've tried to protect them for a long time. I don't sit there and think about trying to make it into a tragedy for them because that's not nice ... they're children. They're busy. They're trying to make friends. They're trying to make new relationships, and I don't need them to worry about something they can't control ... I want their lives to be normal. I don't want them to be fearful or stressed.'

As Seymour and Sally walk to the Brighton Palace Pier, the setting sun casts a pale orange glow over the churning English Channel.

'What did it mean coming here, Sally? Going to these places?' Seymour asks.

'Well, it's been an absolute roller-coaster over here ... This is not a holiday. It's a mission like I've never experienced in my life ... It's such a gamble to come and do this sort of stuff. I can say yesterday though ... going to what used to be Sally's Crafts. The lady who now owns that shop, for her to give me a hug and have tears in her eyes and give me her number and say, "Please let me know how you go with your mum" ... that was such a special moment for me, because I'm standing in that shop going, "Holy dooley, this is where my mum was standing!"

'There's speculation she used that passport to come back into the country. There's speculation it was her that took the money out of her account. That's all speculation, not fact. We don't know for sure if her identity was used to do that, but I know for fact that it's her writing on the postcard and I know for fact it was from that place.

'I'm so grateful for that. It's a really special thing for me to be able to do, and I've wanted to do that for a very long time. I didn't know how I was going to do it, because I didn't want to come by myself. I didn't know how I would feel and what would be the case, so the fact I have a team behind me and we are all out there together, that was really awesome.'

Seymour smiles as his eyes well up. 'Okay you're going to make me cry now, I'm gonna stop.'

CHAPTER 14

Luxembourg

'This guy is going to kill us!'

Sally looks at Seymour, eyes wide with terror. He glances at the speedo – 170km/h – then back at the madman in the white SUV terrorising them on Luxembourg's main autobahn. For 15 minutes an erratic driver has been swerving in front of them as cars hurtle past at breakneck speed. Earlier he was tailgating them for several kilometres, despite there being plenty of empty lane space to overtake them. When he finally did, Seymour made the unwise decision to give him the finger, which he's now regretting.

Finally, their tormentor peels away, disappearing ahead of them, causing them both to breathe a sigh of relief. They smile nervously at each other. 'Shit!' Seymour slams on the brakes. The road-rager is standing in the middle of the autobahn, shirtless and waving his arms, his eyes wild, screaming at the top of his lungs. He is trying to play chicken with their car! Seymour slows and manages to weave around him as he beats his fists on the window.

It's been a chaotic first day in Luxembourg. Paul Walker is stuck in London, his camera gear delayed in customs. They rush to reorganise his travel arrangements, only to be told their hire car is unavailable. Seymour finally secures a vehicle so they can race north in the hope of meeting Fernand Remakel face to face, only to find his house empty and locked. On the muted drive back to Luxembourg City, fatigue catches up with them before their drive erupts into a high-speed cat-and-mouse chase with a crazed driver.

Now they can catch their breath and actually take in their surroundings.

Luxembourg is the last grand duchy in the world and one of the smallest countries in Europe. The main airport resembles a regional terminal in Australia. Driving to their hotel, Seymour and Sally are struck by the lack of skyscrapers. The buildings are a jigsaw of quaint old stone structures and more recent glass and steel boxes. It's also the wealthiest country in the world and a tax haven for the uber rich, who rely on the secrecy and privacy embedded in the law for protection. This continually frustrates the team as they try to access even small, mundane pieces of information from authorities.

It also partly explains the unbelievable rivers of cash that flow through this little country locked in land and time. The constitutional monarch, since 2000, Grand Duke Henri, reportedly wields no real power but has a personal fortune of more than $4 billion, making him the richest monarch in Europe by far.

Seymour chooses an historic bridge overlooking the ancient town to film a piece to camera for one of several stories he is filming on this trip. 'It's so beautiful ... for centuries, nations have fought over this tiny European country, so storied in rich history and so removed from Byron Bay and the Gold Coast, where our journey began. And yet our journey has led here because of one thing, a name: Remakel.'

Seymour has been reading about Jean Claude Juncker, the former Prime Minister of Luxembourg who went on to become President of the European Commission. Suddenly, Juncker appears on the street, flanked by security guards, prompting Sally to rush up to him, Walker racing after her with his camera rolling.

The slightly bemused politician is gracious and listens as Sally tells him about her mother and the possibility that she might still be living anonymously in Luxembourg. They part ways both smiling.

For all their straightforwardness and stern manners, Luxembourgers have an appealing sense of humour, best embodied by their homegrown superhero Superjhemp (Superchamp), who looks like an everyday man in a homemade costume and who gets his super powers from eating runny cooked cheese and drinking beers.

Walker finally arrives with all his gear and they immediately head north again, where the house still sits empty. Dejected, they trek back to the city. Seymour, Sally and Walker set about doing all the other things they plan to squeeze into this trip, including checking on another property in the city that belonged to Fernand's deceased mother and that he now owns.

Since early May, Seymour has been exchanging emails with Douwe Miedema, the editor of the largest newspaper in Luxembourg. Douwe was immediately intrigued by Marion's story and agreed to help with the investigation. He has invited Seymour to the newsroom to meet Tom Rüdell, a senior journalist and editor at the *Luxembourg Word*.

The team arrives at 2 Rue Christophe Plantin and pulls into the carpark of a sprawling, three-storey building with full-length windows spanning the corner facing the street. Inside it looks like all newsrooms; open plan, rows of cubicles swamped with papers and files, cables running everywhere and, in the centre, several meeting tables.

After exchanging pleasantries, Douwe and Tom introduce a young reporter named Sarah Cames, who has agreed to act as an interpreter. It was Sarah who emailed them about the Villeroy & Boch Flora Bella china.

Tom has helped Seymour track down addresses and phone numbers for all the Remakels in Luxembourg. They set up cameras and recording devices, while Walker rigs lights and trains the main camera on Sally, Seymour and Sarah, who hover over a telephone ready to start dialling.

Predictably, no one answers: just voicemails for Fernand's sister and her husband.

Seymour dials the next number, expecting another voicemail. *'Hallo?'*

It's Monique Cornelius, Fernand Remakel's ex-wife. The team snaps alert as Seymour begins speaking, hoping she can understand him.

SEYMOUR: Hello Monique, is this Monique?
MONIQUE: *Ja*.
SEYMOUR: My name is Bryan Seymour. I'm a journalist from Australia. I'm here with Sarah Cames. We're looking for Fernand but we're actually looking for Marion, who we believe knew your ex-husband Fernand.

Monique and Fernand divorced nearly 40 years ago. Despite the lapse of time and the language barrier, Monique is gracious and understands Seymour's English. She initially thinks Seymour is referring to Marianne, Fernand's sister.

SEYMOUR: The woman we're looking for is from Australia. Do you know … was your ex-husband ever in Australia?
MONIQUE: I don't know. You're sure it was Marion?
SEYMOUR: Yes, or Florabella, and let me ask you, when did you divorce your ex-husband?
MONIQUE: Oh, mamma mia! When I was 36, now I'm 70. I don't know, Remakel is old now, in his 60s, 70s as well.
SEYMOUR: Was Fernand playing soccer, playing football when you were together?
MONIQUE: Fernand was playing football, yes. He was a good football player.

Monique says she loved Fernand when they were together and he was a good man, but she's understandably coy about sharing any private details of their marriage. She sympathises with Sally's situation and wishes her well.

Encouraged by making a first contact, the team decides to start doorknocking the home addresses they have for various Remakels, with Sarah tagging along to act as interpreter. About three-quarters of the population speak Luxembourgish, a Germanic language. Almost everyone speaks German and French, as half the workforce, about 200,000 people, commute to Belgium, France and Germany. English is rarely spoken by locals.

As with the phone calls, the doorknocks prove fruitless, so the team holds out little hope for the final address. Then a man opens his front door and smiles broadly. A brief buzz of excitement quickly fades as Nico Remakel explains that he's not related to Fernand and has never heard of him. He is apologetic and gracious.

The next day they rise at 3 am to make the long trek north, just in case Fernand is now home but sets out early.

Seymour engaged a private investigator in Luxembourg to track down current information about the man they are looking for. Privacy is paramount in the Grand Duchy, so there is very little in addition to what they have already discovered through online searches and business records.

A seasoned researcher in the Brisbane newsroom, Erina Flessas, found two addresses for Fernand, the most recent from 2010. They can hardly travel halfway around the world in the hope that he is still living there. Crucially, the PI comes back with confirmation; Fernand still owns the city apartment and the investigator is certain this semi-rural home is his current residence.

The countryside is beautiful. Small villages linked by stretches of road cutting through farmland and mountain ranges, over picture perfect rivers and alongside fields of spectacular yellow sunflowers. The team arrives at a modern two-storey building on a large plot of landscaped grass, just outside a small rural town. Again, the house is empty, prompting Seymour to record a video message of their failure so far to find Fernand.

'Well, we know why Fernand Remakel and his partner aren't home. Because a lot of the houses around here are weekenders. Now we were very fortunate to have a young journalist with us from the *Luxembourg Word* (*Luxemburger Wort*), the main daily newspaper here, who was able to check with a couple of neighbours and find out he spends the odd weekend here but lives in the city. Fortunately, we do have an address in the city. We don't know if it's a current one for him. We're going to drive back into Luxembourg now and knock on another door.'

That address turns out to be an apartment being redeveloped, covered in scaffolding and littered with workers' tools.

After another day of disappointment, they take a detour on the drive back to town to visit the Luxembourg Police: 'We've gone in and spoken to a really nice young officer,' Sally says to camera, 'gave him mum's names, the details of her flights coming in and out of Australia, what was on the customs card, the relation to Luxembourg, the relation to the name Remakel. I've asked if I can give them my DNA to run against any Jane Does. He said they can't get any information on that because it's the weekend, so it might be a case that we'll have to try to work that out somehow, if they say yes, to get my DNA to them.'

There's no need to follow up during the working week. Just as in the UK, the police in Luxembourg are polite but apologetic, as they can only respond to an official request from police in Australia, and the TLV team is not sure Australian police are particularly interested in dealing with their counterparts in grand duchies.

Day three begins with the pre-dawn drive, which is taking its toll on everyone's stamina. The team parks across the valley from Fernand's home to watch for any sign of activity. As dawn breaks, they put a radio microphone on Sally and make sure the camera batteries are charged and the equipment is ready. Still there's no movement.

As the sun emerges fully over the horizon, Sally, Sarah and Walker slip out of the car to make phone calls and find a bathroom. Alone inside the vehicle, Seymour keeps watch over the house. They are facing the very real prospect of a wasted journey and he suddenly thinks about what that might mean. He turns his phone video on and begins speaking.

'All right, well, this is a message I didn't want to record. I've come halfway around the world with Sal and … We've confirmed he's here, but there's no one home. It would be cruel if this man, with this name and all the other things, the date of birth, everything … if he was another Fernand Remakel and not the one we were looking for … But for us to come all this way, for it to be him and for him not to be here when Sal's here seems even crueller … If we don't meet him and put Sal in front of him today or on this trip, surely it's only a matter of time before we find out what, if anything, he knows.

'She's been through so much already, I just hate seeing her go through this as well. Although, as she's constantly reminding me, she's been dealing with this shit for 22 years …. Sal's not giving up and neither are we.'

They knock once more but there's no response, so they regroup on the street to film a conversation.

'Okay, Sal, this is the third day we've come to this house. They're still not here. My question is, "Who are the ones who should be here knocking on this door?"'

'Well, if NSW Police had investigated this the way we have, they would have found what we found, and found that there is a really serious connection to this man in Luxembourg, who has the same surname as what my mum changed her name to, who played soccer the same year as Johnny Warren did.'

Dejected, the crew heads back to the city and the newsroom of the *Luxembourg Word*. Without much hope, they decide to call Fernand. A man answers. It's him.

Sarah begins talking with him in Luxembourgish but isn't sure what to ask. Seymour quickly realises that the plan they had rehearsed in case he answers isn't working; they need to be face to face, to show him a photo of Marion and a copy of the personal ad containing his name and birthdate. Sarah ends the call abruptly and the team races to the car.

Nervous, Sally and Sarah tread the familiar path to the front door. This time, when they knock, it opens. Standing there is a tall, thin man wearing glasses. He's well groomed and unhappy to see them.

SALLY: Hello, I'm Sal. Fernand?
FERNAND: *Ja*, what do you want?
SALLY: Nice to meet you. I've come from Australia. Do you understand English?'

FERNAND: *Nee.*
SALLY: Okay.

Unsure whether he understands, Sal motions to Sarah, who begins
interpreting for them both.

> SALLY: So I found an ad that you put in the newspaper
> in Australia in northern NSW back in 1994, and I was
> just wondering if you can tell me how long you were in
> Australia.

Fernand responds in Luxembourgish.

> SARAH: He says he hasn't been. He wants to stop.
> SALLY: So this is my mum. [She shows him a photograph of
> Marion taken just a few years before she disappeared.]
> SARAH: Okay he doesn't want to talk and he says we should
> leave.
> SALLY: Okay, well this is my mum.

Fernand speaks briefly with Sarah then closes the door. While
they're talking, Seymour and Walker see the garage door open
and a woman emerge. She seems to be in her 60s. She looks at
them, and around the corner at Sally and Sarah, then returns
inside.

As the crew consider their next move, Walker notices Fernand
watching them through an upstairs window, sipping tea and
taking photos. Then a police car rolls up the narrow country road
and stops at the driveway.

Two officers emerge, in no hurry, and Sarah explains who the
camera crew is and what they're doing. Then Fernand appears,
walking towards them with his partner, Marie. He shakes hands
with the police then begins talking with Seymour and the group.
The mood is surprisingly friendly and convivial.

'We thought it would be better to appear in person to show
them what we were doing because we couldn't explain it on the

phone,' Seymour explains. 'It's too difficult. We didn't mean to
scare you. We apologise. We didn't mean to do that.'

Marie explains that they've just returned from a holiday in
Belgium. Fernand says he did play soccer when he was younger,
but he never played against Australia and has never heard of
Johnny Warren.

SEYMOUR: Are you the Fernand we're looking for?
FERNAND: That's what logic should already tell you.
I've been with my wife for 40 years. And that [Marion's
disappearance] was 24 years ago. Why would I go to
Australia? To place an ad? To look for a wife, except if I
wanted to emigrate. But I'm not emigrating.
POLICE OFFICER: So were you ever in Australia?
FERNAND: No. I am … that would be illogical. That should
be clear to them now that it has nothing to do with me. And
that woman that came here, her mother, where would I have
hidden her? If I had her?

Sarah asks Fernand if it was possible that he knew Marion from
Australia and that's how she got the name and Luxembourg in
her head, because back then, you couldn't look stuff like that up
on Google. Both Fernand and Marie reply that they were never
in Australia.

SEYMOUR: So do you know Florabella? Florabella Natalia
Marion Remakel?
FERNAND: I've never heard that name. I guess that's her first
name?
SEYMOUR: Never heard that name, okay. So you're
completely …
FERNAND: I don't know that name.
SEYMOUR: Okay. So you're a completely different man who
happens to be the same age as the person in the ad? It's an
amazing coincidence, isn't it?

FERNAND: You have to explain it like you explain it, not like … these two here [Sally and Sarah], tack tack tack, you'd think you're being ambushed by gypsies.

SEYMOUR: One phone call and then we came here, because we didn't know if you were home and we didn't know if you spoke English. But so you're not – it's an amazing coincidence. Yeah well, we didn't know, we thought it might be. We didn't know.

Fernand turns to one of the police officers.

FERNAND: I'm sure you come across a lot of coincidences where you think it can't be and then it is or the other way around?

POLICE OFFICER: It happens, yes.

SEYMOUR: Very few F Remakels in the world, very few. Hardly any. And the same age. Amazing.

FERNAND: I don't understand English.

The group conversation continues for about 30 minutes. At Sally's prompting Sarah asks, 'She wants to know why you didn't shake her hand in the beginning, and why did you close the door right away?'

Fernand responds by describing how Sally should have approached him. 'Shall I tell you what you should have said? Going forward, you should say, "Excuse the disturbance, I hope I'm not intruding. If I could have five minutes of your time, I would like to ask you a question … My name is such and such … I want to ask you something. We are looking for a person … You don't have to answer me … If you want to help us, then do that." That's how you should do it.'

Protocol and respect are of fundamental importance in Luxembourg. They are proud people who do not bend to accommodate the wishes of others, particularly English-speaking visitors. YouTube travel guide Mark Wolters, of Wolters World, says in 'The Don'ts of Luxembourg': 'Don't expect friendly service, don't expect over-the-top service, don't expect helpful service.'*

Seymour gives his contact details to the police and his business card to Fernand should he wish to get in touch. There's some discussion about a bizarre phone call he received a few weeks ago, which Seymour assures him did not come from the team. As they leave, Fernand is walking backwards, smiling and giving them a thumbs-up.

Back in the city, Sally and Seymour find a quiet nook in an alley off William Square to review what has happened.

'You know, I stood there and I was shaking. I put my hand out to shake his hand and I introduced myself and he completely ignored me. He looked at Sarah and he did not look at me the whole entire time I stood at his front door. And when he asked what it was about and I showed him the ad in the newspaper that I have in my hand, he completely ignored any of that. He looked at the photo of my mum and after that he did not look at me again.

'And you know what, in my world, if you're acting like that, you've done something that you shouldn't have. Like, why would you act so odd? If I showed you or a person on the street, you know, talking about my mum being a missing person, most people go, "Oh my gosh I'm so sorry, that's terrible," you know, "That's a horrible situation for you." He didn't have that reaction.

'I feel emotionless. I feel like I have no emotion any more because it's such a stressful thing to do. I don't want people to think I'm some hard-faced woman who doesn't get emotional. Trust me, I get emotional in my own private world. Because I think my face is out there for the entire world to see now, my whole story is out there for the entire world to see now. Let me tell you, that's a daunting thing. It's not something everyone is comfortable doing in the world. I've done it with a purpose – to try and find Mum.'

'So just lastly,' Seymour replies, 'we did what we came here to do, and that's to find the F Remakel we had identified, a man

---

* 'Luxembourg – The Don'ts of Luxembourg', Wolters World, YouTube, 24 April 2021, <www.youtube.com/watch?v=PqTVsP11GJs>.

that age that could have written that ad, that could have met your mother. He's told us a number of things that we could check, and we will check that. At this stage he remains a person of interest to this investigation. We haven't been able to rule him out.'

'No.'

'Where does that leave you as we're about to get onto a plane and fly away from Luxembourg. Are you satisfied?'

'Yeah, I am. You know why? We have him on record saying particular things, and we can check these particular things with the help of the NSW Police ... I need their help with this. They do a simple check that should take a couple of days, nothing more, and if the information we have proves to be facts, he's done. That's it.'

Seymour and Sandy email Detective Senior Constable Gary Sheehan, apprising him of the trip and the need to follow up with Luxembourg police. His response is disheartening, if predictable, indicating that his hands are tied, 'due to legislative and organisational constraints'.

Walking back to the hotel, Seymour gazes upon a bronze statue of William II astride a horse. King of the Netherlands and the Grand Duke of Luxembourg in the 1840s, he had earlier enlisted in the British Army and was wounded at the Battle of Waterloo. Apparently a bisexual who was frequently blackmailed by his enemies, this father of five lived a secret life and spent much of his time in Luxembourg, Belgium and the United Kingdom.

Little does Seymour know just how much this king had in common with the man they're looking for.

CHAPTER 15

Missing, at Last

It's proving difficult to find a person who isn't missing.

Since arriving back in Australia, Seymour has been sending Fernand Remakel detailed questions.

An anonymous tipster has reached out with some extraordinary claims. Writing in German, she says: 'I was still very young when I met Fernand Remakel in a professional context … He came from a wealthy family that supported him financially. Shortly after our first meeting we became a couple.'

The tipster doesn't give her name, but includes information suggesting she does know Fernand Remakel. 'I was his adviser on certain issues … I believed everything [he said] because I was seduced by his charm and his worldly lifestyle. I maintain – and I also experienced – that apart from using his charm and worldly behaviour, he optimised his psychological knowledge in order to manipulate other people …

'I could not believe I was taken in by a man who only used me to achieve his intended career goal … I listened to the podcast where Fernand Remakel was asked questions – I also speak Luxembourgish – and clearly recognised his voice. When I was with him … he spoke fluent English.'

The team again approaches Gary Sheehan, asking if he has searched exhaustively for any mention of the Remakel name in official records that can only be accessed by police. The response is a curt 'the investigation is ongoing' with no further information.

A major blockage to any breakthrough is the absence of Marion Barter from the National Missing Persons Register – the place where anyone with information can check if a case is that of a missing person and then act. The fact that Marion has never been on the register is an enduring disgrace.

At Sandy and Seymour's urging, Sally starts a petition on Change.org on 4 June 2019. After introducing herself and giving an outline of Marion's case, she writes:

> After years of fighting, she was placed on the NSW missing persons list. But just four years later NSW police removed her from the list and nobody can tell me why.
>
> I believe NSW police have a lot to answer for: why did they remove my mother from the missing person list? Why is there no record of the police searching for her in her last known locations?
>
> This is not just about my mother's case – this is about the justice of due course and a proper investigation for every missing person and everyone who's lost someone they love.
>
> For so many years I felt like I had to fight this battle alone. Now, I'm turning to ordinary people like you to help me to find my mother, so that I can finally find her or find closure.
>
> Channel 7 have made a podcast about my missing mother's case – you can listen to it by searching for *The Lady Vanishes* and find out more information.
>
> Thank you for supporting me.*

The response is immediate and overwhelming. Petitions generally garner a few hundred signatures at most: Sally's quickly grows into the thousands. That's in part due to listener Jennifer Marsh, who promoted the petition on the TLV Facebook page, and Sally Rugg, the executive director at Change.org, who uses all the tools at her disposal to maximise coverage: 'I wanted to let you know that my team and I are looking to put our time into pushing Sally's petition to re-list Marion on the missing persons register.'**

With their help, Sally surpasses her target of 25,000 signatures.

---

* Sally Leydon, 'NSW POLICE: please find my mother, Marion Barter', Change.org, 4 June 2019, <https://www.change.org/p/nsw-police-please-find-my-mother-marion-barter?source_location=search>.

** Email from Sally Rugg, executive director, Change.org, 1 July 2019.

So it's with great excitement that, just over a month later, the team reads an email sent by Shaun Fewings from NSW Police Media:

> A police review of the investigation into the whereabouts
> of a Queensland teacher has determined that information
> will be forwarded to the Coroner and the case reinstated as a
> Missing Person case.
>
> Despite exhaustive inquiries in Australia and overseas,
> detectives from the Tweed/Byron Police District have been
> unable to determine her whereabouts.
>
> As part of the review, it was recommended Ms Barter
> be reinstated on the national register owing to the unique
> circumstances of this case.*

Marion is not being *reinstated* on the national register, as she was never on it. She was only ever on the New South Wales missing persons list from 2007 to 2011. She will now be on the AFP Missing Persons Register. In addition, NSW Police are finally reopening the investigation into her disappearance and referring the case to the NSW Coroner. It's the first major hurdle cleared by the podcast team, just four months after the first episode aired. And, if a coronial inquest does go ahead, Sally will finally be able to access all of the documents she has been fighting for, and witnesses found by the team can be compelled to give evidence.

Sally Leydon is overcome. 'I'm quite elated ... you know, I have a tear in my ... it's a big sigh of relief. My hair is standing on my head and I have goosebumps all over my body ... Oh my gosh ... words aren't enough to express my gratitude for all the people who take time out of their day to worry about me, worry about Mum, have an idea. That's why I work so tirelessly trying to answer everybody's questions. It takes me hours to do that, but I'm more than happy to because I understand these people are taking time out of their busy lives to help me as well, and I'm forever grateful, I really am. I know even if my mum is alive and well and we find her, I'm sure she could appreciate the situation

---

* Email from Shaun Fewings, NSW Police Media Unit, 28 July 2019.

I've been in, and I think that she would be very happy to know that people have really got behind me.'

NSW Police confirms it's 'seeking advice' from the State Coroner to determine whether it has the jurisdiction to 'further its extensive efforts to find the Gold Coast woman'. This seems a face-saving way for police to admit they dropped the ball on this case for years and are only now taking it very seriously.

The first inkling of change comes a few days later, when police visit Sally at her home in Brisbane. Detective Inspector Glen Browne takes possession of Marion's old ballet slippers. If forensics can get some of Marion's DNA from the slippers, they can test it against unidentified bones held by police, including bones found in 2005 at Wallsend near Newcastle, north of Sydney. They can also add Marion's DNA to the National Criminal Investigation DNA Database (NCIDD), which will allow investigators to quickly check her genetic material against any new evidence that turns up or is collected from crime scenes, using integrated forensic analysis.

Detective Sergeant Rachel Lenaz emails Sally to asks if it's okay for the laboratory to destroy the slippers as part of the DNA extraction attempt. Sally says yes. Lenaz also confirms that Sally's DNA is being run against all unidentified bodies and human remains in New South Wales, though this is taking some time. It seems incredible that this wasn't done much earlier, but as Marion wasn't officially missing, there was no need for police to waste time on DNA testing.

The delay in trying to collect Marion's DNA is costly. It's been too long since Marion wore the slippers for forensics to retrieve any genetic material. To rub salt into Sally's wounds, the AFP Missing Persons Register publishes Marion's details as 'Florabella Natalia Marion (AKA Marion) REMAKEL (AKA BARTER)'. The AFP confirms they received the data from NSW Police. Sally requests they change it to 'Marion BARTER AKA Florabella Natalia Marion REMAKEL'.

She also points out a raft of errors in the listing: that Marion was dropped off by her neighbour Lesley Loveday at a bus stop in Surfers Paradise (it was Southport); that 1 July was the date she last spoke to Sally on the phone (it was 1 August); and that there's a 'freckle under right eye' (the spot is actually *in* her eye, in the iris, under her pupil).

One of the most satisfying things to emerge from the decision to list Marion as missing is that police confirm they have never spoken to, let alone sighted, Marion Barter.

A surprising detail in the email from NSW Police is that they have referred material to the Coroner. Police confirm that officers from the Homicide Squad and the Department of Communities and Justice have conducted a review of the case, meeting with Gary Sheehan to go through his investigation in detail. Furthermore, detectives are preparing a comprehensive summary of the case for the Coroner, who has expressed an interest in the matter. A coronial inquest seems inevitable.

There have now been four million downloads of the podcast, with the bulk of listeners spread across Australia, North America and Europe. Marion's story is connecting people across the globe. A listener from Los Angeles sends a tip via the anonymous website with photos of the 1992–93 Luxembourg phone book entries for Remakel.*

The pages reveal a new address for Fernand Remakel, an office in a nondescript, six-storey building in Luxembourg City. A search of tenants reveals two have been there since 1983: a travel agency and another small business. Today it has a bank branch at street level, and a cafe, but is otherwise unremarkable. Maybe it once housed a telephone exchange, or a mail-forwarding service, thus explaining how someone in Luxembourg could manage a phone line and post-office box while living in Australia. Or perhaps it's a dead end.

Reinvigorated, the team launch into chasing the numerous leads that pour in daily. The intense, daily fact-checking that forms 90 per cent of the work falls primarily to Sandy, Seymour and Eeles, with help from the supersleuths.

---

* Email from listener, 12 November 2019.

Among the genuine leads are a plethora of conspiracy theories pursued by members of the public, some of whom seem sure they have cracked the case. Then there are the sightings:

Between 2014 and 2015 I believe I saw this woman. During that time I saw her picture and story on the Australian missing persons Facebook page. I am aware she was never officially on a register but she was featured on the Facebook page which I believe is run by a civilian. I worked at a pub in ██████ which is not far from ██████ which is located in NSW. My co-workers and I 100% believe this was her. At the time I showed them a photo of her on the Facebook page and they were all in agreeance this woman was her or looked shockingly similar. I remember she was with a male and seemed very quiet and reserved almost like she was scared of him. At the time I saw this but just thought they could have had an argument and maybe that was why her behaviour and body language was like that. I did at that time go back to the Facebook post and saw a few people had said they thought they saw her in ██████ Area which I couldn't believe when I saw that it made me 100% feel strongly that this was the woman who came into my workplace. I messaged Sally at that time but felt like she wasn't interested in that theory or lead. So I let it go all these years until now it's in the media again. It's hard for me to accept that Sally was not interested in this sighting and I just know it had to be her. I don't think she wants to be found. I can imagine Sally probably gets a lot of time-wasters with made up sightings or theories so understandable that she may not have taken it too seriously.*

Seymour checks with Sally, who doesn't recall hearing about this lead but says her mum would never have gone into a pub. Seymour contacts all the pubs in the area where the tipster works, but none of the staff are familiar with the case. He adds a trip to the area to the to-do list, but it proves a dead end.

---

* Email from listener (redacted for privacy), 4 July 2019.

Another tipster claims they have not only sighted Marion, but spoken with her in her home.

> I am writing to … advise … of a possible sighting of Marion in ███████████ exactly one week ago.
>
> I attended a woman's apartment to buy a kitten she had advertised on Gumtree. I spoke with her inside for approximately 10–15 mins. I had also had a long conversation on the phone with her the previous night.
>
> Yesterday morning a cousin shared a missing person post of Marion on Facebook, the resemblance was striking. I feel quite positive that it's the same woman, as does my 6yr old daughter. She was wearing tinted reading glasses, which I also noticed around Marion's neck in one of the photos provided. So many of the details align.
>
> She asked me if I'd like to look through some of the many boxes of clothing she makes and sells … seeming a bit desperate for the company. I was picking up a strange feeling from her. She told me she'd been diagnosed with cancer and was downsizing (from 5 cats to 3) to be able to cope. During our phone call the previous night she mentioned she'd been a vegetarian and had kept a healthy diet, being surprised about her diagnosis. She also mentioned that she owns two places, the apartment I was in and a property in ███████████. She had two mobile numbers, which she didn't answer, only replied by text with one.[*]

Sally tells Seymour her mother hated cats, but maybe that's changed. He quickly locates records on the property, and then an individual. The only way to be certain is to knock on the door, but it's a six-hour drive from Sydney so he waits until he's reporting on a story close by. Cats scatter as he approaches the door. A tense moment follows a polite knock, followed by the mildly deflating realisation that the woman standing before him is not Marion.

---

[*] Email from listener (redacted for privacy), 6 August 2020.

Another tip to Sally claims a person with the surname Remakel is working at a shop on the Gold Coast. That too is a bust. A man reaches out to say he was in a pathology clinic when he heard the name 'Florabella' called. Seymour calls him and he recounts how he saw a woman, aged about 75 to 80, about five feet nine inches tall and wearing a bandana and loose-fitting dress and pants. He didn't see her hair and she was not wearing glasses. The websleuths quickly identify a woman with that first name living in the area around the pathology clinic. She passed away in 2016.

Seymour knocks on another three doors, the homes of women sighted by listeners, without luck.

One Sunday, Seymour receives an anonymous tip.

> I have never been one to forget a face and Marion bears an uncanny resemblance to a teacher who taught me grade 4 in the year of 1997 at ███████████ in ███████████, Sydney. I attended the school briefly from June 1997 until December 1997. I recall her wearing large reading glasses and I remember her telling the class she had a baby boy at home and I recall being shocked (from a 9-year-old girl's perspective), and not fully convinced she really was a mum to a baby. I can't begin to try and remember her name. I'm not sure of the appropriate steps required to do so, but it could be worth trying to find out the name/names of the teachers that taught grade 4 students in 1997 at the school.*

The tipster provides an email address and Seymour wastes no time writing to her. She's adamant her teacher was the spitting image of Marion, but she doesn't have a photo.

Seymour drives two hours to the school and enlists the aid of a teacher to locate an archived copy of the 1997 school yearbook. He turns to a page featuring a class of children with their female teacher. She's a middle-aged brunette wearing a demure, floral-print dress and smiling thinly at the camera. Seymour does a double-take.

Close. But it's not Marion Barter.

---

* Email from listener (redacted for privacy), 7 July 2019.

CHAPTER 16

Police Trial

CAS8068

New South Wales Police Force
COPS

Tweed/byron

Case Report - C 31087950

Case Title   : MISSING PERSON - MARION B Case Status : SUSPENDED
Case Type   : MISSING PERSON
OIC   : Not Allocated
Follow Op Freq. : 28   DAYS
Security Level   : FOUO
Source Reports : E 6126286   - OCCURRENCE ONLY
                                    MISSING PERSON
                                    FORENSIC PROCEDURE
Party   : BARTER, MARION   - PERSON OF INTEREST

Case Narr :   C 31087950

T1(f), T3(x), T3(b)

T1(f)   on 7 December 2011
Sally LEYDON, the daughter of BARTER, was
informed of the decision made by the Missing Person
Unit. .
This matter is to be suspended.

Case Narr :   C 31087950
                              T1(f)

So much for a picture paints a thousand words.

The screenshot above is from the heavily redacted file of the police investigation into Marion Barter's disappearance.* Some pages are completely blank apart from the page titles. What little is included is telling: 'Case Status: SUSPENDED'.

The officer in charge, Detective Senior Constable Gary Sheehan, has told the team that the investigation was never shut down and remains active. But this document reveals that he decided to suspend the investigation on 7 December 2011. In an internal memorandum, Sheehan outlined his reasons: 'the evidence available to me strongly suggested that BARTER was not a missing person but had assumed a new identity immediately prior to her being reported missing.'** A series of bullet points, possibly the 'evidence available' to Sheehan, is blacked out.

What else might the police file reveal about the investigation? There's only one way to find out.

2019

'Hi Bryan, don't freak out, but we're taking legal action against the police.'

Sandy is telling Seymour about an external review process via the NSW Civil and Administrative Tribunal (NCAT), because NSW Police won't provide a less redacted copy of their Marion Barter file. After 30 years of FOI applications, Sandy has a good idea of what information should be made available, but also that agencies are usually reluctant to comply. She picks her battles, and this is definitely one worth waging. Not only was the application made by the missing person's next of kin, Sally, but the Information and Privacy Commission (IPC) has backed Sandy's judgement.

Within weeks, the Seven Network has engaged lawyers for Sally and team to make submissions to NCAT. The police also make a submission, and so does the IPC:

---

* Government Information Public Access (GIPA) Notice of Decision, 17 October 2018.
** Detective Senior Constable Gary Sheehan, Memorandum, 22 September 2011.

At common law, a person is presumed dead where the person
has not been heard of for seven years by persons who would
expect to hear from the person if the person were alive. If
a decision-maker finds, infers, or is bound to presume that
an individual whose personal information could reasonably
be expected to be disclosed is deceased, the decision-maker
must weigh the public interest considerations accordingly. If
consultation is required concerning the release of personal
information about a deceased person, that consultation
is to be done by consultation with 'a close relative of the
deceased'.*

The IPC is not a party to this legal action, but it does manage the
process for FOI – or the Government Information Public Access
(GIPA), as it's known in New South Wales. So it's encouraging
that it suggests police could have referred Marion's case to the
Coroner anytime since 2004, but chose not to.

In their submissions to NCAT, NSW Police argue against
granting full access to their file on Marion. Acting Commander
of the NSW Police Force, Chief Inspector Steven White, says he's
deeply concerned that if journalists and the public have access to
the police file, they will aid people trying to disappear: a person
armed with this knowledge could adopt measures designed to
avoid detection and subvert a police investigation into their
disappearance'.** This seems, to Seymour, an odd argument as the
methods police used to search for Marion Barter have failed to
produce any useful investigative outcomes; so how would their
disclosure help someone 'avoid detection'?

Perhaps the most difficult argument to swallow is the apparent
concern police have for Marion Barter's human rights: 'the missing
person has the same right to privacy as any other individual …
Although much of Ms Barter's personal information would be
apparent to the applicant, I believe Ms Barter has the right to

---

* Submissions of the Information Commissioner, Information and Privacy
  Commission (IPC), 20 June 2019.
** Affidavit of Steven White to NSW Civil and Administration Tribunal
  (NCAT), 29 May 2019

ensure her personal information is not revealed to the public through the current proceedings.' But this assumes that Marion may be alive rather than the victim of foul play. It's precisely the kind of thinking that led to a decade of inaction.

The strongest argument that the police have is that the file must remain undisclosed because the investigation is ongoing. But that investigation was wrongly designated from the beginning, ignored for ten years, then suspended in 2011.

Having guided Sally through the external review process, Sandy is confident that Seven's legal team of Richard Keegan and barrister Rico Jedrzejczyk (pronounced *Yen-jay-chik*), will gain access to Marion's file*

In the days leading up to the hearing, the team is too busy investigating to worry about the NCAT case. Seymour emails Sandy about leads he's chasing, including a claim from a Sydney Airport contact that they have CCTV footage of arrivals from 1994 onwards. Unfortunately, this turns out to be untrue. There's no video evidence of Marion returning to Australia.

On 24 June 2019, they front up at NCAT on Goulburn Street in Sydney's CBD, close to the AFP building. It's like a streamlined court. Instead of a judge, there's a tribunal member presiding. Lawyers for opposing parties present their cases and answer questions from the tribunal member. To add to the confusion, the tribunal member for this case, John McAteer, is to be referred to as Senior Member. In addition to lawyers, Jedrzejczyk and Keegan, the tribunal will hear from those representing NSW Police and the Information Commissioner.

The hearing quickly gets underway. It's up to the lawyers representing the Commissioner of Police, who is responsible for denying access to Marion's case file, to prove it's the correct decision.

Jedrzejczyk's command of the brief is immediately apparent, and his sharp and measured approach reflects his confidence. Jedrzejczyk outlines why releasing the file is in the public interest

---

* SC stands for Special Counsel, aka a silk (and in the UK called King's Counsel or KC). They are 'barristers of seniority and eminence'. See 'What is a barrister?', Australian Bar Association, <austbar.asn.au/for-the-community/what-is-a-barrister>.

and points out several instances in the redacted file where police question the thoroughness of their own investigation.

He then reads aloud Gary Sheehan's memorandum, where he states that, 'the evidence available to me strongly suggested that BARTER was not a missing person'.

> JEDRZEJCZYK: You'll see then that there are a series of bullet points. The first is partially released but the rest of the first bullet point is redacted. Beyond that all the bullet points are redacted other than part of the second-last bullet point on page 2.
> SENIOR MEMBER: The first part that was released was clearly known to people close to her. They're factual matters.
> JEDRZEJCZYK: Indeed.
> SENIOR MEMBER: Some of that is public record, such as going overseas.
> JEDRZEJCZYK: Yes, it is. And the reason that I wanted to take you to this document, Senior Member, is that given the context that is referred to here, the key points behind the police coming to the conclusion that Ms Barter was not genuinely a missing person. We say that the information set out in those bullet points – we obviously don't know what it is, but that really goes to the heart of this application.
> SENIOR MEMBER: In some ways if your client had that information, it might summarise the basis of the police decision in November/December 2011.
> JEDRZEJCZYK: Absolutely. That's certainly our case.*

Next, NSW Police Acting Commissioner Steven White takes the stand. He was the acting commander responsible for the Missing Persons Unit when he provided two affidavits for these proceedings.

> JEDRZEJCZYK: Now it's the case, isn't it, Commander White, that the investigation into Ms Barter's disappearance commenced in around October 1997?

---

* NCAT hearing transcript, 24 June 2019.

WHITE: It was around 1997, yes.

JEDRZEJCZYK: And you're aware that the applicant in this case, Ms Sally Leydon, you're aware that she's the daughter of Marion Barter?

WHITE: Yes, I am aware of that.

JEDRZEJCZYK: And you're aware that Ms Leydon has been in regular communication with the NSW Police Force throughout the course of that investigation?

WHITE: Yes.

JEDRZEJCZYK: And you're aware that in some of her communications with police, Ms Leydon has expressed some concerns about the manner in which the investigation has been conducted?

WHITE: I personally haven't received, seen any of those concerns, but that might be a matter for Ms Leydon and the investigating officers.

JEDRZEJCZYK: I see, but do you yourself have some understanding that Ms Leydon has concerns about the conduct of this investigation?

WHITE: I can only give evidence on what I've read in the case file and the COPS [Core Operational Policing System] event, and the documents that are before the tribunal today.

JEDRZEJCZYK: Yes, and have any of those materials given way to any understanding on your part that Ms Leydon has some concerns about the matter in which the investigation has been conducted?

WHITE: I don't see any material in those documents that she's expressed concern. I understand that this hearing today is because of matters in order to gather further information in relation to her mother.

JEDRZEJCZYK: If I can perhaps be a bit more specific. Have any of the materials that you've reviewed given you an understanding that Ms Leydon did not agree with the decision made by the police force to suspend the investigation into her mother's disappearance?

WHITE: I don't recall reading any of those materials in the documents. I might point out that I'm not the investigating officer in relation to this matter.

JEDRZEJCZYK: Yes, I appreciate that. But nonetheless, sitting here today, do you have an understanding that Ms Leydon did not agree with the decision that was taken to suspend the investigation?

WHITE: I didn't see any of that in the materials that I read.

JEDRZEJCZYK: So is the answer that you don't have that understanding?

WHITE: It may be … I don't know that because I didn't read that in the material that I've read.

That one exchange sums up much of the dealings with police in this case. Jedrzejczyk, undeterred, launches into the reasons given by Detective Senior Constable Sheehan to recommend removing the missing person status of Marion Barter:

JEDRZEJCZYK: It says …

Having read the attached file, I am of the opinion that:

1. The intensive investigation by police indicates the missing person Barter has, by choice, changed her name and left her family.
2. The family have apparently accepted that the missing person has voluntarily estranged herself from them.
3. There are no fears held for the safety of the missing person.

Based on these points, I approve the removal of the missing persons status from this file and that it should be recorded as an occurrence only.

You see those words?

WHITE: Yes.

JEDRZEJCZYK: So having read that document, Commander White, you'd agree that at least insofar as this investigation is concerned, and the investigation into Ms Barter's

disappearance, it was the case that the local area command
forwarded the file to the MPU [Missing Persons Unit]
and asked the MPU to make a decision about whether the
investigation should continue. You'd agree with that?
WHITE: That's what they've asked for, yes.
JEDRZEJCZYK: Yes, and in fact that's what was done,
wasn't it?
WHITE: Well, the missing person was removed from the
Missing Persons Register.

This is crucial. Commander White has stated in his affidavit
that police are undertaking further investigations into Marion's
disappearance, yet Sally has consistently been told by police
there's nothing they can do because they don't think Marion is
missing. Now, though, Commander White tells the hearing that
he is aware of fresh police work on the case.

JEDRZEJCZYK: Can I take you to paragraph 5 of that same
affidavit please, Commander White? You say:
I gave evidence that I was aware that the officer that was in
charge of the investigation had continued his investigation
and inquiries into Ms Barter's disappearance. The reason that
I was aware of that was because I had received the COPS
case file relating to Ms Barter's disappearance and observed
that additional entries had been made on the file. I had also
observed that the case recorded on COPS was now active,
having had further entries from January 2019.
    You can see that evidence written there.
WHITE: Yes.
JEDRZEJCZYK: So the COPS entries that you were referring
to in that paragraph were made in January 2019. That's
correct, isn't it?
WHITE: There are a number of entries commencing January
2019.
JEDRZEJCZYK: Yes, and those entries on the case file, which
were recorded in January 2019, they were on the file when

you signed your first affidavit on 29 May 2019, weren't they?
WHITE: Yes.

January 2019. That's three months *after* the team began working
on *The Lady Vanishes* and contacted police for information, and
two months before Seymour interviewed Gary Sheehan. This
appears to confirm police didn't continue their investigation after
2011, but only reopened it when the TLV team started asking
questions.

JEDRZEJCZYK: Can I ask you, is the officer in charge of the
investigation a Detective Sheehan?
WHITE: He is, yes.
JEDRZEJCZYK: But I take it that you yourself have not
spoken with Mr Sheehan in relation to the activities that he's
been conducting?
WHITE: No, I've never spoken to Mr Sheehan.
JEDRZEJCZYK: So when you say in your affidavit 'the officer
in charge is taking further investigative steps when his work
priorities permit him to do so', you actually have no way of
knowing that, do you?
WHITE: I know that from my general knowledge of police
work, and the officer in charge would not only have this
matter to work on. He'd have a number, and he'd be
working on it concurrently.

The hearing then enters a confidential session. Only solicitors
for the police and the Senior Member are allowed in the room as
they consider the very information Sally and the team are seeking
to access. Several months later, NCAT rules in favour of Sally
Leydon and TLV. But the documents the police hand over remain
too heavily redacted to be of any real use.

Seymour emails Sandy a screenshot of the 'documents' with
the caption 'What a sad joke …'

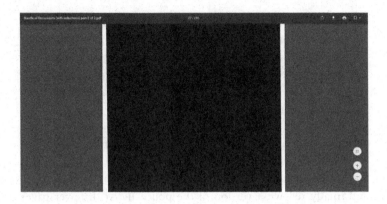

So it's back to NCAT for another round.

It's clear police are now fed up with pesky journalists asking difficult questions. The arguments they make against disclosing any further information pull no punches: 'There are also instances where *witnesses have declined to assist* on the basis of prior interaction with journalists from the podcast.'

NSW Police doesn't say who has declined to assist. And in any case, officers had 22 years before the podcast to approach or speak with anyone they thought might be connected with Marion's case.

> Secondly, as the investigation remains ongoing, it is unclear whether any offences have been committed. The disclosure of this information could alert any potential offenders to what the NSWPF already knows about this case, which could in turn enable them to avoid detection of their involvement in a disappearance and/or to subvert police inquiries into criminal conduct.

Suddenly police are worried that a potential offender may escape capture, despite their repeated claim from the outset that there is no offender, only Marion acting alone.

> I am also concerned that the credibility of witnesses may be undermined, should relevant information be disclosed by

'The Lady Vanishes Podcast' to the public at large or should a
witness be contacted by journalists conducting investigations
for the purpose of the podcast. The credibility of a witness
can be affected where multiple statements are provided, and
inconsistencies arise. The potential of contamination may
also impact on a witness' credibility.

Sandy, Seymour and Eeles have decades of experience reporting
on homicide and missing persons cases and feel these concerns
are unfounded and just plain wrong. They win again in NCAT,
and finally receive a version of the police file with fewer pages
blacked out.

Episode 17 of *The Lady Vanishes* analyses the results. 'Thanks
to the released documents, we now have a much more descriptive
case file, which reveals in part the extent of the investigation and
clears up some of the past anomalies we've been trying to grapple
with,' Sandy says.

They show four periods of activity on the case: 'Firstly, in 1997
when Sally first reported Marion missing. Then in 2007, when
Sally went back to police because ten years had gone by and there
was still nothing from her mother. It was at this time Marion
was finally referred to the Missing Persons Unit … and put on
the NSW Missing Persons Register. In 2009, and then again in
2011, when significant pressure was placed back on Byron Bay
detectives to clear the matter up.

'It's important to note that the police file is also riddled with
errors, and not just minor typos. Marion's name is frequently
incorrect. Several times, they've listed her former surname
as Smith instead of Brown. There's also WILSIN, BAXTER,
BARTOR, BAFRTER, RENKEL and MAJAN. And at one
stage, they even confused her gender, calling her Warren Barter.

'These wrong names weren't inconsequential. They were
often the basis of proof-of-life searches to financial institutions
and government agencies.'

The case file also includes internal police emails that suggest
another reason Marion was removed as the face of Missing

Persons Week in 2007: 'In that particular year, their focus was to be on persons going missing who suffered some form of mental illness … it appears as though not enough thorough checks were made on the missing person, and she did not in fact suffer from any officially diagnosed mental illness. It turned out the [sic] it was only the opinion of family members that she was mentally ill at the time of her disappearance. In order to save the credibility of the campaign for that year, the decision was made not to use this particular matter in the media campaign.'

It wasn't until 2007 that proof-of-life checks even started to be undertaken in relation to Marion. This email from Senior Constable Steve McAlister of the NSW Missing Person Unit is dated 10 July 2007:

Barry, I've had our end dumped on my desk. I read the comments on your case. It's not that she hasn't renewed her driver's licence, she actually surrendered her licence – reason she moved interstate. I have sent off a request to Queensland to have their RTA records checked.

Next time you're on dayshift on a weekday, can you give me a call and we can discuss this and try and clear it up quick. Steve.

But it wasn't cleared up quickly. According to the case file, Lyndal Barker, director of the Salvation Army Family Tracing Unit, forwarded to NSW Police 'all documents held by the organisation that relate to their attempts to locate BARTER' in 1997, and again in 2003:

The documents show applications made by Sally LEYDON and her grandfather John WILSON, but do not show any of the individual inquiries that were made with what agencies. There is an email from the UK branch of the Salvation Army that explains their searches for Marion (whatever they may have been) were not successful.

The documents state that on 13 May 2010, NSW Police spoke with Lyndal Barker about the suggestion the Salvation Army may have located Marion. Ms Barker responds that according to all records available to her there's 'nothing to suggest that was the case'.

The case file continues: 'Check on COPS made, and only information that has been attached to this case is an information report in relation to Crime Stoppers file, which may or may not relate to the Missing Person.' This appears to be referring to the tip-off that Marion was buried in Armidale. There's confusion over the amount of time and resources involved in the unsuccessful search. The file shows only one day of searching with one cadaver detection dog. Investigations continued at a steady pace, but the situation changed on 30 March 2011, when Sergeant Julie Dean from the Missing Persons Unit's Operation Firenze wrote to the Tweed/Byron Local Area Command:

> Section 35 of the Coroners Act, 2009 states, Police have an 'Obligation to report a death or suspected death'. Once satisfied that no further enquiries can be made as to whether a missing person is living or not, the officer in charge of the investigation must report the matter to the Coroner. Depending on the circumstances, this should occur as soon as the investigator is of the belief that the missing person is now deceased, and in any case after 12 months has elapsed.
>
> The Missing Persons Unit is now requesting that a P79B form be submitted via email to the #MPU and to the State Coroner for the above matter or advise why this course of action cannot occur. If this is the case, the original event is required to be updated accordingly.

This email is particularly important, as it shows Marion's case isn't isolated. She's among a significant number of long-term missing people whose investigations haven't been handled properly.

Despite this call to action, Marion's case remains in limbo. But it did appear to trigger a flurry of activity. Several proof-of-life checks were made with financial institutions, government agencies and other police.

Then a breakthrough: Marion's name change. On 5 May 2011, Gary Sheehan advises Sergeant Cath Borton from the Missing Persons Unit, describing it as a 'fair discovery'.

An email from Sheehan dated 22 September the same year gives five reasons why he strongly believes Barter is not a missing person:

1. In 1997, BARTER made a decision to travel overseas. She resigned from her teaching job, sold the family home and informed her daughter that she was going to go to England for an indefinite period of time during which she may seek some teaching work. Records held by the Department of Immigration show that BARTER left Brisbane Airport on 22 June 1997 on Korean Air flight No. 814 to Japan, after which she continued to London.

2. Records held by the Department of Foreign Affairs and Trade show that BARTER made an application for a new Australian Passport on 20 May 1997. This application was in the name of Florabella Natalia Marion REMAKEL, born 3/10/1945, and indicated on the application form that BARTER had changed her name by deed poll, although it did not show in which state or territory or on what date it was changed.

3. Further checks with the Department of Immigration show that on 22 June 1997 when BARTER left Australia, she was travelling on Australian Passport number ███████████ issued in the name of ███████████.

4. Department of Immigration also holds documents showing that on 2 August 1997, Australian Passport number ███████████ was presented by a passenger entering Australia at Brisbane Airport on Cathay Pacific Flight number CX103. The accompanying 'Incoming Passenger Card' showed that the passenger was ███████████, born 3/10/1945, and that she was entering Australia as a

temporary visitor. The card showed that the passenger was residing in Luxembourg and intended to stay at the Novotel Hotel in Brisbane for a period of 8 days. Checks have been made with Novotel Brisbane however records are no longer available for that time period. Police believe that the details about place of residence and duration of stay in Australia are fictitious.

5. The Department of Immigration has no record of Australian Passport number ████████████ being used since 2 August 1997, which expired on 20/5/2007.

Sheehan argues he didn't believe the case fell under the jurisdiction of the NSW Coroner given Barter was not a missing person 'in the true sense of the word' and not a New South Wales resident – her last known address was in Queensland. He indicates later he approached the Coroner's Office for advice about its jurisdiction in the matter, but that advice is blacked out.

On 17 October 2011, Sergeant Julie Dean emailed Sheehan, outlining the position of Chief Inspector Paul Roussos, manager of the Missing Persons Unit, and his recommendation to record Sally's report only as an occurrence.

By now, Sally is world-weary when it comes to managing her expectations. 'I didn't put myself through this and my family through all of this … to come out the other end with exactly the same result, which is not knowing what's happened to my mum … probably silly of me to think so, but I did have a little bit of hope that we'd find some answers faster than we have done, but kudos to everyone who's trying.

'At the end of the day that's going to be what finds us the answers … having people constantly looking … that's going to get us there.'

CHAPTER 17

Strikeforce Jurunga

25 June 2021

There's more than $25 million on offer from the NSW Police for information to solve crimes stretching back to the 1970s, but it has largely failed to entice people to come forward and share what they know.* Even the introduction of $1 million rewards in 2017 hasn't triggered the flood of information investigators hoped for.

At least the announcement of a big reward puts a case in the headlines, and now it's Marion's turn. After more than 20 years of mostly wilful indifference, NSW Police announce a reward of $250,000 'for information into the 1997 suspicious disappearance of Marion Barter'.

'We're trying to piece together all the missing links,' says Detective Superintendent Danny Doherty of the Homicide Squad. 'We still can't explain how someone can disappear off the face of the earth. It's out of character, only that in fact she hasn't been in contact with her family. That's why the reward is important, to try to draw out more information from people that may have it that they may have held back in the past.'

When he's asked about the poor quality of the police investigation to date, he dodges the question: 'It's been a really professional, protracted, complex investigation. I think there are people out there who have some answers for us, maybe be able to fill in those missing links who may have seen Marion Barter, and may know what happened. It's amazing what you can remember.

---

* Chris Hook, 'With $25 million now on offer, do NSW Police ever pay out reward money?', 7News, 30 June 2019, <7news.com.au/news/court-justice/with-25-million-now-on-offer-do-nsw-police-ever-pay-out-reward-money-c-191490>.

Sometimes it's amazing what information and record-keeping people do have.'

More than a year later, the reward figure doubles to $500,000. 'We're hopeful this reward may encourage the flow of new information regarding Marion's disappearance,' says Detective Inspector Nigel Warren of the Homicide Squad at the announcement in Byron Bay. 'We are still working to establish Ms Barter's movements and whereabouts upon returning to Australia in late July or early August 1997, and wish to speak with anyone close to her during that time.'

Sally is standing beside Warren as he announces the increased reward to a bank of TV cameras and reporters. Seymour is standing behind them, filming the press conference.

The events leading up to this moment are extraordinary.

Sandy, Seymour and Eeles are swamped with work for their day jobs. Their plan to file only seven episodes of the podcast evaporates, along with evenings, weekends and holidays. The investigation is surviving on sweat, tears and lots of coffee. Without the work put in by listeners and supersleuths, the story would be way behind where it needs to be.

Seymour visits the NSW State Library many times during this investigation, where he has viewed microfiche of the phone directory for Ballina from 1994. He finds a physical copy of the phone book at the Ballina library while there reporting on another story. There's no listing for the name 'Remakel'. The microfiche might contain the number, and a listing, but Seymour is called away before he can finish checking the entire book.

What he doesn't know is, soon after, NSW Police has the same idea and new investigators assigned to the case will be the first to find a key clue that cracks this case wide open.

Meanwhile, the team hears, via this email from the Police Media Unit, that major changes are underway inside NSW Police:

The NSW Police Force is reviewing the operations of the Missing Persons Unit.

The process involves examining the current structure, staffing and objectives of the Unit.

No determination has been made and there will be no further comment until the plans are finalised.*

This major reform is confirmed by an article in the *Daily Telegraph*:

The NSW Police Missing Persons Unit will be disbanded amid fears families have been living in limbo while their loved ones are actually among more than 100 sets of unidentified remains in the morgue, following years of internal criticism about its leadership.**

Barely one month after *The Lady Vanishes* debuts in April 2019, NSW Police announces that it's disbanding the Missing Persons Unit. The unit has had a string of failures in investigating cold cases, and the public attention now being shone on it due to Marion's case is the final straw.

Among the changes being announced is the establishment of a new unit, named Project Aletheia, with seven detectives and four forensic analysts, along with state-of-the-art technology to properly handle these complex and demanding cases. Aletheia originated in ancient Greek philosophy and means 'truth'.***

The restructuring of the Missing Persons Unit is outlined by Detective Inspector Glen Browne, a police officer with more than 30 years' experience, who has been appointed manager of the new Missing Persons Registry. Several years later, he would reflect upon the handling of Marion Barter's disappearance, saying: 'From the material available to me I hold the view that Marion Barter should have been considered a missing person at the time the initial report was made in 1997. I form this view

---

* Email from Jamie Wallace, NSW Police Media Unit, 6 May 2019.

** Ava Benny-Morrison, 'Missing Person Unit disbanded after mismanagement fears', *Daily Telegraph*, 5 May 2019, <www.dailytelegraph. com.au/news/nsw/missing-person-unit-disbanded-after-mismanagement-fears/news-story/62cc313229ebf9d52224388bb682117c>.

*** 'Alethea', Online Etymology Dictionary, <www.etymonline.com/word/alethea>.

on the basis her whereabouts were unknown and her daughter expressed concern for her safety or wellbeing.'*

Finally, in black and white, acknowledgement that Sally acted correctly yet was let down by a police department that ignored its primary function. Browne goes further, criticising the decision by police to claim that Marion was 'located':

> It appears that in 2011, information was obtained by investigators indicating Marion Barter had changed her name to Florabella Natalia Marion Remakel. Following that, the OIC [officer in charge], Detective Senior Constable Gary Sheehan, submitted a report to the manager of the Missing Person Unit requesting that Marion Barter be re-classified as 'Located' on the basis that she was deliberately avoiding her family and others.
>
> It is my view that Marion Barter should not have been classified as located, as her whereabouts were still unknown and there was still justification to hold concern for her safety or wellbeing.

NSW Police confirms Sheehan is no longer working alone, but declines to reveal the name of the new officer, or officers, involved, saying only in a statement:

> The Homicide Squad's Unsolved Homicide Unit is overseeing the investigation into the disappearance of Florabella Natalia Marion Remakel also known as Marion Barter who was last seen alive on 22 June 1997 under Strike Force Jurunga.
>
> The investigation, which will consider all available evidence, will also include collaboration with officers from Tweed/Byron Police District and the State Crime Command's Missing Persons Registry.**

---

*   Statement by Detective Inspector Glen Browne, 19 June 2021.
** Email from Sarah Burnell, NSW Police Media Unit, 11 December 2019.

When an investigation reaches a level of importance and complexity that requires a specialised approach, police form a dedicated group of investigators called a strike force. The best known in New South Wales is Strike Force Raptor, which targets outlaw motorcycle gangs.* The name of a strike force is chosen by a computer program named Eaglei** from a random selection of words.

'There's a person who doesn't wish to be identified who is working in the Homicide Squad in Sydney,' Sally says. As the next of kin, she is granted inside access to police and their investigation that the journalists on the TLV team are not. 'They say they want to meet me personally.' Finally, after years of ignoring Sally, police invite her to meet with the new team assigned to investigate her mother's disappearance.

Sally and her eldest daughter, Ella, travel to Parramatta, in Sydney's west, where NSW Police is headquartered. Seymour greets her there and then waits as they go inside for their meeting. They emerge seven hours later and Seymour interviews them both for the podcast.

'How did the meeting go with the officer in charge?' he asks.

'Really well … it's been a very big day … I'm feeling extremely confident. They're starting from scratch and are going to look into every single thing and … the new OIC [Officer in Charge] is dedicated to our case, which is great news. She has our own little team helping us. I'm feeling really confident that we're going to be digging really deep and looking into it the way it should have been done 23 years ago.'

'Can I get a high five, Ella? How does that sound?'

'It sounds pretty good I think,' Ella smiles, slapping palms.

'You've lived this your entire life, haven't you?' Seymour asks.

'Yeah, I'm just glad that the podcast and everything that has gone into it has finally led to something and that all of the effort hasn't been for nothing. It's finally eventuated into getting this new outcome for it, which I think is great.'

---

* 'Reporting bikie gang activity', NSW Police, <www.police.nsw.gov.au/can_you_help_us/reporting_bikie_gang_activity>, accessed 2019.

** Brenden Hills, 'Police ordered to use politically correct names for investigations', *Daily Telegraph*, 24 November 2019.

Everyone is a bit giddy with excitement. For the longest time it felt like such a moment would never arrive.

'Most people in similar types of situations, they don't get this meeting,' Seymour says. 'A complete overhaul of the team. Sally, you seem pretty happy ... I want to play devil's advocate, because I've been in a similar situation before – there's a lot of promises going on, then it peters out. What's your impression?'

'This isn't going to peter out. I have a lot of faith in the fact that they've given us a whole day so I can meet the people involved. It's a case that needs full investigation. I've run through my concerns and theories that the listeners have come up with and what *The Lady Vanishes* has come up with. They're all very happy to take it on board, start with fresh eyes and do a full investigation on it. I'm pretty confident that they understand the case is being heavily scrutinised on the podcast, people are watching and listening.

'I was saying to them this morning [when] we got to the check-in, my bags are full of paperwork so I had to hold a lot of it. I got there and the lady said your bag is too heavy, have you got a laptop in there? I said I did, so she told me to take it out, so I said I'm really sorry but I have a lot of documents to take. She goes, "I know, I listen to your podcast. I live in Noosa and I drive down every day. I listen to it in the car." We got off the plane and some lady came up and said, "Good luck finding your mum. I noticed you were on the plane" ... I feel like I've got an army.'

'Given the nature of the police review that was done on this case, was there any discussion about the forensic aspects? The DNA against the remains or something like that? Didn't come up today?'

'No, not yet. They told me the bone was negative, which was the other day.'

'The bone from a woman in the mid 1990s in the Ballina region?'

'Correct, they specifically tested that against my DNA, which gave a negative result.'

'I'm really confident that they won't drop the ball,' Sally says. 'They'll keep on this and they have given me their word that's going to happen.'

Sally's faith in the new police team proves to be well founded. As they launch into the first thorough investigation into Marion's case, changes are also afoot for the TLV team. In July 2020, Eeles leaves Seven News. A month later, Seymour does likewise. While Eeles continues to work on the podcast, Seymour messages the team to let them know he's stepping back from news reporting and the podcast for a while.

Within weeks, the new police team makes major breakthroughs that prove game-changing. The TLV team has no knowledge of this, however. Only Sally has access to the police investigators and she cannot share what she is told, including the identity of the new person of interest.

CHAPTER 18

Speak for the Dead, Protect the Living

Monday, 21 June 2021

The inquest into the disappearance of Marion Barter begins.

Sandy flies to Sydney the day before, but Sally and Chris elect not to come because there's a COVID-19 outbreak in Sydney. Sally instead appears by video link from her Brisbane office.

Sandy arrives at the court complex at Lidcombe in Sydney very early on Monday morning to file a live report for breakfast TV. Heading into the courtroom, she runs into Marion's long-time friend Janis White, the only one in the public gallery who actually knew Marion.

Supersleuth Jenn Marsh and her husband Ken are there, as are Mark and Faye Leveson, who have provided support and guidance for Sally on the road to this inquest. They went through the process themselves after their 20-year-old son Matthew went missing in 2007. His body was found a decade later when his much older boyfriend, Michael Atkins, was given an immunity deal to lead police to where he buried it. Despite the devastation of losing a child so tragically, the pair is determined to help others get justice for loved ones.

Sandy notices the new head of the NSW Police Missing Persons Register, Glen Browne, also walking in, as well as the new homicide investigator on the case, Detective Senior Constable Sasha Pinazza. She looks like someone not to be messed with. She's joined by her partner in this case, DSC Leza Pessotto.

State Coroner Teresa O'Sullivan, who presides over the inquest, has a good reputation. When she walks into the court, she appears calm and exudes warmth and self-assurance. Her counsel assisting, Adam Casselden SC, looks serious and no-nonsense. He's joined by his junior, Tracey Stevens. Representing Sally Leydon is barrister Bradley Smith. With him is Richard Keegan, who knows the story well, having been there from the start and legally cleared everything before publication. After the inquest was announced, Sally expressed concern to Sandy about the prospect of Seven discontinuing its legal support. Sandy argued Sally would require representation, and successfully convinced her bosses to see this through to the end.

Appearing on behalf of the NSW Police is barrister Kim Burke.

There's plenty of media interest, with three TV camera crews outside the court complex and a gaggle of journalists in a designated media room watching the case via video link. They can report on the evidence that's presented by witnesses during the inquest and on the brief of evidence as it's submitted to the Coroner, but they're not allowed to record proceedings in any way. Sandy is also not permitted to make any recordings or do interviews within the court complex.

The inquest is due to start at 10 am but doesn't get underway until around 11.45. At the last minute, NSW Police submit a bundle of documents that Sally and her lawyers don't have time to go through. Sally looks flustered by the delays and appears on the audio-visual link overlooking the courtroom looking tired.

Casselden opens proceedings by stating the known facts and outlining how the inquest will play out. He acknowledges the loss and emotional turmoil Sally and her family have experienced in not knowing what happened to Marion. He says the last two known movements by Marion are possibly:

1. Cancelling her car insurance policy with RACQ on her red Honda Civic Breeze, which she lent to Sally on 7 August 1997
2. Using her Medicare card at Grafton on 13 August 1997.

The first person to give evidence, via audio-visual link, is Detective Senior Constable Gary Sheehan, who took charge of the case from December 2009 until 29 September 2019. He seems anxious and says he's been on sick leave for about a year. He says he was allocated the case when the officer who had control of it, a Detective King, went on long-term sick leave and never returned to work.

One of his first actions was to call Sally Leydon for a conversation because of the ambiguous nature of the details on the police software COPS. He says there had been virtually no action on the case from late 1997 to 2007. When asked whether it was appropriate for the matter to be listed as an occurrence in COPS on 22 October 1997, Sheehan replies that initially he was 'non-judgemental' but later came to the opinion that it should have been a missing person's report.

It's revealed that the occurrence listed by Senior Constable Graham Childs is scant on detail. The court is told that Childs' shift supervisor, Michael Pearce, marked the file: 'No further action at this stage until person has been reported missing'. But reporting a missing person is precisely what Sally thought she'd done when she went to police in 1997.

Sheehan says he took a lengthy and detailed statement from Sally Leydon at Tweed Heads station, which she read and signed.

Questions then focus on the Medicare statement discovered by another officer, Steve McAlister, which reveals Marion's Medicare card was used for treatment from a Dr Evans at Grafton in northern New South Wales on 13 August 1997. Sheehan admits that information seems to have 'slipped through the cracks for ten years' and he's 'very surprised' about that. He tells the Coroner, 'That was part of my investigation that I found extremely frustrating.'

In June 2010, Sheehan noted on Marion's file: 'Her Medicare card was used at Grafton Shopping World for an initial consultation which happened 11 days after her passport was scanned at Brisbane airport.' Under cross-examination, he explains that after examining the Medicare docket he tried to find a doctor with the name D.M. Evans in the Grafton area in 1997. The TLV team later learns that Evans was not a medical doctor but an optometrist.

Sheehan says he tried to trace the money Marion sent to the UK by contacting both Barclays Bank and Interpol, but received no response from either. He also tried to verify Sally's reports of money being drained from her mother's Australian bank accounts with Colonial State Bank, but due to the passage of time couldn't find any remaining records.

He was unsuccessful in finding Betty Brown, who'd worked for the Salvation Army Family Tracing Unit and had been contacted by Marion's father, John Wilson, in the late 1990s. He also mentions discovering that Marion Barter's passport returned to Australia just weeks after she left, and that on 16 May 1997 she had changed her name to Florabella Natalia Marion Remakel. This was a major find, but it turns out Detective King had already made an application for this information and it was in Marion's file. When asked about this, Detective Sheehan responds that he 'probably overlooked that'.

After discovering the name change, Sheehan concluded Marion purposely estranged herself from her family: 'The fact she had sold Sally her car, sold her house at Southport, resigned from her job ... told people she was heading overseas, had been spotted in a car with a man by Sally and when asked about it brushed it off, and the information that sums of money were taken out and that was at the time that she had returned to the country.'* It's all circumstantial but he believes it was enough to justify changing the case from 'Missing' to 'Found'.

Between September and October in 2011, Sheehan advised the Missing Persons Unit that Marion Barter was *not* a missing person: 'I believe that Sally had accepted the information I had told her,' he wrote, 'but I don't know if Sally has ever believed that her mother has voluntarily estranged herself.'

When asked if there's actual evidence that it was Marion who returned to Australia on 2 August 1997 using Florabella Remakel's passport, or someone else, he says: 'To my eyes, on the

---

* Evidence notes by Alison Sandy, 21 June 2021.

incoming passenger card, I was of the belief that the handwriting was Marion's, but I am no expert.' He tells the Coroner that handwriting experts cannot make a positive identification.

'I had no reason to believe otherwise,' Sheehan says. 'There was no proof that it wasn't her. At the time I made that decision, it wasn't a decision I had made alone. I had spoken to colleagues, and they had concurred. I had submitted a report to the Missing Persons Unit and the reply I got was that it should be marked as "Located". So I felt that what I had discovered had been vindicated. It's unfortunate, but I believe I had sufficient information to make the decision that I did.'

When asked what evidence he used to determine that it was Marion, and not someone else, who made the withdrawals of money from her bank accounts, he replies, 'It coincided with a period of time that I believe Marion had come back to Australia. Unfortunately, everything I was relying on was circumstantial at best, due to the ravages of time.'

So why did postcards written by Marion keep arriving from the UK after the date her passport returned home? 'She wanted to give off the opinion that she was doing as she said but was covertly arranging a new life,' Sheehan says.

What about the date of Marion's phone call to Sally, 1 August, the day before the passport returned to Australia? 'I'd like to accept that, and this is no criticism of Sally, I don't believe Sally is telling me untruths deliberately.' Is Sheehan really suggesting that Sally is mistaken about the date?

On suspending the investigation, Sheehan says, 'I had no information that Marion had met with foul play in Australia or overseas … It's not the job of NSW Police to work out why but to figure out what happened.'

'Do you still believe today that Marion has changed her identity to start a new life?' Casselden asks.

'I do and I think she went to great lengths to do so.'

Over the following two weeks, other officers involved in the case appear, most notably former Byron Bay constable Graham Childs. Now retired, Childs appears in person and tells the Coroner he has no recollection of Sally and Chris reporting Marion missing in October 1997. Nor does he have any independent memory of making enquiries regarding Marion Barter or ever being involved in a missing persons investigation.

Records show that Childs made an occurrence entry in COPS regarding Sally's initial report, but notes on Marion's description and bank account transactions were not entered. When asked if the matter should have been written up as a missing persons case from the start, Childs says, 'No, I don't agree with that.'

The police records show that reference had also been made to Marion's 'personal safety' due to 'fears for her welfare'. Asked why wasn't the matter upgraded on that basis, Childs says, 'I believe if that was my comment it may have been poorly worded because it appeared at the outset there was no sense of urgency. It would appear from the information from all parties that I may or may not have contacted that there was insufficient evidence to make it a missing person at the time.'

They then come to the phone call to Sally Leydon during which she claims she was told by a police officer that Marion had been located and wanted to be left alone. Did Childs make that call? 'No, not at all. If I had made that phone call, that would be an incident that would be in my memory.'

A witness of particular interest is former investigations manager for the Commonwealth Bank of Australia Graeme Smith. He tells the court he was first made aware of Marion Barter after media enquiries to the bank's communications team. 'As I've been around a long time, it was thrown my way to see what I could find out in regards to old records in Ms Barter's name.'

He reached out to the investigating police officer, Detective Senior Constable Gary Sheehan. 'I did find that Marion had accounts with Colonial State Bank – before the merger with the Commonwealth Bank.' He cannot say whether these accounts were subject to frequent withdrawals of $5000 over a number of weeks in late 1997 because he could only go back as far as 2004, a few years before the merger. 'We are trained about customers withdrawing large amounts in small periods … if they went to the same teller time and time again then that should be a trigger. It wouldn't be so noticeable if the person visited multiple branches.'

He's asked whether a total of $80,000 being taken from an account in October 1997 would raise an alarm. 'It'd be subject to what the withdrawal was for. No red flag if they were buying a property. Then no concerns at all.'

He says keycards at that time had a withdrawal limit of $800 per day at automatic teller machines, so a customer would have had to go into the branch for a larger amount. Marion had a Mastercard account that had been held by the bank's fraud team after she'd reported her purse stolen in 1994 and cancelled her credit card. The account was opened in 1985 and officially closed on 9 April 2010.

There is also a Visa card statement that was in the care of Barclays Bank at Rye in the UK. 'It appears to me that this was a recorded mailing address for Ms Barter at the time,' Smith says. He confirms that to access this money at Barclays Bank, Marion would likely have had to provide a number of elements of identification. When he investigated it, this account was still accumulating fees, so he took steps to close it. Marion also had a high-performance cash account that was opened in June 1997 and closed after several years due to inactivity, with the money sent to unclaimed funds. In total, Marion had about $14,000 remaining in the account.

Smith says there had been no activity on the accounts, other than fees, for as far back as he could trace to the early 2000s. He'd never come across a case quite like it. 'I've dealt with missing persons matters before, [but] none sort of match this frame where there is a large sum of money left behind.'

Three other witnesses give evidence on Tuesday, 22 June, including David Martin, who worked at the Colonial State Bank and then the Commonwealth Bank until 2018. In 1997, he was manager at the Ashmore branch of Colonial State Bank on the Gold Coast, which apparently recorded the final withdrawal from Marion's bank account: $80,000 on 15 October 1997. He provided authority to operate an account for Marion Barter and says he remembers her well. 'As soon as I saw a photo I recognised her. We weren't a large branch. If she was coming in to make withdrawals, you got to know your clients more intimately than if there were 25 staff.'

He can't recall, however, his last time dealing with her. He confirms that to withdraw $5000 at a time, a customer would have had to enter a branch. 'Myself and the lender knew Marion well, we knew her by sight. If she was at another branch, she would have to provide identification, such as a passport or driver's licence. 'If it was more than $10,000,' he says, 'it was a suspicious amount and would have to be reported.'

If that was the case, he says there would have been a significant cash transaction report. 'Under AUSTRAC [the federal government's Australian Transaction Reports and Analysis Centre], it's to do with money laundering. The idea was that if the money was over $10,000, the information would be collected and passed on file for review by the authorities. I believe there was a property sold and funds put into a high-performing interest account, but there was a restriction that only $5000 could be withdrawn a day.'

Martin says he had no recollection of police from either Queensland or New South Wales getting in contact with him in 1997 or 1998. Nor was he approached by the Salvation Army Family Tracing Unit.

When asked if there was ever a security officer at Ashmore, he says there wouldn't have been. That particular piece of evidence is revealing when considered in conjunction with the evidence of Betty Brown, the director of the Queensland branch of the Salvation Army Family Tracing Unit in 1997. The 90-year-old gives her evidence over the phone, telling the Coroner her role was to look for people with whom family members had lost contact. In 1998, she received handwritten letters and information about Marion Barter from Marion's father, John Wilson, but says she has no independent recollection of it.

Mr Wilson's letter is read aloud to prompt her memory, but she responds, 'I have never heard any of that – that is all new information. It isn't in my memory and I certainly do not have any recollection at all.'

A letter that Mrs Brown herself had written to Mr Wilson on 18 March 1998 is provided to the court:

Dear Mr Wilson,
Just a short note to confirm our recent phone conversation
and say that I have been talking at length to Police Missing
Persons, who in turn contacted the security officer at
the Colonial State Bank at Ashmore at Southport and
after lengthy conversations were able to advise that it was
definitely your daughter Marion, who went in and withdrew
the balance of the money at Ashmore on 15/10/1990 and
spoke of starting a new life.

There's conjecture about why the letter mentions 1990 rather than 1997, which is most likely a typographical error. Of particular interest is that the letter refers to 'Police Missing Persons' having contacted the 'security officer' at the Colonial State Bank in Ashmore.

Mrs Brown makes it clear she can only talk about the general procedures of what would likely have happened because she can't remember the case: 'I would normally have rung the bank, but I said Police Missing Persons had spoken to the bank. Looking at a copy of the letter I sent, it appears I had a lengthy conversation with Sergeant Trudi McKechnie from Police Missing Persons, who also had a discussion with the bank at Ashmore, and so felt that I didn't need to do that.'

Betty Brown says that in her job she only provided police with the 'basic stuff, not the background emotional stuff'. And likewise, the police didn't tell her everything. When pressed on what information wasn't provided, she replies, 'I don't know because they didn't tell us.' Many in the courtroom giggle at this. It's hard not to like matter-of-fact Betty. She says the Salvation Army would likely have tried to send a letter to Marion through social security and, had she chosen not to reply, Betty would have accepted that she had the right to be left alone.

The next witness is retired dentist Raymond Walduck, or John, as he prefers to be called, who appears via audio link. He was the one who signed as a witness to Marion's application for a new passport in the name Florabella Remakel, while he was working for the Queensland Teachers' Union Health Society in Brisbane. While he accepts he treated Marion at times during that period, he says he can't remember her. He does, however, have a vague recollection of signing that passport application because the name 'struck me as strange'. Grafton optometrist Evans, who apparently saw Marion when she returned to Australia on 13 August 1997, can't remember her either.

One witness of note is Marion's former boss, Dr Bruce Cook AC. Now retired, Cook was headmaster of The Southport School from January 1988 to December 2003. 'I believe Marion was first and foremost a highly skilled and excellent teacher at the junior primary level,' he says, 'a caring lady and artistic lady. She was very highly regarded by me and the parents and boys in her class and the staff at her school.'

'Is it your view that Marion was well liked by staff as a whole?' Casselden asks.

'Yes it is, on the whole. You'll see in the statement there are some reservations there, but on the whole.' Cook adds that he has no recollection of any tension at the time. 'Since rereading her resignation letter, which says there were things she'd like to discuss with me, I suppose there were issues there that I wasn't aware of. There were changes to the prep school that may have caused some tension with certain members of staff.'

At the end of 1996, Cook conducted an appraisal of Marion's teaching objectives when she mentioned a possible exchange to England: 'We talked about the possibility of an exchange and we talked about it being to a Lakes District school. In fact, St Anne's at Windermere. The teaching exchanges were a relatively normal part of our operation and it was something that was seen as being of great professional relevance and a way of improving, and learning new insights from other countries and other schools.'

Cook has Marion's first resignation letter but he can't remember receiving it. 'I don't think it would have been a shock, because it's a large school and there's well over 130, 140 teachers. I'm sure I would have been very disappointed, but I wouldn't use the term shock.' He adds, though, that it was unusual for a teacher to resign mid-term. 'I got my diary out of archives for 1997 and I saw an appointment with Marion at 2.30 on 15 April that year, which could well have been to talk about what was going on, but I honestly have no recollection. It may have been to express concerns, or tell me what she planned to do in the future. Perhaps Marion felt the school was being moved in a new direction she wasn't comfortable with. I honestly don't know.'

When questioned about a second resignation letter dated two months after the first, he replies, 'This letter is a surprise to me because it wasn't in her school file. I'm not quite sure where New South Wales Police got that letter from.'

The team works feverishly to keep across the evidence accumulating in the coronial inquest.

CHAPTER 19

Dead End

It may as well be called a 'Pandemonium'; the global pandemic hits hard and makes the work of the TLV team more difficult. The first COVID-infected person was discovered in Australia on 25 January 2020, in Victoria. By March, the pandemic forces the nation's borders closed and the first lockdown is instituted, in what quickly becomes an intensely difficult and traumatic time.

The Zero-COVID policy adopted in Australia sees militaristic quarantines in place through to late 2021. Eeles has taken time off from her new role with the Australian Broadcasting Corporation, Australia's national public broadcaster, to focus on the inquest. Concerned about sudden COVID lockdowns, she was reluctant to go to Sydney for the inquest and has instead dialled in to listen to proceedings.

In the weeks before the inquest began, the team discussed creating a single episode for each of the inquest's two weeks, wrapping the evidence into a neat weekly package. It quickly becomes apparent that in order to present as accurate an account as possible of the flood of witness testimonies, many more episodes will be required. Sally is the only one with access to the 'file', the police brief of evidence, which is keeping her and Joni busy.

Then Sandy finds herself having to book an urgent flight home after hearing just a day or so of evidence. There's been a COVID outbreak in Sydney, and there's a deadline for Queenslanders to return home. While Sandy rushes to the airport, Eeles remains dialled in, keeping across everything that's going on in court.

When Marion's second-youngest sister, Bronwen, is called upon to testify, she appears annoyed to still be discussing her sister's disappearance. Asked about Marion's personality, she replies sarcastically, 'Heavens, you don't ask hard questions.' She continues, 'I haven't seen her for 24 years. She was a loving person. She was my sister. She cared about people. She was very nice to people, kind to people, and concerned about people. She loved her job, teaching little kids. She was very good at it. I don't think there was any mystique about her. I mean how well do you know anybody? She could be impulsive about some things and not other things.'

Between 1995 and 1997, Bronwen Wilson lived on North Stradbroke Island off the southern Queensland coast, a couple of hours' drive from the Gold Coast. 'I went down to visit her a couple of times and stayed with her at her house, and she came up to the island several times to stay with me. I also saw her up at Moffat Beach [on the Sunshine Coast] at the parents' house quite often. We didn't call each other very often as sisters, only for birthdays or news we wanted to convey.'

Bronwen is candid when asked whether they were close. 'Um, it wasn't *not* close … We didn't live in each other's pockets, but I didn't with any of my sisters. It didn't mean we weren't close or didn't stick up for one another or love one another. I was closer to Deirdre when we were growing up, and probably in the early years when she lived in Lismore and Evans Head, because she was closer than Marion or Lee were.'

Marion and Bronwen didn't talk about men: 'I guess that's because I tend not to be interested in hearing about personal relationships, if you're talking about her love life. If I didn't know anything it wasn't a problem talking to the rest of the family, particularly parents. They agonised about anything, and I didn't want to agonise with them. If I didn't know anything I couldn't give them any information to agonise about, could I? They agonised about things in that they talked about things endlessly … Because she'd been married three times maybe. My parents didn't think people should get divorced, perhaps an old-fashioned attitude, so they didn't understand.'

Bronwen was aware of Greg Edwards, the school groundskeeper, and didn't believe it to be serious, but she couldn't say if Marion had been seeing someone before her departure overseas in 1997. 'It could be quite possible that she was. I didn't pick up on anything to do with her having anybody in her life. Anybody new.'

Bronwen was visiting her parents the day Marion brought Owen around during Sally's engagement party in June 1997. 'It probably was the last time I saw her. I knew she was going and I was excited for her ... She told me she was going to be away for a couple of years and she wasn't going to be in contact with people. Not to expect to get lots of letters or hear from her. I think people have got the right to have their own space if they feel they need it.'

Marion didn't mention going with anyone and Bronwen offered to take her to the airport. 'But she wasn't interested in doing that. She said she wanted to spend a couple of nights at the hotel in Brisbane and get her head together because everything had been so rushed. I was a bit peeved about that because I like taking people to the airport, seeing them off.'

She remembers Marion being very upset about resigning from The Southport School: 'When we were up at Dad's birthday, we went for a walk on the beach and she was terribly, terribly upset. She told me she'd been betrayed at that school. She didn't tell me any details. She wouldn't tell me. I did ask her but she wouldn't tell me. She was just terribly upset. She was crying. And it left her with no option but to tender her resignation.'

According to Bronwen, the episode prompted Marion to travel overseas. 'Yes, because her whole world was falling apart, wasn't it? It just seemed logical to me ... she was heartbroken.'

When concerns for Marion were raised in late 1997, Bronwen was blindsided. 'Yes, my father was really upset because Sally had rung up. Sally just caused a whole lot of hysteria about it. It was only about three months after [Marion] left.'

Then, 'Everything became hysterical,' Bronwen says. 'I just thought it was over the top. It was all anybody could think about, talk about, and all [Marion] wanted to do was go away and have some peace and quiet. I was annoyed. I was really cheesed off with the missing person thing. Because she said she was going away for two years. I thought that was fair enough. I'd accept that. Maybe I was really naive.'

But did Bronwen really think Marion would deliberately miss her daughter's wedding? 'Yes. If that's what she wanted to do, I don't think it would be unusual at all, because she didn't want to go, obviously.'

Bronwen signed a ten-page statement to police, dated 3 September 2020, at Tweed Heads in northern New South Wales. In it, she said, 'Marion used to think that she could mould men. She definitely tried to change Ray but failed. Marion just never seemed to manage to be happy. Everything that she wanted to do in life, to be happy and stay happy, had to do with having a man in her life. Marion was telling me on the phone one time that she had to hurry up and find a man before she turned 50 because men weren't interested in you after that. She told me I'd better hurry up and find a man too.

'I remember our father used to joke and call her "Marrying Marion". I'm not sure that Marion found this all that funny. She really didn't have much of a sense of humour. I don't think any of us were brought up with much of a sense of humour.'

Bronwen says her sister remained open to the idea of another marriage: 'Marion told me that her relationship with Ray was the happiest six years of her life. Despite everything, she said, "I've done it three times and I'd rock up for the fourth any day." [She] spoke to me about feeling that she had spent her life pursuing the wrong things and that doing so had not made her happy. She didn't tell me what she planned to do to change that, and I didn't ask her. It said to me that Marion was looking to change the direction of her life somehow. I got the impression that she was sick of everything in her life. Sally was hounding her about how much money she was giving her for her wedding and what furniture she could have, because she needed it now. Stuart still managed to hound her. Marion didn't say so, but it was my thought that he would contact her every time she was single to try and get a foot in the door.'

There's also mention of Marion's relationship with her parents after the incident at Christmas in 1996. 'It wasn't nice between Marion, Mum and Dad. There was definitely an escalation in tensions over that Christmas, and I know Marion wanted to do something about it. She wanted to have words with Mum and tell her what she thought, but I don't think that ever happened.

'Mum was more the issue for Marion than Dad was. My mother's attitude was that she could say whatever she liked. It didn't matter what you did or said, she was always right. Marion and I were always the outcasts with Mum. Deirdre was always Mum's favourite. I was Dad's favourite, so he offered some protection for me. I felt guilty. I felt that I didn't stand up for Marion enough.'

At a dinner Bronwen had with Marion and their parents shortly before her trip, 'Marion was telling us about her impending trip to Europe and Mum thought she'd express that she thought it to be a waste of time, money and effort. Mum said, "You might learn to enjoy life more, Marion, if you drank."

'The next time I saw Marion was maybe only a fortnight before she went away … I remember being peeved with Marion because we had spoken about doing alternate weekends at Mum and Dad's place to help while Dad was sick. I was peeved when Marion went away, because that left me with the responsibility. I overheard Marion say to Dad, "I wouldn't be doing this if I didn't think you would be okay."

'Marion said goodbye to all of the neighbours in a way that seemed as though she was going away for a while. This ended up being the last time I saw Marion.'

Bronwen also refers to Marion's distinctive eye, which would explain the appointment with the optometrist in August 1997. 'Marion told me that she had a melanoma in her eye. It was only after she moved to Queensland that she discovered it. It was quite pronounced, but she didn't seem particularly concerned about it. It was a very brown mole in the coloured part of her eye, in the bottom part of the iris, dead centre, like a swelling.'

Finally, Bronwen touches on Marion's name change. 'The name that Marion chose, Florabella Natalia Marion Remakel, means nothing to me. It seems to me that it would take a bit of planning to change your name and get a new passport. It wasn't like Marion to be a terribly independent person in doing things.

It seems strange that she would be doing it alone. If she changed her name and had all those other plans, I just don't see that as being valid. That makes me feel less positive about the outcome, because it doesn't seem like such an innocent act and you wonder what was behind it.

'I still believe that she left herself a way to come back, and I always felt that she would except for the fact that Dad and Sally went down the missing person route. If it had been me that was doing as Marion was doing, I would never have come back. The whole thing makes me feel very sad that my sister felt she had to do what she's done and I miss her. She added a "grace" to life.'

Monday, 28 June 2021

Sally takes the stand in the inquest. She's nervous, but her evidence is calm, measured and precise. She answers in detail every question put to her by Adam Casselden SC. But the mood takes a sudden turn for the worse when the lawyer representing NSW Police, Kim Burke, stands up. While answering some basic questions about her early reports to police, Sally explains that Detective Senior Constable Sheehan told her Senior Constable Childs had taken notes and written them up at a later date.

Burke is apoplectic, 'Are you seriously suggesting that Graham Childs has fabricated the date?'

The Coroner weighs in to defuse the situation: 'It is a very serious circumstance when there's a suggestion. It's never been suggested by anybody representing the family that there was an issue in relation to the date of the COPS event. It was never put to him [in court] that he had fabricated the date.'*

Burke then grills Sally about whether she read the statement she provided and why she signed it if there are errors.

SALLY: It was a very busy day and I do not remember going over that statement with a fine-tooth comb, no. Probably at that point I trusted what I said to him had been documented properly, yes. I actually don't remember reading the statement.

---

* Transcript, NSW Coroner's Court, 30 June 2021.

BURKE: You were satisfied with him typing it up and you
signed it.

SALLY: I did sign it, yes. ·

BURKE: In your evidence, you mention errors – for instance
Westpac is mentioned.

SALLY: There are a number of errors in that document.

CORONER: Ms Burke, I don't know where this is going.

It's not what it seems, Burke tells the Coroner, who then asks her
to get to the point. Questions regarding Marion's bank accounts
follow, specifically how Childs would know the details, including
a bank manager's name and phone number, unless Sally provided
them.

'What about the COPS event in that narrative created by
Mr Childs,' Burke asks, 'where it records that the POI [person of
interest], who was her mother, has travelled to England and did not
contact her upon return. You gave that information to Mr Childs.

'I am telling you I did not know that information,' Sally says.

As for whether the bank officer from Sally's phone call put a
stop on Marion's accounts:

SALLY: I don't recollect her telling me she put a stop on the
card in the initial phone call.

BURKE: You provided that information to Mr Childs?

SALLY: I'm also of the opinion he could have rung the bank
and found it out himself.

BURKE: You told him, not the bank.

SALLY: I don't recollect that, no.

Burke presses her on whether she's referring to a note in the police
computer system or in the notebook:

BURKE: If you go down to the next sentence, 'believes she's
capable of behaviour of this nature'. Certainly discussion
between yourself and Mr Childs in respect to what type of
person your mother was.

SALLY: That's not my words. No, I went to the police
because she missed my brother's birthday. It's completely the
opposite of that statement.

Burke then brings up Chris Leydon's earlier evidence to the
inquest that early on he was concerned that Marion's bank account
had been defrauded rather than that she was in physical trouble.
Smith interjects:

SMITH: My recollection was that was his view, not confused
that it was Sally's view.
CORONER: That's right.
SALLY: That's what he said, yes.
BURKE: Do you recall, that was your concern, wasn't it?
SALLY: No, it was not.
BURKE: The call from the police within a week …
Mr Smith, I can see you're nodding your head, it's really
disturbing me.

Once again, the Coroner steps in: 'Just quieten down the tone all
round. It's a very accusatory tone and it's not helpful.'

'I'll back off,' Burke says, 'and we'll go through it step by step.'
She asks Sally about the call she received telling her Marion no
longer wanted anything to do with her family, and specifically
whether she can confirm it was officer Graham Childs who made
that call.

'I said just before I believed it was him. I can't verify it.'

More queries follow about bank documents sent to the home
of Lesley Loveday. Then Burke bombards Sally with questions
about exactly where she searched for Marion in Byron Bay in
October 1997.

Again, the Coroner reins Burke in:

CORONER: It's not for you to try to understand that really.
That's the evidence. You can make submissions. I don't think
we can go over this any more. We haven't got endless time.

BURKE: I'm entitled to take as long as I can.
CORONER: Move on, please.
BURKE: I'm trying to be fair as well.
CORONER: Move on please, Ms Burke.

Burke asks Sally why she approached Queensland Police about the case and is shown an exhibit confirming she went to Morningside Station on 25 November 2016. 'Notes identify you describing your dissatisfaction with the New South Wales Police Force and you wanted the Queensland Police Service to take over. Do you remember that?'

'I was a bit tired,' Sally replies. 'Detective Sheehan said he couldn't do anything else. They actually said they couldn't do it because the case was still active in New South Wales, because New South Wales had carriage of the case and therefore it was up to NSW Police.

The next morning begins as the previous day ended:

SALLY: I'm sorry, there's been a lot said in the last three days. My brain's hurting.*
BURKE: Is it more likely than not, that your concern ... was more about the money coming out of the bank account.
SALLY: I'd like to say, I think I have said numerous times, I was concerned for my mother. It had been weeks and months since we'd spoken to her. My concern was for my mum's welfare.

Finally, Smith takes over, returning the focus to Marion and Sally's relationship. 'We didn't really have a normal family life,' Sally says. 'Because ... between my mum and my dad there were five marriages and five divorces. She was caring and she cared about me. I think I was robbed of the opportunity ... to have an adult relationship with my mum. I was probably a bit self-absorbed, with things going on with me at the time – building houses and getting engaged. She loved me and I loved her.'

---

* Transcript, NSW Coroner's Court, 1 July 2021.

Sally says that if she'd known about Ashmore bank manager David Martin, and that money had been withdrawn from that branch, she would have gone there rather than all the way to Byron Bay.

When Smith repeats a comment from Sally's aunt Deirdre, that Marion just wanted a clean slate, Sally breaks down:

> SALLY: I find it terribly upsetting, to be terribly honest with you. I'm not a slate, and neither is my brother. The whole thing is very stressful.
> CORONER: Are you okay, Sally? Do you need a break?
> SALLY: I just want to finish, Your Honour.

Afterwards, Sandy says to Sally, 'At one stage, it felt like you were on trial.'

'Yeah, for sure – and Chris. There were questions we were expected to remember, like when we booked our holiday to go skiing in … I had to make it clear that … I wasn't taking notes or keeping diaries of those events, because *she wasn't missing to us at that point*.

'I think everybody felt the pressure in the room. It wasn't pleasant. And I don't think anybody was particularly enjoying that situation … I'm really grateful for the Crown solicitors and the Coroner herself, because I was allowed to give my evidence. I wasn't cut short. I was given an opportunity to say what I thought was important to finding out what happened to my mum.'

At the end of the inquest, the Coroner announces she needs more time. Another round of public hearings will take place the following year, in February 2022. Eight months seems an eternity to wait.

During those months, Sandy rings in to listen to one of the directions briefings, which are held just to provide information or instruction on the pending legal proceedings, and discovers an additional lawyer representing a man she's never heard of. At this stage, she's not advised of the relevance of this mysterious man, but understands he must be significant if he has a lawyer.

CHAPTER 20

Bombshell

1 February 2022

It's a stiflingly hot beginning to the last month of summer. The coronial inquest into the disappearance of Marion Barter is scheduled to resume on Valentine's Day, 14 February, for just five days.

In late 2021, Sandy receives word that proceedings will now start earlier each day, and last twice as long. Sally is the only one privy to what is going on, but although she has been kept in the loop by Strike Force Jurunga, she's not allowed to divulge anything. 'I've learnt a lot. That's probably all I can say,' Sally tells Sandy in an interview the week before the inquest resumes.

'Are you encouraged?' Sandy prompts.

'To find her? Probably not,' Sally concedes.

'Are you encouraged to find out what happened to her?' Sandy persists.

'I have a pretty good understanding of what's happened,' Sally responds. 'There have been developments and I'm really looking forward to sharing that with everybody who's been listening and supporting me for the last three years … I can also say that we definitely wouldn't be sitting here if it wasn't for the podcast and for the supersleuths helping.'

'How confident are you that this … inquest will really make a difference?' Sandy asks.

'I definitely think it will make *a* difference. I don't know if it's going to be *the* difference between finding her and not. We'll just have to wait and see.'

'The new team, do you think they're doing a good job?'

'... From what I know and what I've seen, I think they're doing a good job.'

This week's hearings are taking place in Byron Bay, but because of COVID-19 concerns, only State Coroner Teresa O'Sullivan, and her counsel assisting, Adam Casselden SC, are in the small Byron Bay courthouse. Everyone else who's tuning in via audio-visual link is scattered around the country, including Sally Leydon, who sits alone in her office in Brisbane.

This time, there's a dedicated YouTube link that anyone around the world can access. Thousands of people end up tuning in to the remaining days of the inquest. All of the relevant legal parties and witnesses can be seen at once, with their names printed on the screen. Because it's available on YouTube, the evidence can be watched over and over. But recording the proceedings for publication is prohibited by law. For this reason, the podcast has to rely heavily on voice actors to recreate the scenes played out in court.

Sally does a live TV interview with the presenters of Channel Seven's breakfast show, *Sunrise*. As always, she is well spoken, but this time particularly, she looks like she needs a hug. She tells her interviewer that she is crossing her fingers the inquest will lead to her finally finding her mum.

When Sally posts on her Facebook page the idea of placing billboards around northern New South Wales, outdoor advertising company oOh!media responds. They offer to build billboards and the Seven Network agrees to pay for them. Giant images of Marion's face and the reward offer of $250,000 appear along the roads Marion herself used to drive. 'It might spark somebody's memory as we're approaching the inquest,' Sally says. 'We've had people stopping and taking photos and sending it to me.' The billboards are up until March, and some electronic billboards also go up in shopping centres in Lismore and Grafton.

'We need to spread the word further ... particularly on the ground.'

One of Sally's supersleuths, Jenn Marsh, and her husband Ken, have been driving up and down the coast putting up posters.

Bundles have been sent to others who responded to the callout, offering to put them up in their local areas.

Sally also does an interview with a journalist from a local newspaper, the *Northern River Times*, in an effort to reach an older demographic of people. 'It was a full page in the local paper there, which is delivered to everybody and it goes all the way down from Grafton up to Tweed [Heads] and out to Tenterfield, which is near Armidale,' Sally says.

Sally is frustrated that COVID restrictions again mean she and her family can't physically be in the courtroom. 'I've put a request in that if we do face to face the second week that I do have the opportunity to bring my family, because this is important for them as well,' she explains. 'It's been interesting conversations at the table, particularly with my younger daughter. She's started talking a lot more about Mum and feels that she's connected with Mum in some way through this journey. Chris can get a little heated under the collar sometimes and get a bit frustrated with things. It's kind of weird. I should be the one really stressed and I feel like I'm trying to keep everyone else not stressed about it. We're in it together, and hopefully we'll come out the other side all right.'

The inquest resumes at 10 am Australian Eastern Daylight Time, with the Coroner and Casselden visible in the Byron Bay courtroom. Bradley Smith, the barrister representing Sally Leydon, appears via video link, as does Kim Burke, representing NSW Police. There's also another legal face, Bridget Kennedy, who is representing a man named Ric Blum.

Casselden announces that there are applications to be made, requesting that the court be closed to the public until 2 pm, after which he will make an opening address and call the first witness to the stand. The Coroner obliges.

When proceedings resume slightly after 2 pm, Casselden briefly explains that evidence will be delivered in person and via audio-visual link over coming weeks. He sums up evidence from the previous year's hearings, then tells the court that police have received a witness statement and interview from Ric Blum, a

Belgian national who moved to Australia in the late 1960s and has lived in a number of states. 'Mr Blum has informed investigating police that he placed the advertisement in 1994 under the name of Fernand Remakel,' Casselden continues referring to the advertisement in *Le Courrier Australien*. 'He says that his purpose was to seek a French-speaking friend.' The court hears that according to historical Queensland driving records, Blum obtained a driver's licence with the name 'Remakel' well before the disappearance of Marion Barter.

Then comes the first bombshell: Ric Blum knew Marion Barter.

Blum informed investigating police that in the 1960s, when he was in Switzerland, he met a woman by the name of Marion Warren in a hotel lobby. He told them that Marion's husband played soccer for Australia and was there as part of a football training camp, and they had a fleeting relationship at that time.

The court hears that back in the 1960s, Blum was known by the name Willy Wouters. In fact, this Ric Blum has had many aliases spelt various ways, including Frederick De Hedervary, Richard Lloyd Westbury, Willy Wouters and Fernand Remakel.

From their respective work spaces, Sandy, Seymour and Eeles are astounded with what they're hearing. There are audible gasps, screams and several expletives as they listen to the events playing out. There's a mad flurry of text messages with plenty of exclamation marks.

Bombshell number two: Ric Blum knew Marion Barter in the 1990s.

Not only did Blum tell police he had a dalliance with Marion in the 1960s, but he admitted to a second relationship with her. Blum claims that in 1995 or 1996, he answered a personal advertisement in a local Gold Coast newspaper for a woman seeking companionship. After a phone call, he says he found out that the ad was posted by Marion. They met up, had dinner at a restaurant, then went back to her house at Southport. The court hears that the pair spent three or four nights together.

Bombshell three: Ric Blum spent time with Marion Barter in the weeks before her trip overseas in 1997.

Blum told police Marion shared with him personal information about her family and her role as a teacher at The Southport School. Casselden says Blum even recounts an occasion when he visited The Southport School with Marion after she resigned, to pick up some books.

The court is then told that Blum also knew that Marion had sold her house, because he agreed to store wooden tea chests of her belongings at his home at Wollongbar, and she had a removalist deliver them. Marion Barter sold her Southport home on 25 April 1997 and moved out six days later, on 1 May. Wollongbar is a small town of about 3000 people located between Lismore and Ballina in northern New South Wales. It's about half an hour's drive north to get to Byron Bay, and an hour and a half to Southport on the Gold Coast.

After this, the bombshells are too numerous to count.

Casselden tells the court Ric Blum knew Marion was planning a trip to the UK: 'Mr Blum says that about one week after these boxes were delivered, Marion came to collect them. He said she was accompanied by a man in his 50s. He says that this man was tall and wearing a white hat, in blue uniform with gold markings, like bars on the sleeve. Mr Blum says in his statement that he took him to be a navy officer or pilot.

'Mr Blum has informed police that Marion told him that they were travelling to Europe together to go on the *Orient Express*. According to Mr Blum, Marion told him that she was going to the United Kingdom and that she wanted to open a private school in England. He said this was the last time he saw Marion.'

There is so much to unpack.

Sally has consistently said many of her mother's belongings were stored at the Gold Coast hinterland property owned by her husband Chris's grandparents, and were never touched by Marion again. Some boxes, however, likely containing expensive artworks and antiques, had gone missing. Despite extensive searches of local storage companies, they've never been found.

Marion also had a crush on a pilot on while working at The Southport School. According to friends and former work colleagues, he was the father of a child she taught. But he was not aged in his 50s at the time and they did not have a relationship as he did not reciprocate her feelings.

There's also the mystery of the 'tall' man spotted in Marion's car by Sally and Chris shortly before Marion left the country. When asked later about the encounter, Sally recalls Marion downplaying the incident, saying the man was a friend she knew from a local art gallery. None of Marion's family members or friends believed she was travelling with anyone to the UK. And she had told no one of any plans to start a private school.

Casselden then tells the court about Blum's travel movements in 1997, which dovetail neatly with those of Marion. Records show Blum travelled to Japan on 17 June 1997, five days before Marion made her way to the UK on Korean Air. His incoming passenger card shows he returned to Australia on 31 July 1997, two days before Marion, or someone using her passport in the name Florabella Remakel, returned to Australia.

The significance of this is heightened by Sally having received a letter on notepaper from the Hotel Nikko, Narita in Japan, from Marion dated 22 June 1997, which according to the postmark was sent from Tonbridge in the UK eight days later. In this letter, she asked her daughter to return a set of kitchen scales to TSS which Sally maintains was strange because if Marion was going to 'disappear', why would she care if the scales got back to the school or not? While there is no record Marion ever having stayed at Hotel Nikko, Blum confirmed he had been there.

Casselden tells the court Blum denies having anything to do with Marion after she went overseas. 'Mr Blum … informed investigators that he never saw Marion coming back from wherever she went. He denies having any interaction with Marion in Australia after August the 2nd, 1997. Blum also informed police that he was unaware Marion was a missing person, had no knowledge of her name change, and had never received any money from her.'

The evidence put forward by Casselden is the result of persistent digging by Detective Senior Constable Sasha Pinazza, the officer in charge of the Homicide Squad's investigation. She tracked Ric Blum down by starting with the personal ad published in *Le Courrier Australien* in 1994, which was included in the case file transferred to the Homicide Squad in November 2019. Detective Pinazza did a search across jurisdictions for the Remakel name, and came up with a hit: a Queensland driver's licence issued in the name Fernand Nocolas Remakel.

Apart from the 'o' replacing the 'i' in Nicolas, that's the exact name of the man the TLV team tracked down in Luxembourg. They always suspected a connection and now here it is. Except that the personal ad and the Queensland driver's licence do not belong to the *real* Fernand Remakel they met in Luxembourg, who truly never met Marion. Ric Blum stole Remakel's identity, right down to his birthdate.

It turns out Ric Blum lived not far from Fernand Remakel in Luxembourg in the early 1980s, and knew all about him. Blum was infatuated with Fernand's ex-wife, Monique Cornelius, the very same Monique Cornelius who Seymour and Sally spoke to on the phone during their trip to Luxembourg.

The Queensland driver's licence for the fake Fernand Remakel was issued on 24 August 1988 and linked to an address at Mount Warren Park, a suburb of Logan, a city south of Brisbane and north of the Gold Coast.

Detective Pinazza also conducted inquiries into the Lennox Head post-office box and Ballina phone number listed in the ad. The investigation, including a laborious search of the 1994 Ballina White Pages, yielded nothing. When Pinazza and her colleague, Detective Senior Constable Leza Pessotto, began checking the 1995 Ballina White Pages on 15 October 2020, however, they found a match on page 52 – Ballina Coin Investments Pty Ltd at Tamar Street, Ballina.

A request to search records of the Australian Securities and Investments Commission (ASIC) for the business delivered results within hours. The directors of Ballina Coin Investments Pty Ltd from 2 September 1994 to 28 January 2000 were Frederick David De Hedervary and his wife, Diane De Hedervary.

Inquiries into those names found that Frederick De Hedervary is presently known as Ric Blum, a Belgian national born on 9 July 1939, who married Diane in February 1976 and was granted Australian citizenship on 25 March 1976.

The detectives' investigation finds Blum is linked to 30 known aliases across Australia and internationally, one of which is Fernand Remakel. All of his identities are recorded in a statement made by Detective Pinazza on 8 December 2021.*

Name	Date of birth
Anthony Grech	25/07/1951
Atilla Dupont	
Bernard DuPont	04/03/1944
Charles Guyon	04/04/1947
Christopher Du Pont	04/03/1944
Christopher Stein	04/03/1944
David Freddy	09/02/1937, 9/06/1932
Fernand Nocolas Remakel	02/12/1947
Francis David De Hedervary	09/07/1939
Franck Melan	19/09/1938
Freddy David	09/06/1942
Frederick David De Hedervary	09/07/1939
Frederick De Hedervaru	09/07/1939
Frederick De Hedervary	09/07/1939
Frederique De-Haverdary	09/07/1939
Gaetan Le Bouriscot	17/10/1939
Guy Divio	01/01/1901
Philippe Dint	14/03/1937
Remy Lajoy	27/09/1938
Ric Blum	09/07/1939
Rich Richard	09/07/1939
Richard Lloyd West	09/07/1939
Richard Lloyd Westbury	09/07/1939
Rick Richard	09/07/1939
Rick West	09/07/1939

---

* Statement of Detective Senior Constable Sascha Pinazza, 8 December 2021.

Name	Date of birth
Roger Lazoney/Lauzoney	01/02/1945
Willy Coppenolle	09/07/1939
Willy David-Coppenolle	09/07/1939
Willy Wouters	09/07/1939
Wouters Willy	09/07/1939

Their inquiries also lead them to two women living in New South Wales. Both have incredible stories of love, loss and trauma involving a man whose names are on this list.

CHAPTER 21

*The Cozener**

24 December 1998
NSW police pull up outside the Ballina home of 'Frederick De Hedervary'. An officer serves him interim orders for an application for an apprehended violence order (AVO) issued by Sydney divorcée Ginette Gaffney-Bowan.

13 January 2000
Recently divorced Janet Oldenburg provides a comprehensive statement to police in northern New South Wales in which she makes serious allegations about a man she identifies as 'Rick West', but who may be known to others as 'Rich Richard' or 'Richard Lloyd Westbury'.

26 July 2010
A typed letter from Belgian widow Andrée Flamme is forwarded to the attention of Australian authorities, outlining a string of alleged misdeeds by Belgian turned Australian 'Frederick De Hedervary'. She also provides his contact details.

Ginette, Janet and Andrée's stories share similar accounts of deception, theft and fraud at the hands of a man with many names. But he's neither investigated nor charged.

---

* The noun 'cozener' is defined by the *Oxford English Dictionary* as 'a deceiver, cheat, impostor'.

3 February 2022

Ginette Gaffney-Bowan, 76, is the same age as Marion Barter, if she is still alive. Her face appears from Sydney on a screen alongside those of the lawyers who will be asking her questions.

It's less than 16 months since Ginette recounted her story about Frederick De Hedervary to Detectives Sasha Pinazza and Leza Pessotto, who attended her home on 22 October 2020. They found her apprehensive about providing a signed statement outlining her relationship with the man from whom she sought police protection more than 20 years earlier.

Ginette was born in Algeria, schooled in France and moved to Australia via New Caledonia in 1972. Not surprisingly, she speaks with a distinctive French accent. In the 1980s, she was married with two daughters. By the late 1990s, she was a single mother, divorced and running a childcare service from her home in the Sydney suburb of Greenwich. The business operated five days a week, from eight in the morning until six at night. She took only two weeks off a year, at Christmas.

While she was financially independent, she was very lonely and vulnerable: 'I was extremely busy, extremely. Extremely down, because my ex-husband was always harassing me and I had no friends. So I was really just on my own.'[*]

She placed an ad looking for companionship in an English-language newspaper in late 1998, and received a phone call from a French-speaking man, Frederick De Hedervary. He told her he lived at Lennox Head but often visited Sydney, and would like to take her out to dinner. Ginette reveals how quickly he moved to gain a foothold in her life: 'When he brought me back home, we stood in front of my house. He said he had lost his home, and that I had a nice home, it was like his. He put on a very sad face and I felt sorry for him.'

Ginette had a garden studio, separate from the main house, where students sometimes stayed. Because De Hedervary claimed to visit Sydney often, Ginette offered him use of the studio. While he departed that evening, he did come to stay soon after.

---

[*] Transcript, NSW Coroner's Court, 3 February 2022.

By Ginette's recollections, her dealings with De Hedervary added up to a matter of weeks. She tells the court she did not ask for rent, nor did he offer to pay any. She doesn't believe he had a key, as the studio was not lockable and the main house was often open because parents were always coming and going for the childcare service she provided.

She called him 'Frederick' or 'Fred'. Sometimes he would pop over to the main house to say hello in the late afternoon. Once he cooked for her. On weekends, they would chat into the evenings. But she denies ever having a romantic or sexual relationship with him.

'He made a business proposition – buying and selling old coins. I had been looking for a while to start another business. I must have told him, that's why he suggested this business. I assumed he had an interest in coins because he seemed to know a lot about it. He said it was an easy business and very rewarding financially … He said he needed money for the start-up, for things like fax machines.'

Ginette says she handed De Hedervary her card and the pin number to access her bank account, and $30,000 was withdrawn. Adam Casselden SC asks her what De Hedervary spent it on and she can only recall a fax machine, for which she never saw a receipt. To her knowledge, there were never any coins bought. While there was no discussion about what role she'd play in the business, she says she assumed it would be a partnership.

Casselden asks Ginette whether she had forgotten forming an emotional attachment to De Hedervary, citing the December 1998 AVO, which stated there were plans for marriage. Ginette says she hoped for a close connection, but it was clear early on that there would not be: 'When I placed the ad, I was looking for a friend. Hopefully it could become much more than friendship, but the behaviour he had did nothing for my emotions. All he was interested in was belittling and the business.'

Some weeks into the relationship, De Hedervary suggested Ginette sell her house. Casselden reads from her statement: 'He said, "if I sold my house, he would go to find a beautiful, spacious apartment in Paris".'

'He was manipulating for me to sell my house so we could go to France and get a unit. I said I would not sell my house, it's for my children. He did not like that. I told him Australia is my daughters' home. After the second time, he left it because I was quite adamant about it. He wanted to get hold of my money. I think he was surprised. He thought I was stupid.'

The court hears that Ginette believed De Hedervary to be single until one time, while they were driving, he received a phone call from a woman. Ginette then had a feeling he might be married, but she never asked, so was never sure.

She appears embarrassed when asked about nude photographs, mentioned in her statement, that Frederick had taken of her:

GAFFNEY-BOWAN: I am afraid he caught me at a very low time in my life. I don't understand how he got me undressed. He was partly clothed when he took photos of me but there were no sexual relations. His mind was on taking the photos to blackmail me. He was impotent.

CASSELDEN: What happened to those photos?

GAFFNEY-BOWAN: He said that he would be showing them around. He blackmailed and threatened me. He wanted me to do what he wanted me to do, like selling my house for the money.

The court is told De Hedervary threatened to put garbage all over Ginette's garden and have her childcare business closed down, so she contacted the Belgian consulate to report him. Then she called the police. 'What was it to your mind ... after he took photos ... what was he seeking from you?' Casselden asks.

'Money, that's all he has been after all along. I got scared. I was becoming very scared so I contacted the police.'

She sought the AVO after De Hedervary threatened to 'get' her family in Australia and overseas. After that, she says she didn't hear from him again. Around the same time, however, an anonymous complaint was made to the Department of Community Services about Ginette's home-based childcare service. It mentioned certain aspects of her house that only a few people knew – and De Hedervary was one of them.

Ginette tells the court about several possessions that went missing from her home while she was shopping one Saturday and De Hedervary was staying in her garden studio. They include a gold nugget given to her daughters by their father, an 18-carat gold chain, pure silver coins from Argentina (a present from a friend in the 1970s), cassettes of French songs by a Belgian singer, and a book from the bedside table. 'He was the only one in my home,' she says. 'I personally have no doubt, but I cannot give you specific proof.'

Ginette admits she knew very little about Frederick De Hedervary before letting him into her life. She knew he was Belgian, had an interest in old coins and lived at Lennox Head, and that's pretty much all. She didn't even have his phone number or the correct spelling of his name. 'He was just collecting information from me,' she says. 'I believe that Frederick made a job of zeroing in on vulnerable females to steal from them. From the moment he came into my home I was belittled, I was openly threatened. He tried to separate me from my daughters so I [would] have no one, not even my own children, close to me. I believe he could easily emotionally destabilise as well as financially ruin a person without any care on his part, as long as he benefits from his actions.'

When the TLV team is allowed access to the brief of evidence for the first time, they discover a little more to Ginette's story. It reveals Ginette Gaffney-Bowan told police that after ending contact with Frederick, she told a friend at her church about what had happened and was astonished when her friend said that another of her female friends had also been 'taken advantage of by this man'. Ginette tried to track the woman down, but said she had since passed away.

4 February 2022

A new day arrives, along with another woman who has serious allegations about Ric Blum. Appearing on screen is 73-year-old Janet Oldenburg.

Born in England, Janet moved to Australia in 1963 but still retains a reasonably strong English accent. In the 1990s, the mother of two sons was living on an 11-hectare property just outside Woodburn in northern New South Wales. Woodburn is a small town with a population of less than 800, about a 30-minute drive south of Ballina. Janet's closest neighbours lived half a kilometre away.

Janet was married to Michael Oldenburg, a coins enthusiast. In the mid-1990s, the couple attended coin auctions together in Ballina. In these coin-collecting circles she met a man named Ric West, from whom her husband made some purchases. She later came to know this same man as Rich Richard and discovered he changed his name by deed poll to Richard Westbury.

They are all Ric Blum.

In May 1998, Michael Oldenburg left Janet and she was shattered. He'd been the primary breadwinner, so now she had to rely on social security. Money was tight. More than a year after the separation, in June 1999, Janet received a phone call out of the blue from Blum.

She hadn't been to a coin auction since her husband left, and had only seen Blum on the odd occasion at the shops. She was in the midst of an unpleasant property settlement and a bit suspicious: 'He said: "You're a very nice person and I don't like what's being done to you." I said: "Has this anything to do with Mike?" He said: "Yes, it's about your settlement." I said: "What about it?"'*

Janet recalls Blum asking to see her so they could discuss the matter over coffee. It was four months before she heard from him again, in October 1999, by which time Blum had a business proposal. She told Blum she had no money to invest in a business, but he insisted he was looking for a business partner and they should meet up. Janet was single. Her two sons, then in their 20s, were not living nearby. She saw it as an opportunity to secure some work and gain an income.

Janet says she believed she would be doing administrative work. They agreed to meet the following day at a cafe in Evans Head, a ten-minute drive from Woodburn. At that stage, she had no idea

---

* Transcript, NSW Coroner's Court, 4 February 2022.

where Blum lived, although he later told her he was staying with friends in East Ballina. He never gave her his phone number.

At the cafe Blum ran through his business proposal. 'He was going to teach me how to use the computer because I knew nothing about it. I'd have a computer and fax machine at my place. He wanted me to look at his emails, take orders for coins and post them off. Also, go down to Sydney and do some bidding for him at coin auctions. He wanted to help me out because of my predicament. Give me some work. And I knew there was money in coins.'

The business never eventuated, however, and Blum did not leave a computer or fax machine at Janet's home. He did invite her to London for a coin auction, though, telling her he'd pay for all expenses.

Janet tells the court she was starting to have feelings for Blum. She was 51 years old at the time, lonely, vulnerable and concerned about her financial position. 'I'd had a husband who took care of everything and then suddenly he left. I did feel very emotional, but I was trying to get over it. It was difficult.'

Shortly before her first meeting with Blum, Janet was granted sole ownership of the family home at Woodburn and a Nissan Patrol vehicle on 15 October 1999. Three days later, Blum asked Janet to start life afresh with him in the French Riviera, saying he'd had feelings for her for three years. 'I felt uplifted,' she says, 'to start a new life, a new beginning. That was pretty much where the relationship began. We talked about the trip a couple of times and other locations like Algeria and Spain – because the weather would be nice and warm and I could have servants to look after my house so I wouldn't have to do anything.'

Casselden tells Janet that Blum has since told police investigators he had no plan to settle in Europe with her. 'Sorry, I can't believe he said that because it's true,' she says, 'he did say that. He was telling me all these things.'

The court hears the pair started a sexual relationship, but at no time did Janet know that Blum was married with children: 'He told me he was single.' She did see documents with the name Richard Lloyd Westbury, but he said he was now going by the name Rich

Richard. 'People change their name by deed poll all the time,' she explains. 'Didn't pay any attention to it. There was his passport, that was all done in the name Rich Richard. The driver's licence was in the name of R. Richard. And he had a photo on it.'

So Janet then began referring to him as Rich Richard. 'He told me that he was worth about $12 million through his coin dealings. And he also owned 20,000 acres in Nymboida [south of Grafton] with red cedar growing on it. I got together with him for a relationship, not the money, so I just brushed it off. I didn't really pay any heed to that. I didn't have any reason not to believe him. I did put my trust in him fully until the end of the relationship.'

Before their trip overseas, the pair arranged new passports. Janet says Blum wanted her to change her natural dark brown hair to blonde for the passport photo, but the hairdresser was not keen to make such a radical change. They discussed attending a coin auction in London and spoke of visiting Bali and Amsterdam.

Casselden asks whether Blum raised the notion of becoming power of attorney in each other's affairs.

OLDENBURG: Yes. He brought the subject up. He said if anything happens to him, I would be taken care of and so would the boys.

CASSELDEN: Did you know it could authorise a person to sign documents on your behalf?

OLDENBURG: No I didn't realise, no.

CASSELDEN: Did you obtain legal advice about this proposal?

OLDENBURG: No.

CASSELDEN: Was the power of attorney witnessed by a Justice of the Peace at the Lismore Courthouse?

OLDENBURG: Yes.

CASSELDEN: Did Rich Richard provide you with a power of attorney over his affairs at this time?

OLDENBURG: No. I think we both signed the same document. He took care of that and put it in his bag when we went overseas. That's the last I saw of it.

The court is told that before the trip Blum brought black tubing to Janet's house and asked her to put her valuables in it so they could be buried, just in case the house was robbed while they were away. They went through Janet's jewellery and put into the tubing a wedding ring, an engagement ring, a gold ingot, a jade necklace, a couple of gold bracelets, one with opals, a silver necklace and Janet's grandmother's wedding ring. 'I presumed he buried it as he said. I didn't see him bury it.'

The pair flew out on 2 December 1999, taking with them many official documents, including the title deed to Janet's Woodburn house, her birth certificate, her Australian citizenship certificate, her marriage certificate and the power of attorney document. At Blum's suggestion they also took the keys to the Woodburn house and $1000. When Casselden asks if Blum explained why, Janet replies, 'It was because we were going to settle in Europe somewhere.'

The court hears Blum paid for the flights and accommodation and told Janet he was taking $10,000 in cash and traveller's cheques. She says she wasn't even sure of their itinerary when they took off, but knew they planned to return to Australia and relocate to Europe later. She told her friend and sons about the trip and fully expected to be home for Christmas.

The first stop was Bali, before they flew to Amsterdam, where Blum had arranged a ferry to England. Despite being tourists, they did not do any sightseeing in either Bali or Amsterdam. 'I trusted him. He knew everything.'

Richard arranged to leave some of their luggage in storage at Amsterdam airport, which they'd pick up on the way home.

CASSELDEN: How long did you believe you'd be leaving your luggage at Amsterdam?
OLDENBURG: When he finally did some business in England, we'd go back to Amsterdam and collect the cases.
CASSELDEN: Rich Richard left a suitcase at the airport in Amsterdam. Do you know what was in it?
OLDENBURG: I have no idea, I don't know.

CASSELDEN: Why did you decide to leave them at the airport in Amsterdam and not travel with them like you did in Bali?
OLDENBURG: Because he said it saves lugging cases all over the place, we can just travel freely.

Janet never ended up going to London or France. Instead, when they got to England, Richard and Janet hired a car and drove to Sussex to look at rental properties. The stark parallels with Marion's story jump out, from travelling through Sussex to the unplanned and chaotic nature of her movements.

CASSELDEN: Where did you go?
OLDENBURG: I don't recall any names of any towns or anything.
CASSELDEN: Any sightseeing?
OLDENBURG: We didn't do any sightseeing, only that he was looking for a place to rent. And we looked through a window at a little house for rent but then decided not to so that was the end of that one.
CASSELDEN: Did the plan change to relocate to England?
OLDENBURG: I can't answer that one, what was in his mind at the time.

On 11 December 1999, when the pair was in Dover, 'Rich Richard' suddenly informed Janet she should go to spend time with her cousin in Manchester, even though she hadn't made any plans to spend time with family.

'Did this come to you like a bolt out of the blue?' Casselden asks.

'Yes, it did. He wanted to go over to France and do business. I wanted to see my cousin anyway. He suggested I stay there because he had business in France. He said he had to see a couple of people over there and he'd be in touch with me later.'

Janet stayed with her somewhat surprised cousin, John Mills, from 11 December to at least 16 December. Now in his 80s and still living in Manchester, John tells Sandy about the unexpected arrival in December 1999. 'We were just having a normal morning and out of the blue, Janet phoned saying she was getting a train to Manchester and could she come up for a few days?'

'So I said, certainly, of course you can. I picked her up in Manchester that evening. She had very little luggage and she had very little money. I hadn't seen her for donkey's years. The last time I saw her, I believe, was before she went to Australia in 1963, '64. She told us that she'd flown to Amsterdam with this "tricky dicky" fellow. Janet was very taken with him at that time, and she was very trusting of him.

'She was saying that they were looking for a place to live on the continent and I thought, that's a bit unusual, to say the least. The fact that she left her luggage in Amsterdam, and that he left her and put her on a train to Manchester … I certainly smelled a rat. But then my wife and I kept it to ourselves because Janet was so full of him.'

Janet tells the inquest she didn't hear from Blum for two days. She couldn't call him as she didn't have a contact number or know where he was staying. What she did know is he retained possession of all of her important documents, including the title deed to her Woodburn home.

'Did you have any suspicions about his intentions?' Casselden asks.

'Nup, no idea.'

On 13 December, Blum called Janet at John Mills' home.

CASSELDEN: Did he say, 'I'm still in England, I'll get the night ferry, catch a train to Brussels and then to France, ring you on Wednesday night'?
OLDENBURG: Correct.
CASSELDEN: Did you ask why he hadn't called previously if he was still in England.
OLDENBURG: No.

Three days later, on 16 December, Blum contacted Ms Oldenburg again, telling her he'd been bashed and robbed by six men armed with baseball bats at a train station and he was in hospital with two broken ribs at Lille, in France, near the Belgian border. He said his passport and all of her personal documents had been stolen, along with her house keys. He claimed he had to contact the embassy for a travel document and then asked if Janet could stay in England until 29 December.

'Why could he not get you on a flight prior to 29 December?' Casselden asks. 'Did you have any sense he did not want you to return to Australia quickly?'

'Not me, my cousin did. He thought something was wrong and that's why he got me back on a plane quickly.'

John Mills recalls that after that phone call, he and his wife finally expressed their concerns about Blum's behaviour: 'We decided that something was wrong, and that she should get back to Australia as soon as possible because she had property, and I understood that he had access to the house,' he tells Sandy.

Janet tells the inquest, 'I arrived in Woodburn at seven in the morning on the night coach.' She collected a spare front-door key she'd left with a friend and arranged for a locksmith to cut new keys for the house. Blum hadn't told her when he was likely to be discharged from hospital in France or when he'd contact her or meet up with her again.

CASSELDEN: Had you started to become suspicious?
OLDENBURG: No, no I hadn't.
CASSELDEN: You still trusted him fully?
OLDENBURG: Yes.

At around 11 am that same day – Monday, 20 December – Blum turned up unannounced at Janet's Woodburn home. She had presumed he was still recovering in hospital and didn't know she had found her own way home.

CASSELDEN: You confirmed that you had not seen him since nine days prior in Dover ... What was his reaction?
OLDENBURG: The expression on his face was sort of

shocked. I couldn't work that out. I thought he was just
weary from walking up the driveway. It was a hot day.
CASSELDEN: Did he have any injuries?
OLDENBURG: No, and I asked him how his ribs were and he
said he took the bandages off because it was uncomfortable.
CASSELDEN: Did he show you the injuries?
OLDENBURG: Not that day. I noticed he didn't have any
bruises and he was walking around okay, so I thought he was
better.

Blum didn't say how he managed to get from a hospital in France
to Australia in four days, despite apparently having no passport.
He only stayed for half an hour.

CASSELDEN: Did he return your house keys?
OLDENBURG: Yes, he did.
CASSELDEN: The ones he said were stolen in Lille?
OLDENBURG: Yes, the same.
CASSELDEN: What was his explanation?
OLDENBURG: He said the French police sent the keys, and
my title deeds, by courier.

Janet says Blum returned her title deed at a later date and she put it in
her filing cabinet at that time. Her other personal documents were
never returned. Nothing more was said about relocating to Europe,
but Janet still trusted him, and there were further discussions about
selling her house. When she contacted a local real estate agent, she
found the title deed for her property missing from the filing cabinet.

OLDENBURG: That's when I started to get suspicious, really
suspicious. About Ric or Rich.
CASSELDEN: Why?
OLDENBURG: Because he gave them to me a few days before
or whatever and I know I put them in the filing cabinet and
all of a sudden they're missing and he's the only one who's
been in the house.

CASSELDEN: Did he have any keys to your premises?

OLDENBURG: I did notice that on some doors there were little keys, about three and I used to leave them sitting in the door and there was one missing. That was weird.

CASSELDEN: Was anything else missing from your house at this time?

OLDENBURG: I went to dig up the jewellery and it was gone. It wasn't there.

The missing title deed was never found, so Janet had a new one issued in January 2000.

The Coroner hears Janet last spoke with Blum on 5 January 2000, when she asked him about the jewellery and he said he'd send it back. She received a package two days later containing some of the jewellery. A silver necklace and her grandmother's wedding ring were missing and she reported it to police. When Casselden says Blum has since told police he returned the jewellery, Janet laughs and says, 'He didn't.'

Janet tells the court she hasn't seen or heard from Blum since early 2000 and has never tried to locate him. She's shown a recent photo of a white-haired man and says, 'Yeah, that's him. Ric West. Rich Richard.'

Janet also reveals that she would often pick Blum up and drive him around. She'd drop him off near the Big Prawn in Ballina. She never had the opportunity to introduce him to anyone she knew, other than once briefly when she popped by a friend's house. Even then, he did not get out of the car. Janet's friend saw him through the window in the front passenger seat. This is eerily reminiscent of Sally and Chris seeing a tall man in Marion's car.

Sandy catches up with Janet about an hour after she finishes giving evidence. She's just how she appeared at the inquest: kind and polite, but also quite cheery.

'He's a very convincing, cool, calm character – smooth,' she says, 'and he was very logical in everything he said, so I believed everything. He reckoned if our relationship dissolved, the power of attorney would too. I was very naive back then, so it sounded logical to me at the time.'

Janet did eventually find love again with Ron, a retired university professor. She's glad *The Lady Vanishes* is shining a bright light on Blum.

The inquest is far from over. More testimony comes from two former Queensland police officers, Paula McKenzie and Trudi McKechnie.

In late 1997, when McKenzie worked with the Queensland Missing Persons Unit, she made notes in her official diary about long phone calls with Marion's father, Jack Wilson, in December, and likely Sally in late November, as Sally's former phone number is listed in the notes. The Coroner hears diary entries detailing Marion's return from England in 1997 without contacting family and accessing $95,000 from her bank account, which was out of character. McKenzie tells the court the diary was used for basic notes while the official daily running sheets contained more detailed information. The running sheets for this period are, however, no longer available.

One diary entry on 25 November 1997 states: 'Marion missing from England believed to be back in the country. Inquiries being conducted in the Byron Bay area.' A note from the day before shows McKenzie had been in contact with a woman from the Colonial State Bank, and she tells the court she clearly remembers the phone call: 'She advised me that Marion had been in the bank to withdraw the rest of her money … Marion had said she did not want her whereabouts to be disclosed to anybody, and I can remember her informing me that it was definitely Marion in the bank and they didn't have any doubts.'*

McKenzie is asked what evidence she had from the bank officer to confirm that it was indeed Marion. 'The bank won't supply anything other than that the person that is there has the right to their own privacy and we were lucky enough to be getting the information we're working with, with them to even be replying to us. The teller was just so insistent that that was definitely her.

---

* Transcript, NSW Coroner's Court, 1 February 2022.

And that was it … that was the information I had to go with – the bank teller. But I still believe that it was correct.'

When asked if there were any checks to ensure that someone wasn't masquerading as Marion Barter at the bank, McKenzie says, 'Now that is something that the bank has to prove, as they are the ones that were giving her her money and closing her account.' McKenzie claims the bank officer told her she had been very thorough in confirming Marion's identification as it was such a large transaction. 'I presume she remembered her because she was so determined in the way she was telling me that she knew who Marion was and that she knew that she knew her.'

On 1 December 1997, McKenzie notes in her diary: 'Missing person located safe and well. Whereabouts not to be disclosed.' Police guidelines, then and now, require officers to sight and/or speak with someone before determining they are located.

Trudi McKechnie managed the Queensland Missing Persons Unit from the late 1980s until her retirement in 2001. In 1997, she worked alongside six police officers and an administrative assistant on all the missing persons cases in Queensland. They also helped the Red Cross and Salvation Army with inquiries. Cases were allocated to whomever was on shift, and any information that came in was added to the files, which were kept in the office.

She tells the court she has no independent recollection of Marion Barter's disappearance, but it was common to contact banks for information on missing persons' accounts, and certain checks were needed to verify if someone had been found. 'I used to always maintain that we needed to talk to the actual missing person or that the missing person needed to have been sighted for them to be located.'

When asked whether her former co-worker, Paula McKenzie, should have done more to verify that Marion Barter had been located rather than rely on the word of a bank teller, McKechnie defends her colleague: 'I think that she would have acted appropriately. She was an accomplished investigator, and if she was satisfied, having spoken to the bank teller that they had verified that it was Marion Barter, I would have accepted it.'

Graham Smith, the former investigations manager with the Commonwealth Bank, returns to the stand. This time, he's quizzed about Frederick David De Hedervary.

Records relating to applications to the Commonwealth Bank for safe custody envelopes and a safe custody box are tendered as evidence in a bundle of documents. A handwritten note, in the name Frederick De Hedervary, is on one of them. 'So that's an authority that has been lodged,' Smith says. 'It's an automatic funds transfer for the payment of safe custody lodgements and that relates to a safe custody lodgement that was made at Ballina on 14.10.1997, with a reference number of 3810.'*

On that date, De Hedervary paid $13 to secure a safe custody envelope and keep it at the Commonwealth Bank in Ballina. The safe custody lodgement is made to a joint account in the names of Frederick and Diane De Hedervary. On a different page in the bundle of documents is another authority, which cancels the same safe custody holding on 27 October 1997, only 13 days after it was opened.

Smith confirms that only Frederick De Hedervary could access the safe custody envelope. He agrees that cash, jewellery or documents could easily be stored in the A3-sized envelope. Coincidentally, on 15 October 1997, one day after he paid for the envelope, an $80,000 withdrawal was made from Marion Barter's bank account.

Smith also reveals that on 27 July 1999 there was another authorisation for De Hedervary to acquire a safe custody lodgement, which was cancelled one year later in August 2000. In September 2005 a safe deposit box was acquired, and surrendered two years later in 2007.

When Sally Leydon is called again as a witness, the lights and air conditioner in her office have stopped working due to electrical storms. Despite her discomfort in sweltering conditions, she ploughs on. The questions focus on Ric Blum's statement. She agrees that she's read a police statement he made in June 2021, and has seen transcripts of a recorded interview with Blum made in

---

* Transcript, NSW Coroner's Court, 2 February 2022.

September 2021. She can't say whether the man now on a screen in front of her matches her memory of a shadowy stranger in her mother's car at a Gold Coast service station one night in 1997. 'Mr Blum has very white hair now,' she says. 'My memory of the man is that he was tall and dark … but it was also night, which made it appear dark.'*

She also casts doubt on Blum's suggestion that he responded to a personal ad placed by Marion Barter. 'I did not believe that when I read it. It's been addressed before, but my mum had a lot of partners. She never had any problem finding partners, so she wouldn't need to put an ad in the paper.' The only man she recalls her mother seeing in early 1997 is Greg Edwards, the school groundsman.

Sally is then quizzed about personal matters, including her late brother's occupation and where she met her husband Chris. She's asked whether these pieces of information are included in the podcast, as investigators are trying to determine if Ric Blum has listened to *The Lady Vanishes*.

'Did your mother have a relationship with a naval officer or pilot?' Casselden asks.

'I only know what I was told by her friends in 2018. I had three people tell me. Barbara [Mathie] believed she liked the father of a boy she taught who was a pilot. Janis White, my mother had told her about a man she was interested in who was a pilot but that it was one-sided. And a parent that my mother was friendly with remembered the little boy of the pilot.'

The TLV team works around the clock collecting notes, reviewing transcripts of evidence and writing well into the night. As soon as Eeles completes a script she messages the rest of the team. Voices are recorded beneath pillow tents in bedrooms and among clothes in cupboards – anywhere that's fast and convenient for producing decent-quality audio.

Wrighty is up at dawn each morning to get a jumpstart on the edits. Nearly three years after the first episode aired, *The Lady Vanishes* is breaking new ground.

---

* Transcript, NSW Coroner's Court, 2 February 2022.

CHAPTER 22

Speaking in Tongues

At long last the TLV team is allowed access to at least some of the brief of evidence compiled for the Coroner by NSW Police. They're not allowed to copy anything, but can inspect the files at the Coroner's Court complex in Lidcombe under strict conditions. As Seymour is the only team member in Sydney, he makes the 45-minute drive out west.

Once he signs in, he is taken to a small, empty meeting room on the first floor. An old Dell laptop is open on the conference table. The clunky machine takes a while to come to life, but finally the home page appears with the folders he's been waiting for months to access. It takes him two days to view the single 2356-page pdf file, which has no index or coherent structure. The collected documents reveal that detectives have been busy chasing up leads, including tips and 15 reports through the NSW Crime Stoppers network, such as:

- The claim in 2002 that Marion was buried in Armidale, New South Wales, followed up eight years later by Detective Sheehan.
- Possible sightings of Marion in Mullumbimby, Riverwood, Tyalgum, Byron Bay, Campbelltown and Coffs Harbour in New South Wales, Margate in Tasmania, and even in Western Australia.
- A 'premonition' from an informant who approached police at Penrith, New South Wales, in May 2019, about where Marion was buried. They provided the longitude and latitude of a remote, rural area south-west of Byron Bay.

A local detective sent to examine the ground could find
no evidence of a grave, while the nearest residents were
cleared of any possible connection to Marion or the case.

The brief also includes the statements given to police by Ginette
Gaffney-Bowan and Janet Oldenburg. Apart from the statement
from Gaffney-Bowan when she applied for the AVO against
De Hedervary, both women were interviewed by detectives more
recently. Ginette's interview revealed that:

- After ending contact with Frederick, she told a friend
  at her church about what had happened – and was
  astonished when the friend told her one of her female
  friends had also been 'taken advantage of by this man'.
  She tried to track down the woman but said she and her
  husband had since passed away.

Janet Oldenburg's evidence at the inquest covered much of what
was contained in her interviews with police, with a couple of
additional pieces of information:

- When she questioned Ric (aka Rich Richard and
  Richard Lloyd Westbury), about why she had to take her
  title deed and identification documents to Europe, he told
  her it was so they could buy a property in her name in
  Europe, where they would spend their new life together.
- When Janet asked why not have the house in both
  names, Ric told her, 'In case something happens to me,
  you won't have to pay capital gains tax.'
- In 2000, the detective who interviewed Janet, Andrew
  Campbell, was already suspicious of Frederick and his
  motives, writing on 14 January 2000, 'A motive for
  Rich to steal the items including the documents is
  unclear at this point, however several scenarios along
  the lines of using her identification documents for illegal
  transactions or to assist him to enable another female to

assume Ms Oldenburg's identity for whatever purpose is being considered.'

There's plenty more in the brief, and Seymour takes copious notes in shorthand and on his laptop before finally calling it quits, to the relief of the staff member charged with watching him the entire time.

14 February 2022 – Valentine's Day

Ric Blum and his wife, Diane De Hedervary, arrive at the Ballina Courthouse at 8.40 am. They haven't come far. They've lived in and around Ballina for decades.

The tall, white-haired Blum is slightly stooped. A disposable blue Covid mask covers much of his face. He's carrying handwritten notes in a clear folder while pushing his wheelie walker. The front of it is emblazoned with the manufacturer's logo, 'Hero'.

When Sandy approaches with a microphone and a camera crew trailing close behind, Diane quickly moves out of shot but remains relatively close to her husband.

'Hi Ric, can you tell us about your relationship with Marion?'

Blum chooses to ignore Sandy. Perhaps he's been instructed to. The couple acknowledges her only once, when she tells them where the bathrooms are.

When another man walks past, he makes eye contact with Blum and nods, which Blum reciprocates. Sandy approaches him and the man introduces himself as Don McKenzie. He says he lived next door to Ric Blum and his wife in the mid-1990s at Ballina, until the couple moved away. Blum went by the name De Hedervary then.

Don has already spoken to police and was shocked to hear of his former neighbour's link to the Marion Barter case. He remembers Blum travelling overseas a lot but says that he kept pretty much to himself. 'A complete surprise, he didn't splash money or anything like that. Very ordinary people, I'd never have expected it.'

There's standing room only as the few chairs are quickly taken and Coroner Teresa O'Sullivan takes her seat. Adam Casselden SC stands facing the bench.

Ric Blum's wife shuffles to the stand, six days before her 50th wedding anniversary. She mostly looks down, avoiding the eyes of strangers.

> CASSELDEN: Have you known your husband by other names?
>
> DIANE: Willy Wouters, Frederick De Hedervary or Ric Blum.
>
> CASSELDEN: Were there any others?
>
> DIANE: Ric West.
>
> CASSELDEN: Any more? What about Richard Lloyd Westbury? Why did he go by different names?
>
> DIANE: I don't know. I asked him but he said it was legal. I haven't done it myself so I don't really know why. I didn't understand why. He had no reason for it. I didn't gain any explanation.
>
> CASSELDEN: Did you not press him as to why he kept changing his name?
>
> DIANE: He said it was all above board and legal. I did say it was weird.
>
> CASSELDEN: You accepted that?
>
> DIANE: In the end.
>
> CASSELDEN: Were you concerned that he changed his name?
>
> DIANE: I was concerned. I always got the same answer, there was nothing wrong with it.
>
> CASSELDEN: Did your children know their father was changing his name?
>
> DIANE: No. I didn't tell them. We kept our name and he changed his.*

Diane repeatedly pleads ignorance as a long list of deceptions is put to her. She didn't know about Blum's 'affairs', and his trips abroad on their meagre income were to visit family and collect small instalments of an inheritance left by his mother. They never had much money to spend or to do anything. She assumes her

---

* Evidence of Diane De Hedervary to the NSW Coroner, 14 February 2022.

husband was staying with family to save money and claims that she 'doesn't know about airfares'.

As Casselden's questioning fails to elicit any insightful responses, he frustratedly resorts to listing a string of aliases Diane's husband has used.

> CASSELDEN: Anthony Grech, Atilla DuPont, Bernard DuPont, Charles Guyon, Christopher Du Pont, Christopher Stein, David Freddy, Fernand Nocolas Remakel, Francis David De Hedervary, Franck Melan, Freddy David, Frederick/Frederic David De Hedervery, Frederick De Hedervaru, Frederick De Hedervary, Frederique De-Haverdary, Gaetan Le Bouriscot, Guy Divio, Philippe Dint, Remy Lajoy, Ric Blum, Rich Richard, Richard Lloyd West, Richard Lloyd Westbury, Rick Richard, Rick West, Roger Lazoney/Lauzoney, Willy Coppenolle, Willy David Coppenolle, Willy Wouters, Wouters Willy. Apart from the four you mentioned you don't know the others?
> DIANE: No.
> CASSELDEN: Does this come as a surprise?
> DIANE: Yes.

Diane doesn't look surprised. If anything, she seems bored.

> CASSELDEN: You can't recall why he used different names at different times?
> DIANE: No.
> CASSELDEN: Was it to obtain financial benefit?
> DIANE: I don't know.

It seems Diane doesn't know a lot of things.

> CASSELDEN: Did you learn that he'd been married?
> DIANE: Not then, no. I found out later. Probably between that period of 1970, '74. I just knew he'd been married once, that's all.

CASSELDEN: Do you know her name?

DIANE: No I don't.

CASSELDEN: You only understood there was one marriage … have you learned anything recently?

DIANE: That he may have been married three times before.

CASSELDEN: How did you find out?

DIANE: Just through the conversations with my daughter.

CASSELDEN: When did you find out? Did he tell you?

DIANE: Just in the last month or so.

When Casselden asks if she has been listening to *The Lady Vanishes*, Diane says 'not really', then clarifies that she hasn't listened to it, but her daughter, Maite, told her about it.

Diane maintains she first became aware of her husband's relationships with other women after police approached him a few months ago and he came clean about several affairs. She claims to have no historical knowledge of Monique Cornelius, Janet Oldenburg or Ginette Gaffney-Bowan, and seems less perturbed about them than she does having to be questioned about it.

When questions turn to Marion Barter, Diane is curt and dismissive.

DIANE: I had never heard of her before. I was surprised by the whole thing. I asked if he knew her. He said, 'Yes, he had known her.' He had met her 50 years ago. He said he caught up with her once or twice, that was all. Just that they got together somehow – he never really told me details. I don't know how he caught up. I think she put out a message in the newspaper or something, I don't know. He answered an ad.

He told me that they'd had a relationship again. They caught up a couple of times but he felt torn because he was married and she had another relationship, and he said that was that. Said she was up in Queensland – I think somewhere around Southport. He said that he had no idea that she was a missing person.

CASSELDEN: I imagine it came as a great surprise to you
when you realised your husband was being questioned about
Marion Barter?

DIANE: Yes.

CASSELDEN: What did he say about his last interaction with
Marion Barter?

DIANE: He said he's seen her in Queensland, he'd answered
that ad and he had a couple of days with her and then it was
over and he came back.

CASSELDEN: Did he say anything about Marion Barter's
personality?

DIANE: She was basically … it is a bit awful to say it … she
was pretty keen on men.

CASSELDEN: What else did he say to you, after he spoke to
the police?

DIANE: He just said they had a sexual relationship but it
wasn't right because he was married with children and she
had another relationship, so they just called it quits.

CASSELDEN: In such circumstances where police have spoken
to your husband, did you not want to know a bit more about
this missing person Marion Barter?

DIANE: He didn't even know she'd gone missing … He
hadn't heard from her since that time they caught up … He
had gone to Queensland and been with her for two days or
two nights and then left.

CASSELDEN: Did he tell you the last time he saw her was in
Queensland?

DIANE: Yes. I heard she was a teacher … I heard that on
the podcast … on the TV they were talking about her.
Obviously I was upset. I found out he had affairs with her.
How do you think I felt? It wasn't very nice for me. He told
me she was a teacher in Queensland.

CASSELDEN: Did he say anything to you about whether she
was living with someone or owned her home?

DIANE: No. He said she was in a relationship at the time that
he caught up with her.

CASSELDEN: Did he say who that person was?

DIANE: No.

After several hours of sustained questioning, Diane sums up her position: 'I was upset when it happened. He explained he'd been in those relationships. It was all very stressful. He was advised Marion had disappeared. He knew nothing about it. I had a surprise he even knew her … that just brought up the other women, he told me about the other women. The whole thing has been upsetting.'

Day seven of the inquest marks the first appearance of a man who will soon be very familiar to millions of people. Ric Blum takes his seat in the witness stand as Casselden squares up to him. Sally is watching intently from the public gallery.

He confirms his name and that he's a pensioner. He says he believes his birth date is 9 July 1939 and that he's read the brief of evidence and has made notes, which he forwarded to his solicitors.

CASSELDEN: At any time prior to today, have you listened to a podcast known as 'The Lady Vanishes?'

BLUM: No.

CASSELDEN: Have you at any time prior to today, followed the disappearance of Marion Barter on social media such as Facebook or anything like that?

BLUM: Until the police interviewed me. I never knew —

CASSELDEN: [Cuts him off] Have you been, at any stage prior to today, following news reports in relation to the disappearance of Marion Barter?

BLUM: I only watch ABC and SBS when I watch TV. I never watch the commercials.

CASSELDEN: Have you seen any part of your wife's evidence before Her Honour in the last few days?

BLUM: No.

CASSELDEN: You have accepted, have you not, that you had a sexual relationship with Marion Barter in the 1990s and a previous sexual encounter with her in the 1960s in Switzerland?

BLUM: That's right.

CASSELDEN: Mr Blum, Marion Barter's family is present in court today. Are you aware, from reading the brief, that there is some evidence that suggests that in mid-October 1997, Marion Barter was located safe and well?

BLUM: Police told me that when she came back, she stayed in a motel in Brisbane for a week.*

Casselden appears slightly aggravated. He's becoming impatient with Blum, who is maintaining a look of confusion and surprise on his face.

CASSELDEN: Do you know anything about Marion Barter wanting to start a new life and her whereabouts not to be disclosed.

BLUM: I read somewhere that the police in Queensland said that she went into a cult society.

CASSELDEN: I'm asking you, yourself, whether you have any personal knowledge about Marion wanting to start a new life and not having her whereabouts known?

BLUM: No, honestly. No.

Unlike his wife Diane De Hedervary, who had to be prompted repeatedly to provide adequate information and responses to questions, Blum often provides additional, uncalled for, extraneous information. He seems to talk 'around' questions, possibly to avoid providing specific answers. Casselden frequently has to repeat questions.

When asked about his birth name, Blum says he 'doesn't know', but that it was recorded as 'Willy Coppenolle'. He then explains he believes his father was a man named Désiré David who was executed during the war. He ended up with the surname of his stepfather, André (Abel) Wouters, making him Willy Wouters.

Even simple facts seemingly cause Blum confusion. He is adamant he was first contacted by police in September 2021,

---

* NSW Coroner's Court transcript, 16 February 2021.

when in fact police first reached out to him in June and he provided a signed statement dated 9 June. Even after being shown his signature, Blum denies speaking to police before September.

He admits, however, that when he was first approached he denied even knowing a person by the name of Marion Barter:

CASSELDEN: Was it that you were caught by surprise?
BLUM: No. It's because my wife was there.
CASSELDEN: Did you take some time to come to the view that you should contact police about having knowledge of Marion Barter and holding a previous licence under the name of Fernand Nocolos Remakel.
BLUM: I didn't take any time because I didn't. Until that moment. I didn't know that Marion disappeared.
CASSELDEN: But you *did* know when the police first contacted you, having had at least two sexual encounters with Marion in the 1960s and one in the '90s?
BLUM: Yes. Yes.
CASSELDEN: And you knew when police first contacted you that you had previously held a Queensland driver's licence in the name Fernand Remakel.
BLUM: Yes. Correct.
CASSELDEN: Why did you not admit to the police that you had previously held the driver's licence?
BLUM: I did not initially because my wife was interviewed by the other detective and I didn't want to say anything, that's all. My wife never knew anything. I didn't want her to be asked that.

Ric Blum admits using 13 different names. Casselden suggests he has used 30 aliases, but Blum denies this. He does admit, however, to multiple convictions for fraud in France and Belgium:

CASSELDEN: Have you not cured the problem you believed you had by changing your name in 1976 from Willy Wouters to Frederick De Hedervary – yes? If you accept that, could you please answer my earlier question as to why you have, on a number of occasions since 1976, changed your name here in Australia. Why?

BLUM: I cannot give a reasonable explanation.

CASSELDEN: Is it because you were committing acts of dishonesty here in Australia and did not want your identity to be revealed?

BLUM: Because it's legal to do so and because, probably because it was a fantasy. I don't know, I can't explain. But I never committed anything now. I don't know why I did it. Because it was easy to do it, because it was legal to do it and I was never asked any questions.

CASSELDEN: And do you have a passport now? You should, in the name of Ric Blum?

BLUM: Yes.

CASSELDEN: Why did you choose the name Blum?

BLUM: No specific reason.

CASSELDEN: From 1976, when your first Australian passport was issued, and to the present time, did you tell any family of a change of name and your passports?

BLUM: No it never came up.

CASSELDEN: Why were you so secretive to your family as to your identity? Did you not have any conversation with any family member to the effect of, 'I just changed my name to Richard Lloyd West. So you're not startled when someone calls me Mr West in the street, I shall now be known as Richard Lloyd West from here on'? ... Why the secrecy? Why the non-disclosure to your family of your new name?

BLUM: Nothing specific.

CASSELDEN: No specific reason. Do your children know that you've had all these different names or aliases?

BLUM: No. They didn't know. They know now.

Casselden goes through the various dates Blum changed his name.

CASSELDEN: Do you see how a reasonable person can draw
the conclusion that the reason you have changed your name
so many times is for some dishonest purpose?
BLUM: As I said to you, not in Australia.

When he's questioned about why his wife knew some of his aliases
but not others, Blum produces a piece of paper and says, 'Well, she
was born with craniosynostosis.' This condition is a birth defect
affecting infants that causes problems with normal brain and skull
growth. It's difficult to see what relevance it has to Diane now,
but Blum seems to be implying his wife has a memory deficiency.

There's nothing in Diane's memory about his extramarital
affairs, says Blum, because he didn't tell her about them.

'What about Monique Cornelius?' Casselden asks.

Seymour's ears prick up. Monique is the ex-wife of Fernand
Remakel in Luxembourg. He had spoken with her on the phone
when he was there with Sally. *This* is how Ric Blum is linked to
Fernand Remakel.

BLUM: That was only a platonic relation I had with
Monique. She's a fantastic person. She used to visit. Her
parents used to live near the factory. And she used to come
to the factory many, many times. She came to our home.
My wife doesn't remember that but she came to our place
to see the baby. And I said to my wife this morning – I said,
'You've got to remember Monique.' I wasn't having a sexual
relationship with Monique when my wife was having a new
baby.

Blum explains that he and his wife lived in Luxembourg in
the early 1980s for a few years, and ran a furniture store in
Noertzange. He says they left Luxembourg because his relatives
opened a bigger factory in Ellezelles, Belgium, and the operation
in Luxembourg ceased. Blum says the family then moved to
England and he looked after furniture exhibitions in Ireland,
Scotland, Paris, Genoa and London, which meant he had to travel

a lot. Eventually they moved back to Australia, a decision Blum now seems to regret.

Casselden refers to a statement Monique Cornelius made to NSW Police in October 2021, when Blum was spelling his name Frederic without the 'k'.

CASSELDEN: Were you known as Frederic De Hedervary in Luxembourg?

BLUM: That's possible.

CASSELDEN: And did you meet Monique Cornelius by chance in Luxembourg City.

BLUM: No, we met at a book sale.

CASSELDEN: You see ... she claims that she met you by chance in Luxembourg City.

BLUM: I know that. I think she was 'having the mickey' of whomever she told. I know her too well.

CASSELDEN: She says that you sat down at the same table to drink a coffee in a bistro.

Casselden then reads from Ms Cornelius' statement:

CASSELDEN: 'He talked to me and we had a good and interesting conversation. He told me, among other things, that he was working for the British Embassy in London, as a special agent.'

BLUM: I never said anything like that.

CASSELDEN: You never said to Monique Cornelius that you were working as a special agent in the British Embassy.

BLUM: No. Why would I say that?

CASSELDEN: Ms Cornelius goes on to say, 'I believed him. I was young and dumb. In the end, Frederick asked me if we could see each other again. I agreed.'

BLUM: [Interrupting] She is not —

CASSELDEN: [Continuing statement] 'We saw each other every now and again to eat out, or go out together to an event.'

Again Blum interjects quite passionately in Monique's defence:

> BLUM: She's not young and dumb. She was a teacher at the time.
> CASSELDEN: She lived alone in an apartment at the time you knew her in Luxembourg, and was she separated from her husband when you knew her?
> BLUM: I don't know if she was separated or divorced. But she wasn't living with him – that's for sure. And what —
> CASSELDEN: Was his name Fernand Remakel?
> BLUM: Yes.
> CASSELDEN: He was either married or separated from Ms Cornelius.
> BLUM: No, he was living with another woman but I've never met her, but that's what Monique told me. She is a super intelligent person. She speaks Luxembourger German fluently, English fluently, Italian fluently. She was super intelligent.
> CASSELDEN: She says that you really 'wanted and insisted a lot on doing a long sailing boat trip with me. He even told me that he had already bought the boat for us.'
> BLUM: I never, never owned a boat in my life. I just said to you and I swear by it. I think she 'took the mickey' because I know. I know.

The court hears Monique was very well connected in Luxembourg and helped Ric, or Frédéric, as she knew him, make contacts in relation to the furniture business.

Blum starts to stutter feebly at this point. 'Well I depended on her for lots of things, you know, like, with the, with the trademarks and all that sort of thing to do with the furniture, and she, she knew everything and everybody – everybody to know in Luxembourg.'

'She goes on to say …' Casselden says, 'in relation to doing a long sailing boat trip … that "he said it would be only the two of us, the sun and the sea". That sounds more than a platonic relationship, Mr Blum.'

Blum agrees he socialised with Monique. She introduced him to important people, took him to posh places and went to a concert with him.

> BLUM: She introduced me to all the people who you had to know in Luxembourg.
> CASSELDEN: Monique Cornelius says, 'He always told me he loved me.'
> BLUM: Yes.
> CASSELDEN: Did you invent extraordinary stories, Mr Blum, when you socialised with Monique Cornelius? Did you tell her about participating in a war in Asia?
> BLUM: A war in Asia. No.
> CASSELDEN: She says, 'He could tell and invent extraordinary stories about participating in a war in Asia.'
> BLUM: Yes, I've read.
> CASSELDEN: She goes on to say, 'He was coming to my place whenever we set a time. And after a few hours, he would leave. We were never living together and that suited me.'
> BLUM: I went to her place two or three times.
> CASSELDEN: And you maintain that your relationship with Monique Cornelius was purely platonic?
> BLUM: Exactly.

Blum speaks with a heavy accent – often struggling to find the right words and muddling his grammar.

> CASSELDEN: Did you send her letters from Australia?
> BLUM: I send a few postcards on special occasions. I sent maybe one or two letters – only talking of Australia. When I went to live in Tasmania, I sent a letter to explain that it was the most southern part of Australia.
> CASSELDEN: She goes on to say at the end of her written evidence to New South Wales Police, 'At the end of our relationship, he confessed to me that he had a wife in

Australia.' It suggests that the relationship may have been more than a platonic relationship.

BLUM: No, sir. She came to my place when my wife gave birth. She came to my place to see the baby. Honest to God.

CASSELDEN: And after that line, she says, 'For me, that was the end of our relationship. I told him never to approach me again.'

BLUM: No, no, I didn't see her again. But because we, you know, I left Luxembourg.

CASSELDEN: And then her final words, 'He disappeared and that is very good this way.'

'Why, Mr Blum,' Casselden then asks, 'did you appropriate Fernand Remakel's name and obtain a Queensland driver's licence?'

Blum can offer no explanation.

CASSELDEN: You returned to Australia in 1986. Why did you appropriate Fernand Remakel, use his name and acquire a Queensland driver's licence in 1988?

BLUM: No, no explanation.

CASSELDEN: None at all?

BLUM: No.

CASSELDEN: No fantasy?

BLUM: Fantasy?

CASSELDEN: You didn't wish to be Fernand Remakel?

BLUM: Nooo.

CASSELDEN: An international soccer player for Luxembourg?

BLUM: Nooo.

CASSELDEN: Formerly married to Monique Cornelius.

BLUM: I didn't want to be him.

Casselden then asks why Blum held the licence in Fernand Remakel's name from 1988 until December 1997.

BLUM: Was it ten years? Suppose.

CASSELDEN: And it needed to be renewed in 1992.

BLUM: No, I only got one licence. I didn't renew it. No.

Records reveal he did renew the licence and it expired in 1997, just a few months after Marion Barter disappeared using the name Florabella Remakel. Why did he decide to stop using this name at precisely that time?

The inquest winds up for the day and Blum is told to go to Byron Bay courthouse at 10 am the following morning to continue his evidence.

As one of the last known people who saw Marion alive, Blum is the key witness and Casselden is going to take his time with him.

CHAPTER 23

Tangled Web

20 February 2022

Shortly before 10 am, Ric Blum is dropped off in a shopping centre car park and begins shuffling his way to the court. Sandy again tries to get him to answer a couple of questions, but he stares resolutely ahead and says nothing. He seems more alert and upright today.

Casselden begins by asking him about the time he and his family lived in England, after they left Luxembourg in the 1980s.

CASSELDEN: You mentioned that you resided at Burwash [East Sussex]. And when you and your family were living in Burwash, did you take the time to explore the countryside nearby?

BLUM: Not really. No.

CASSELDEN: Did you go to Tunbridge Wells in that period of time?

BLUM: Tunbridge Wells. Yes, my daughter went to hospital.

CASSELDEN: You were familiar with that area around Tunbridge Wells?

BLUM: No, just driving, because I went probably three times to the hospital once my daughter was there.

Casselden returns to Blum's use of the Remakel name:

CASSELDEN: Why did you seek to obtain from the Queensland Department of Transport and Main Roads a licence in the name of Fernand Nocolas Remakel?

BLUM: No specific reason.

CASSELDEN: If you had no special reason or special purpose,
why have it in your pocket?

BLUM: Because it was the only … ah … only use it once in
Sydney and that was it then and I had it in my wallet, you
know.

He says he only used the licence once.

CASSELDEN: Is that the ad in the *Le Courrier Australien*?

BLUM: That's right.

CASSELDEN: Do you say, after six years, the first time and
only time you ever used it was on that occasion?

BLUM: That's right.

CASSELDEN: And that's your honest evidence today?

BLUM: Yes.

Blum then claims he lost the driver's licence, probably after 1992,
even though he remains adamant he didn't renew the licence.

BLUM: I thought I lost the licence at one stage because I
didn't have it any more, but that's what I did, sir.

CASSELDEN: When was the last time you recall having the
licence?

BLUM: Um [big pause], I can't recall … I can't tell you more
than that.

CASSELDEN: Was it before 1992 or after 1992?

BLUM: Probably was after … I can't recall, sorry.

CASSELDEN: Are you making this up, Mr Blum?

Adam Casselden exaggerates Blum's name, which he pronounces
'Bloom', as he becomes increasingly frustrated with the man's
obfuscation.

BLUM: Sorry?

CASSELDEN: Are you making this evidence up, Mr Blum?

BLUM: No.

There's a long pause. The tension in the silent courtroom is palpable. All eyes focus on Blum.

CASSELDEN: Why did you renew the licence in 1992 if you had not at that time ever used it?

BLUM: I can't ever recall renewing it. I said it before. I mean, it's on paper but I can't … I can't remember having a renewed account … I can't.

CASSELDEN: And do you know why it was that you let the licence in the name Fernand Nocolos Remakel expire in December of 1997?

BLUM: Because like I said before, I lost it. I didn't have it.

CASSELDEN: Did you receive a notification from Queensland Department of Transport and Main Roads notifying you that this licence was due for expiry?

BLUM: No.

CASSELDEN: How long before December 1997 do you believe that you had lost this licence?

BLUM: As I said before, I can't remember, sir.

CASSELDEN: Let's explore that. Where were you living when you believe you may have lost this licence?

BLUM: I was living in maybe, I was living in … maybe in Wollongbar … I just went into my wallet one day and noticed that the licence wasn't there and I thought I lost it. That's all I can say.

CASSELDEN: I take it you didn't report the licence stolen?

BLUM: Obviously not.

CASSELDEN: And it's never resurfaced?

BLUM: Not as far as I know. No.

CASSELDEN: It seems rather convenient that you lost this licence in 1997, isn't it?

BLUM: Well, that's the way it is. I don't think it was in 1997. But anyway.

The time period is obviously crucial to the mystery of Marion Barter's disappearance.

CASSELDEN: You went overseas, did you not, in the middle of 1997?

BLUM: Probably did.

CASSELDEN: Was it in your wallet when you went overseas in the middle of 1997, Mr Blum?

BLUM: No.

CASSELDEN: Quite certain of that?

BLUM: I'm pretty … pretty certain of that, yes.

CASSELDEN: And why are you so certain on that topic when you've been less certain on others in relation to questions about this licence, Mr Blum?

BLUM: Because, going overseas, I checked whatever I took with me. And in my wallet, the licence wasn't there.

Blum says he used his New South Wales driver's licence to obtain an international driver's licence whenever he travelled overseas.

CASSELDEN: Is it your evidence today that you believe your licence was lost, shortly, to your knowledge, before you departed in the middle of 1997? Is that honest evidence you're giving today?

BLUM: It's honest. Yes. Yes. Look, I'm prepared to take the polygraph. You know, if you want to.

No one in court bats an eyelid. Polygraph [lie detector] tests are not admissible in court, although police can use them in their investigations.

CASSELDEN: In what name did you obtain an international driver's licence?

BLUM: In the name of my New South Wales licence.

CASSELDEN: And what name is that in, Mr Blum? What name is the New South Wales driver's licence in?

BLUM: The name is Blum.

CASSELDEN: And what was it in the mid-1990s?

There's a long pause.

> CASSELDEN: Do you remember or have there been too many
> changes of name?
> BLUM: That's right.
> CASSELDEN: Do you remember what name was on your
> NSW driver's licence in 1997? If it assists you, Mr Blum,
> your passport was in the name Richard Lloyd Westbury.
> BLUM: In that case my licence was in that name.
> CASSELDEN: And did you ever use the Fernand Remakel
> licence to obtain an international driver's licence to use
> overseas?
> BLUM: I obtained the national driver's licence on that name
> in Luxembourg.
> CASSELDEN: And when did you do that?
> BLUM: That's before I left Luxembourg and that's the licence
> I use to get the one in Queensland.
> CASSELDEN: And why did you do that?

Here, Adam Casselden breaks into a broad smile, both hands resting on the lectern. He's directly facing Blum, who leans forward with his hands crossed in front of him.

> BLUM: No, no. No.
> CASSELDEN: Were you wanting to live a fantasy? In relation
> to the name Fernand Remakel?
> BLUM: No, no, not a fantasy.
> CASSELDEN: Why then, in circumstances where you say you
> only used it once?
> BLUM: Yes. Because like other, other names that are
> changed ... I can't exactly explain ... I don't have a, a
> pragmatic answer to that.
> CASSELDEN: Was it because you were going to use the
> licence for wrongdoing?
> BLUM: Well I did ... I put an ad in the paper.
> CASSELDEN: And you say apart from that ad, no other use?

BLUM: That's right.

CASSELDEN: What identification did you need to present to obtain the international driver's licence in the name Fernand Remakel in Luxembourg?

BLUM: Just the, um, Auto Club.

CASSELDEN: At any time after you obtained either the international driver's licence in Luxembourg or the driver's licence in Queensland, did you pass yourself off as Fernand Remakel?

BLUM: That's right, I never used it.

CASSELDEN: Did you ever invent a story that you were in truth Fernand Remakel?

BLUM: No.

Here, Blum lets out a chuckle, as though the suggestion is comical. Casselden doesn't see the humour.

CASSELDEN: You never introduced yourself to anyone as Fernand Remakel?

BLUM: No. As I've said before, I'm prepared to take the polygraph if you want to.

CASSELDEN: You were prepared, though, to be known as Remakel, because he placed the advertisement on the 10th of December 1994.

BLUM: That's right. That's what I did.

CASSELDEN: And did anyone answer your 1994 ad in the *Le Courrier Australien*?

BLUM: I never got an answer, no.

CASSELDEN: Are you sure about that?

BLUM: Positively sure.

CASSELDEN: And had you got an answer, what were you going to say to them as to your identity?

BLUM: I can't forecast that.

CASSELDEN: But had you got an answer?

BLUM: I know, understand.

CASSELDEN: … would you not have had to continue the tale that you were Remakel?

BLUM: Well, the question never occurred. So I couldn't answer you that … I don't forecast my answer.

Casselden breaks down the ad:

CASSELDEN: You were not single, were you, on the 10th of December 1994?

BLUM: No I wasn't.

CASSELDEN: In 1994 you were not a multiple homeowner, were you?

BLUM: No.

CASSELDEN: In 1994 you were not genuine, were you, Mr Blum?

BLUM: No, I've said it already.

CASSELDEN: In 1994 you were not very morally aligned, were you?

BLUM: Obviously not.

CASSELDEN: And you were not, as you have said a moment ago, looking for a permanent relationship?

BLUM: No, I wasn't.

CASSELDEN: Nor were you looking for marriage?

BLUM: No.

CASSELDEN: Why did you include the word 'marriage'?

BLUM: Why? Because it's part of the whole thing and the whole thing was a lie. That's all.

CASSELDEN: And why were you hell-bent on publicly lying?

BLUM: No … Can't answer that.

CASSELDEN: Was it because you were seeking to obtain a personal or financial benefit by deception from any person who happened to answer the advertisement?

BLUM: No. No sir.

Casselden moves on to Blum's income and finances. Blum explains that his only source of income was two disability pensions, one from the Belgian government and one from the Australian government, while his wife received a pension as his carer.

> CASSELDEN: And apart from the three pensions that were coming into the household, there was no other income stream?
> BLUM: No.
> CASSELDEN: No inheritance from your side of the family?
> BLUM: Yes, I got money every time I went overseas from my family.
> CASSELDEN: And why would you receive money from your family every time you went overseas?
> BLUM: Just because it was part of my, part of my inheritance and because I produced zillions during the time I was working with the [furniture] company.

Blum explains that the inheritance from his mother wasn't paid out all at once, but in coupons that could only be redeemed periodically. He claims he received large amounts when his mother Maria Coppenolle was still alive, and after she passed away he would travel to see family members and the family accountant.

> CASSELDEN: In terms of the inheritance, what was your understanding of your inheritance that led to money being provided to you on each occasion you went overseas by the family?
> BLUM: She had invested, even after her death.
> CASSELDEN: When was that?
> BLUM: I can't exactly remember. But even after that I was receiving money from the old accountant because she left, I don't know what you call that, either she bought shares or bank … what do you call that? Anyway on the papers, there were coupons that could be cashed at a certain date every year. And so when I went overseas, I went to see Armand, who was the old accountant who set up after she was dead.

When she was alive she would just give me some money. But
he gave me the sale of those coupons every year.

On average, Blum says he netted more than €20,000 per visit in
cash, worth about AU$29,000 at the time.

CASSELDEN: What would you do with the cash?
BLUM: I would come back to Australia and declare that to
the customs.
CASSELDEN: And you did that in the 1990s?
BLUM: Yes, always did declare to the customs whatever I
came with.
CASSELDEN: And you mentioned the figure of €20,000 a
moment ago, is that the sort of figure that you might receive
in the 1990s?
BLUM: Yes, that's right. Always declared.

The morning adjournment is called, and when the inquest
resumes, Blum revises his earlier evidence: 'The amounts of
money … I told you they were in euro but they were in Belgian
francs. My mother never knew euro. She died before euro came
in. Because of the enormity of it in my head when I was in the
toilet … the bond thing she did with the accountant, the same
thing she did when she was alive … she never even knew euro. It
was in Belgian francs and Belgian francs was 45 to one.'

This is a baffling claim. According to the Reserve Bank of
Australia, in the mid- to late 1990s, 20,000 Belgian francs would
have been worth only about AU$700, not $29,000, which means
he would not have had to declare the amounts to Australian
Customs on his return. Yet Blum made a point several times
of saying he *did* declare the amounts. Blum then claims that he
collected the last of his inheritance in 2012, a sum of €50,000,
which was stolen after he returned to Australia.

Seymour discovers a police report filed by Blum in the brief of
evidence. In it, Blum claims that he was robbed of the money in
the car park of the Pacific Fair shopping centre on the Gold Coast.

There is, however, no CCTV footage to support the account, and the crime scene was teeming with shoppers who did not report seeing anything. This so-called Gold Coast mugging has shades of similarity with Blum's account of another attack in Amsterdam in 1999.

The reason for his numerous overseas trips is not explained. He travelled at least once a year to Europe between 1990 and 2012. Sometimes there were up to five trips in a 12-month period. The lengths of the tours vary too, from a couple of weeks to five months. If he was travelling to collect money from his family, then the cost of the trips far outweighed the small amount he says he was getting. This begs the question, how could he afford all these trips on a pension?

CASSELDEN: If I understand your evidence correctly from today, you formed an acquaintance with a director from Japan Airlines who had an office at Amsterdam airport and that he would provide you with discounted airfares. And that is why you commenced to fly with Japan Airlines.
BLUM: That's right.
CASSELDEN: And do I understand also correctly that your acquaintance with the unidentified individual endured for perhaps ten or 15 years?
BLUM: Yes.

When attention turns to Ginette Gaffney-Bowan and the AVO she took out against Frederick De Hedervary in 1999, Blum denies any knowledge of it and even claims a court document he's shown confirming the AVO must have been forged.

He denies taking $30,000 from Ginette and then rejects Janet Oldenburg's allegations that he talked her into starting a new life with him before stealing from her. Specifically, he denies suggesting to Janet they start a new life on the French Riviera, telling the court that Janet, who was 51 years old at the time, had a dream to be a belly dancer on the stage in Europe and he travelled with her to assist with meeting talent agents to book dancing gigs.

Blum says Janet used a feather boa and 'bewitched him' with her dancing.

Blum then claims he had lined up a meeting in the town of Deal, in Kent, with an elderly talent agent who used to represent the ballet dancer Rudolf Nureyev. The planned meeting, he says, didn't happen.

(When Sandy checks in with her, Janet Oldenburg laughs uproariously at the suggestion she planned a career in belly dancing, dismissing Blum's story as a total fabrication.)

Blum tells the Coroner that the power of attorney was Janet's idea and he never had possession of the document. He offers no explanation as to why she would do this. His evidence is one long, blanket denial of all of Janet Oldenburg's claims. He also changes parts of his story from what he said in his September 2021 police interview, including telling Janet in 1999 that he was beaten and robbed at Amsterdam airport and needed to spend a few days in hospital at Lille, France.

Now Blum says he never went to hospital and never said that to Janet. Again, he cannot explain why his story has changed. Blum denies digging up Janet's buried jewellery or holding onto her personal papers, saying she has 'a fertile imagination'. Similarly, Blum rejects Ginette Gaffney-Bowan's claims of theft, blackmail and threats as crazed accusations made 'because she was completely drunk'.

Casselden produces a letter from an Andrée Flamme, now elderly and living in Belgium, who wrote to the Queensland Governor in 2010, raising 'concerns about Australian-born Belgian, Frederick De Hedervary who is wanted by Belgian police'.

This was to be the final day of the inquest but, as has been apparent for several days, there is so much more to examine. Blum is informed he will be required to return to the witness stand in two months' time, in April 2022.

The final questions of the day focus on Marion Barter.

CASSELDEN: Mr Blum, would you tell your honour the last time you saw Marion Barter?

BLUM: The last time I saw Marion Barter was in her
home ... in Southport or near Southport.
CASSELDEN: And was she in good health – the last time you
saw Marion Barter?
BLUM: Oh, yes. She was in good health.
CASSELDEN: And what were the last words you and Marion
Barter exchanged on this last occasion that you saw her in
her home itself?
BLUM: The last words?
CASSELDEN: Yes the last things you and she said?
BLUM: Can't recall.

Blum repeats his claim that he had a fleeting sexual affair with
Marion in 1968 in Switzerland.

CASSELDEN: How did you come to reacquaint yourself with
Marion Barter in 1997?
BLUM: I saw an ad in a paper from a lady looking for a
relationship – possibly in the *Gold Coast Bulletin*. And I
answered the ad ... I kept the ad.
CASSELDEN: You kept it?
BLUM: I kept it on my desk for a few days.
CASSELDEN: You kept it in the family home? You weren't
concerned about your wife seeing the ad, Mr Blum?
BLUM: She did. She knew or I told her. She knew that I had
that relationship.
CASSELDEN: She knew?
BLUM: Not at the time of the relationship but she found
out afterwards. I told her – I told Marion that I wasn't
continuing the charade because I had a wife and two
children. And after that, yes, I told my wife.

And the other reason Blum claims he called things off with
Marion?

BLUM: Because she was ... she was insane. I couldn't keep up with her sexually. She was voracious. She was voracious and hungry for sex. Nonstop.

CASSELDEN: How did you go about making contact? How did you respond to that advertisement?

BLUM: I respond ... I respond to a phone number ... No ... I wrote a note. I wrote a note and I gave my phone number and she rang me.

He said he sent his note to the office of the newspaper but can't recall which alias he used for himself.

'Was it Fernand Remakel?' Casselden asks.

'I said before I never use that.' He also can't remember what he wrote about himself.

'Did you disclose that you're an invalid pensioner, now 60, living in rental accommodation?' Casselden asks.

'I'm not sure.'

Blum is asked what drew him to the newspaper ad.

BLUM: Because it was a personal ad and what mainly the others were ... all people offering sex.

CASSELDEN: Was it a lonely hearts type ad?

BLUM: That's right.

CASSELDEN: Someone who is searching for companionship.

BLUM: Exactly.

CASSELDEN: Someone who may have been at that moment in time, a little lonely?

BLUM: Perhaps.

CASSELDEN: Even vulnerable ...

BLUM: I don't think she was. I don't think so.

Blum says he believed he saw the ad in 1997 and kept it for about a week before answering, supplying his home phone number. He heard back a few days later. 'I got a phone call,' he says. 'And then she gave me a meeting point.'

Blum says he did not have a mobile phone but would sometimes give people the number of a public phone booth when he was

expecting a call. He couldn't recall how many times Marion may
have phoned him at his Wollongbar home or whether someone
took a message from Marion and got him to call her back.

He says their meeting place was arranged by Marion. According
to Blum, he had to take a bus to the Gold Coast, then a train,
and Marion would be waiting in a red car in the car park of the
railway station. It was dusk on a Friday evening when they met.

Blum says they went to an Asian restaurant, one with red
Chinese lanterns, on the side of the Gold Coast Highway, possibly
at the entrance to Surfers Paradise.

'And when did you first come to realise that the woman who
met you at the car was one and the same woman you'd had a two-
night fleeting affair with?' Casselden asks. 'Was it immediate?'

'Yes.'

Blum goes on to describe their reunion: 'She jumped on my
neck.'

The Coroner looks up and intervenes directly.

CORONER: She what, sorry?

BLUM: She jumped on me and wrapped her arms around my
neck. Yes.

CASSELDEN: It was some many, many years since you met
her for the first time in 1968 – and you claim that she
immediately recognised you.

BLUM: Yes, I would say.

CASSELDEN: … and jumped on your neck?

BLUM: Yes, I would say.

CASSELDEN: In a public car park on the Gold Coast.

BLUM: Yes.

CORONER: It must have been an incredible surprise.

BLUM: It was a surprise, because I never thought that I would
meet her again, if I can put it that way.

CORONER: And a coincidence?

BLUM: And a coincidence. You know I just couldn't believe it.

Neither can the TLV team.

CHAPTER 24

The Three D's

27 April 2022

A drizzling rain settles over Byron Bay courthouse. This time Sandy, Seymour, Eeles, Sally and her husband have travelled to attend in person.

Nearly a dozen supersleuths and supporters from across Australia and the world have turned out in force: Joni, Jenn and Ken, Kellie, Kristina and her husband Gavin from the UK, and Mandy, a former work colleague of Marion's.

While the COVID pandemic restrictions have eased, people are still required to sit apart and wear face masks in the courtroom.

Ric Blum arrives alone, his white beard longer. It's his fourth day on the stand and he's due to appear for two more days this week.

At his last appearance, Blum claimed he reconnected with Marion on the Gold Coast in 1997 after he answered a personal ad she placed in a newspaper. But when Casselden asks him about that reunion, he says Marion answered *his* ad! Casselden points out that in February, Blum told the court that when answering Marion's personal ad he had given the publisher his phone number so that she could contact him.

'I don't think I gave my phone number ...' Blum says.

'Mr Blum, in February, you gave sworn evidence that you gave your telephone number to the publisher. And then Marion Barter, at that stage unknown to you, had contacted you in answer to your note responding to her advertisement. Do you wish to change your evidence this morning?'

The questioning continues in this vein for some time, until Casselden finally says. 'Would you like to see the transcript of your evidence, clear evidence, not once but more than once, that she telephoned you to arrange a meeting?'

The next points of dispute centre around how many times Blum saw Marion Barter during their 1997 relationship, when and where he'd seen her and how long the relationship lasted. After a fair bit of toing and froing, Blum seems to suggest that he'd seen Marion a total of four times between February and June 1997.

He tells the court he spent just one night with her and that was the time he first met her. He met her again in February after she'd picked him up from the railway station and they had dinner at an Asian restaurant on the Gold Coast. He claims he travelled by bus on two other occasions to the Gold Coast to meet with Marion and during one of those times he accompanied her to her former workplace, The Southport School, to collect some books. The third time he saw her he says was the 'last time' in Southport, when he apparently called their relationship off.

But then he tells the Coroner he saw Marion for the final time when she turned up at his Wollongbar home in June 1997, with a man, to collect some wooden antique tea chests he was storing for her.

CASSELDEN: You're quite certain today, it's your sworn evidence, that the last time you saw Marion Barter was in June at your place in Wollongbar?

BLUM: That's right.

CASSELDEN: Why then did you tell Her Honour in February of this year – on oath – that the last time you saw Marion was in Southport? ... If I could take you to the transcript, Mr Blum —

BLUM: The last time I saw her in Southport was on the third occasion ... when she went she went to school to pick up some material that she had left.

CASSELDEN: I'm about to read a passage. Evidence given by Mr Blum on the 18th of February 2022: 'The last time I saw Marion Barter was at her home in Southport – maybe it was inside. Oh, I can't know I can't remember. Question: Before you parted ways on this last occasion in her home in Southport – What was she doing by way of work? Answer: I believe she was packing the house.' Do you see, Mr Blum, stark differences between what you've just said now on oath and what you've told Her Honour on the 18th of February 2022?*

Blum is adamant that at their final meeting Marion had come to collect the boxes from his home in Wollongbar, but clarifies the last time he 'spent time' with her was in Southport. This kind of semantic reconstitution of events is a regular feature of Blum's evidence.

When quizzed about when he'd told his wife about his affair with Marion, Blum says he'd told her in 1997, completely contradicting what his wife told the court in February. Diane De Hedervary said the first she'd heard of her husband's affair with Marion was in September 2021, when police started asking questions.

Then Blum makes a startling revelation. He's breathing heavily and speaks slowly as he says, 'Since I was last here I have been diagnosed, I have been diagnosed with Parkinson's disease … I … I … everything … everything is blurry in my head.'

Blum is asked if he needs a break and is told by the Coroner that he can request one. He chooses to continue giving evidence.

When asked if he told Marion his surname was Remakel, Blum takes a lengthy pause before answering. 'Well … she did answer that ad.'

Seymour and Sandy struggle to believe what they are hearing. Just a few minutes ago he claimed he had answered Marion's ad, changing what he said in February. Now he's reverting back to the original version he told police.

Casselden homes in on the comment.

CASSELDEN: Mr Blum … you've just said now … 'she answered that ad'. And so is that another slip, Mr Blum, in the sense that you had placed —

---

* Evidence from Inquest, 27 April 2022.

BLUM: Oh no.

CASSELDEN: Let me finish, please. And that she has answered your advertisement of a kind similar to the ad you placed in 1994 in *Le Courrier Australien* publication?

BLUM: Yes, she answered.

CASSELDEN: Did I hear you correctly just now – that she did answer?

BLUM: Yes she did.

CASSELDEN: Which ad are you referring to that she answered? I want to be very clear on this. This is an advertisement that you placed.

BLUM: That's right.

CASSELDEN: So the evidence that you've given this morning that you answered an advertisement placed by her is false?

BLUM: I was confused.

CASSELDEN: And when you told New South Wales Police Force detectives that it was you that answered an advertisement, were you confused then?

BLUM: Obviously, as I told you before … I am not right in my head anymore.

There is a distinct change in the atmosphere of the courtroom. Then this happens.

CASSELDEN: I thought I put it to you fairly and squarely a little while ago. The evidence that you are now seeking to give is that *you* placed the advertisement …

BLUM: No sir – she did —

CASSELDEN: [cutting Blum off] And that Marion Barter answered your ad.

BLUM: She answered my ad.

CASSELDEN: Thank you, stop there. She answered my ad.

So the story changes back again. Casselden is exasperated, especially when Blum agrees that the statement he gave police about the issue is false but then can't explain why he hasn't sought to have it corrected.

> CASSELDEN: Which statement do you wish to stand on today, Mr Blum?
> BLUM: The version that you said and I answered.
> CASSELDEN: We seem to be going around in circles, Mr Blum. You seem to be blowing in the wind as to which version you wish to tie your colours to.
> BLUM: I am not blowing in the wind. I'm just not … as I said … I'm just not right in the head … but I am for certain that she answered the ad that I put in the *Courier*.

Is he referring to *The Courier Mail*, the mass-circulation daily tabloid newspaper in Queensland? Or does he mean *Le Courrier Australien*? Casselden does not seek clarification. The rest of the day is spent detailing Blum's claims that Marion asked him to store several tea chests for her. Despite claiming he'd already broken up with her, he says he agreed to keep her things in the garage of his family home.

> CASSELDEN: Do you see how strange it would be for Marion to lean on you to store your belongings when she had other options available on the Gold Coast at no cost to her.
> BLUM: No.
> CASSELDEN: For a man who didn't want drama … can you see how careless it is to store the belongings of a woman you'd had an extramarital affair with?
> BLUM: As I said, I made sure I was alone.
> CASSELDEN: Where was your wife?
> BLUM: I can't remember – maybe shopping. Maybe at the pool.
> CASSELDEN: Your son? Your daughter?
> BLUM: Can't remember.
> CASSELDEN: Can you offer any explanation as to why she just didn't simply leave them with a friend that lived nearby in Southport?

Blum stumbles and stammers before muttering he 'wouldn't know'.

The point of Blum's story about minding Marion's things is revealed when he says Marion returned to collect them with a man dressed as an airline pilot. This brings another, unidentified, mystery man into the story right before she vanished.

The only pilot the TLV team can think of is the pupil's father Marion was keen on. When they track him down, he confirms his son was in Marion's class but they had nothing to do with each other. He also says he would never wear his uniform unless he was actually flying a plane.

Blum gets confused again when asked about the flights he took to and from Europe within days of Marion leaving and returning.

CASSELDEN: Did you tell her a tale of starting a new life in Luxembourg with her as your wife?

BLUM: No sir.

CASSELDEN: Using your alias Fernand Remakel?

BLUM: No sir.

CASSELDEN: Another coincidence? Did you know that she'd changed her name before she took that flight?

BLUM: No. Maybe she did. I honestly can't remember.

CASSELDEN: Can't remember or don't wish to remember?

BLUM: No, I can't.

CASSELDEN: Did you assist Marion Barter in changing her name by deed poll?

BLUM: No.

CASSELDEN: But you knew how to do that?

BLUM: Yes.

CASSELDEN: And you knew how to change a passport?

BLUM: Yes.

CASSELDEN: And how to change a driver's licence.

BLUM: Yes.

CASSELDEN: Did you assist Marion Barter in changing name in May 1997 to Florabella Natalia Marion Remakel?

BLUM: No sir.

CASSELDEN: Did you assist Marion Barter in attaining a new passport in that name.

BLUM: No sir.

CASSELDEN: Are you able to explain how she came to change her name to Remakel?

BLUM: No.

The Coroner then weighs in.

CORONER: Mr Blum, you now know that your and Marion's departure dates in 1997 were within days of each other and you knew when Marion was about to travel overseas because she told you when she was leaving. You knew when you were leaving, I take it. She told you —

BLUM: [angrily cuts Coroner off] *Yes*, I understand!

CORONER: [Continuing on calmly] She told you 'I'm leaving in three weeks' when she collected the boxes. Given your relationship with Marion, did you mention that 'hey, we're both abroad at the same time?'

BLUM: No, no I did not. No, never discussed it. Never saw her.

CORONER: I just wanted to ask. It's quite a coincidence that you left within days of each other given the relationship you'd had. It just strikes me as unusual.

It's also quite the coincidence that the initials of Marion's new name FNMR are so close to FNMER, the initials of Blum's adopted name Fernand Nocolas Marie Ernest Remakel.

Asked the reason for his trip to Europe in 1997, Blum says he went to spend time with his friend Alfonz, to visit coin fares and horse shows. Alfonz has since passed away, so he can't corroborate Blum's claimed movements during the time Marion was overseas.

The next morning, as Blum makes way to the courthouse, Sandy joins him on the footpath again to try to get him to speak: 'Hi Mr Blum, or is it Mr Bloom? I just want to pronounce it correctly, is it Blum or Bloom? The reason I ask is because you made a big deal of how to pronounce Remakel, so I thought you might like to make sure – because that's a name you hardly ever use – so I thought you'd like to make sure we pronounce Blum or Bloom right.'

No response.

'So what this inquest seems to have established, Mr Blum, is that you're a liar – do you deny that? The question that everyone wants to know now is are you also a killer? Capable of violence? Monique Cornelius seems to think so. Did you know that? Why would she be afraid of you, Mr Blum? Should she be afraid of you? Are you capable of violence? Why won't you answer any questions, Mr Blum?'

Resolute and determined, he trudges into the court for his fifth day of giving evidence. Straight away, he changes his story about the ad that led to him meeting Marion in 1997. He now says *he* answered an ad placed by Marion. Seymour jokes his pen has run out of ink just covering the varying versions of this one simple fact.

When asked if he answered any other personal ads Blum replies, 'I don't think so,' but then says he answered an ad placed by Ginnette Gaffney-Bowan in 1998, despite giving evidence in February that there was no ad, he met her at a coin fair.

The whole point, says Casselden, is that Ric Blum was answering ads and meeting women for a reason. 'Is it because you were trying to obtain some personal or financial benefit by deception down the path?'

'I didn't obtain anything,' Blum replies.

At the morning break, Blum walks past the open door of the small media room and looks at Seymour and Sandy. There's no look of confusion; he meant to come there and he flashes them a gloating smile as though he's won.

Back on the stand, he's questioned about a business named Renov Pubs registered in Belgium. The company was registered in 1968 by Frederick De Hedervary. Since 25 May 2021, the business number has been linked to Ric Blum and is still active.

Blum denies any knowledge of the company.

Then he's shown an update on the register for Renov Pubs made on 11 April, just two weeks earlier. Blum, incredibly, maintains he knows nothing about it.

'You can't shed any light why two weeks ago Ric Blum has had some involvement with a register related to Renov Pubs?' Casselden asks.

'The last business I was involved with was my family, say 40 years ago in Luxembourg, and afterwards when I was maybe with the same family, the same postcode … in Ballina.'

Then Blum says: 'Somebody's been using my name.' Now he's claiming *he* is the victim of someone stealing *his* identity and using it to register companies – without any explanation as to why anyone would bother.

The next set of documents Blum cannot deny, as they are in his handwriting. They are letters written in French he sent to Monique Cornelius during their brief affair in the early 1980s in Luxembourg. Casselden reads the English translations aloud for the court and online audience.

CASSELDEN: [Reading] 'Hello my beloved one, to my heart that I received your letter … only I am Frederick, not Fernand, what is important is the theories that life and her problems. If my sentiments are found to echo in your heart … if you one day decide to marry me, my father will say to you' … and then you go on. Do you maintain that at this time you were in a platonic relationship with Monique?
BLUM: Yes, I did. Those letters were infatuation. I wasn't in Luxembourg, I sent them some, some, some, some, 40 years ago. I can't remember.
CASSELDEN: You then go on to say … [Reading] 'I love you, Monique, and you are an authentic magician who possesses the gift to beautify every moment – you are not only my woman, not only mine, but the whole adventure … you carry with you a perpetual renewal which allows the biggest lovers never to become monsters … with you I know the beauty of a big love and nothing of these little grudges …'

BLUM: As I said before, it was all infatuation … I don't have any reason to lie, I don't have any reason to lie, it won't change anything if I say yes or no …

CASSELDEN: Well if I need to, Mr Blum, I'll go through line by line …

BLUM: No, it's okay!

CASSELDEN: Do you still maintain that you did not have any sexual relationship with Monique Cornelius?

BLUM: I do, I do.

CASSELDEN: May I continue? … [Reading] 'I am crazy and I scream I have made it, oh you beautiful bastards, I have made it. Monique, I am crazy because you are the heaven I turn to after every storm … Monique, I am crazy … and I have to tell you one more way, and I know that you accept the compliment … it is a strain and so explicit of our wild nature, but never mind Monique … you are a song in a man's testicles. Do you still maintain that you did not have any sexual relationship?'

BLUM: Yes.

Casselden, who has always been serious and proper in his conduct, ignores Blum's apparent embarrassment as he protests that he knows what he wrote and gestures to Casselden that he need not continue.

CASSELDEN: You continue to say … [Reading] 'I want to say in my maternal language, that's to say, my enchantress, I have never in my life made love like that with anyone before. I feel completely drunk with it. You have somehow put a spell on me and I find it magic even just touching your arm, you make the whole thing so lyrical, so beautiful.' Again, Mr Blum, do you maintain that you did not have sexual relations with Monique Cornelius?

BLUM: I do. As I told you before, it's all perfidious, I never had a sexual relationship with Monique Cornelius, never did, and it's … I don't deny writing the letter but it's all part

of my ... I used to read and jot things every day, and that's all there is to it. I have, I have, my, my counsel – at the beginning of this ... told me I should always tell the truth ...
CASSELDEN: You're going off on a tangent. You've answered my question. You still maintain you did not have a sexual relationship with Ms Cornelius?
BLUM: No.
CASSELDEN: I'm doing this as a matter of fairness ... you go on to say in your letter: [Reading] 'Monday, I leave for the UK and Ireland. A few days to buy our boat, I will look at a 40 foot, 12 metres, sloop which will suit us perfectly for what we want to do. Me, I simply want to get to know this country, which is as sweet as your smile, pretty like your eyes and warm like the love that I have for you. I am intimately persuaded that you will not regret your decision to leave with me and to start a new life.' I could name Janet Oldenburg. I could name Ginette Gaffney-Bowan. It seems from your correspondence with Monique Cornelius that you were suggesting to her to marry and start a new life ... and all this while you were married, with no intention, I suggest to you, to leave your wife.
BLUM: No sir, I never had an intention to leave my wife.
CASSELDEN: What was the point of it all, Mr Blum?
BLUM: It was just, as I said to you, infatuation, I can't explain any other ways ... things you think yourself, things you don't normally discuss or divulge, yes I admit I've written the letters, but if it was, if it was, if it was, if it was true there'd be no difference to say no, because, because like my counsellor said, tell the truth all the time ...
CASSELDEN: Mr Blum, you're going off on a tangent again. Do you accept that you ended this letter to Monique Cornelius in August of 1980 with the words ... [Reading] 'Bye for now my love, take care of yourself because I love you insanely, sleep but my heart watches, a million big kisses and hugs.'
BLUM: Yes, I said that I sent those letters, yes, I'm not disputing that.

CASSELDEN: And there's nothing of substance beneath your words, it was pure fantasy?
BLUM: Yes.

Blum is flustered. Asked why all these women would lie, he says, 'Probably because they're that type of women.'

BLUM: What harm did I cause to any of them?
CASSELDEN: Mr Blum, if we take Ms Gaffney-Bowan as an example, she was looking for friendship and marriage … in circumstances where you did not disclose you were married, there is a deception being imposed by you in relation to your true intentions.
BLUM: It wasn't a deception.
CASSELDEN: You've answered a woman seeking companionship, you don't disclose to her that you're in a permanent relationship of many years, of which there are two children … that, with the greatest respect, is a clear deception!
BLUM: Oh well, it's a deception.
CASSELDEN: And do you accept that a woman who has placed an advertisement looking for companionship and sometime after that has entered a relationship of sorts … and finds out that she has entered a relationship with a married man, that that could cause harm or hurt to her?
BLUM: Yes, there's thousands of them on the internet every day.
CASSELDEN: Will you answer my question, Mr Blum?
BLUM: I never thought it was deceiving.

The TLV team's collective ears prick up as Mr Casselden turns to a crucial detail.

CASSELEN: Did you acquire a second car for the use of your family in August of 1997?
BLUM: No, I only had the one car. Which other car are you talking about?

CASSELDEN: I am suggesting that you acquired a second
motor vehicle on the eleventh of August 1997.
BLUM: No.

Blum's wife Diane previously confirmed the purchase of the car,
which was made nine days after Marion returned from Europe.
Mr Casselden produces documents proving Blum owned a Nissan
Bluebird station wagon and the purchase of a Mitsubishi Magna
on 11 August.

Blum recovers his memory when questioned by Bradley Smith.

SMITH: Why did you buy it?
BLUM: I bought it because I couldn't have the previous
car registered. It was a rust bucket, so I sold it for a few
hundred dollars. It was a rust bucket. There would have
been a few months left on the rego when I sold it. I don't
know if they, the new owner, used it. Don't know. Can't
remember.

Mr Blum says the Mitsubishi was bought to replace the Nissan
Bluebird which could not be registered.

BLUM: I had the Bluebird until I got the Mitsubishi. And
after a few days I sold the Bluebird as I had an inspection,
and I couldn't get the Bluebird registered.

A vehicle register also shows a Toyota Corona linked to Mr Blum's
name at the same time, although he says that was the car he bought
for his daughter when she started work.

SMITH: So, it seems that in August 1997 you had three cars,
is that right?
BLUM: I didn't have three cars.
SMITH: Did the return of Marion Barter on the second of
August 1997 have anything to do with your purchase 9 days
later of the Mitsubishi magna?

BLUM: No. Why would she have anything to do with it.
I never saw her when she came back.

The inference is obvious. If Blum had been using two cars during
the time between Marion returning and disappearing and, if he
was still involved with her, there might be physical evidence in
the car they used. But this is all speculation which cannot be
verified as both cars are long gone. And so, Blum is directed to
the question that everyone is waiting to hear him answer. A video
appears on a big screen overlooking the court. It shows the police
interview detectives did with Blum on 14 September, 2021. Blum
is seated at a table facing the camera.

FEMALE DETECTIVE: Mr Blum, did you murder Marion
Barter?
BLUM: Are you kidding?
FEMALE DETECTIVE: No, I'm not kidding. And I expect you
to answer my question. Did you in any way harm Marion
Barter?
BLUM: No.
FEMALE DETECTIVE: Did you have any interaction with
Marion Barter after she returned to Australia on August 2nd
in 1997?
BLUM: No.
FEMALE DETECTIVE: Do you know where she is?
BLUM: No.

Casselden stops the video and turns to Blum.

CASSELDEN: Were the answers that you just gave truthful
answers?
BLUM: Truthful answers, yes.
CASSELDEN: And you're quite sure of that, Mr Blum?
BLUM: Yes, I'm quite sure of that.
CASSELDEN: Present in court today, as they have been
most days, is the family of Marion Barter. The family, and

in particular Marion's daughter Sally Leydon, have been
searching for Marion Barter for nearly 25 years.

BLUM: I understand that.

CASSELDEN: Is there any additional information that could
assist Marion's family and New South Wales Police in
locating Marion Barter?

BLUM: Well I wouldn't know where she is, but I never saw
her after, after the day she came and pick up boxes. I never
saw her again, and as I said before, the police told me that
she was living in a motel.

During the lunch break, Blum shuffles off to the small room
where he sits alone and waits to be called back in. He's right
next door to Seymour and Sandy. He makes a phone call and
speaks very loudly, as though he wants them to hear what he is
saying. They're not eavesdropping, but it's clear he is talking to
his wife Diane and he says, 'There is nothing, they are lying.'
Either Blum is telling the truth and everyone else is making up
fantastic stories about him, or he's lying to the Coroner under
oath.

When court resumes, a different lawyer stands to ask the
questions. Bradley Smith, representing Sally, wastes no time
querying Blum's claimed mental lapses, in spite of his ability to
recall in great detail things that support his versions of events.

SMITH: Despite what you said yesterday about your
Parkinson's giving you headaches and making your brain
go foggy, you'll recall Mr Casselden asked you about your
trip to Europe in 1997 and you told Her Honour in minute
detail yesterday – I suggest to you, you were sharp as a tack –
you visited your cousin Jean-Pierre with your friend Alfonz.
You spent four weeks in Montpellier. You had no difficulty
recalling any of that detail, did you?

BLUM: No, I answered to the best of my knowledge …
because that was, that was, that was … that was the last time
that I saw my friend.

SMITH: Do you have a vivid memory of that trip because
you need to explain why you were in Europe at the same
time as Marion Barter?
BLUM: No. It has nothing to do with Marion Barter.

As Blum leaves the Byron Bay courthouse, Eeles, who's often
away from the action, takes the opportunity to approach him:
'Mr Blum, are you an honourable man? Do you have a conscience?
Do you realise that in the eyes of the entire world you are seen as
a liar trapped in his own little world of lies? You keep accusing
everyone else of lying, but you are the liar. Why don't you be
the person that you want to be, that person who is honourable,
who has self-respect, because right now you are coming across
as a very sad, pathetic little man? Why do you not tell the truth?
Where is Marion?'

Yet again, Blum refuses to answer any questions. And he's
silent, too, as he returns for his final day on the stand.

'Do you agree with me,' Smith asks, 'that the very first time
you set foot in Australia, the very first thing that you did was
dishonest?'

Blum pauses and shrugs. There's no denying the fact that when
Blum first arrived in Australia in May 1969 he stated he had never
been married, when he was, in fact, married to his third wife. On
his application for residency, he said he never had a serious injury,
apparently forgetting his chronic illness after being thrown and
dragged by a horse when he was in the Belgian Gendarmerie
in 1960, for which he has collected a disability pension ever
since. He also failed to disclose his extensive criminal record to
immigration officials.

That's not all he has lied about.

'Do you now accept,' Smith asks, 'that between 1994, when
you changed your name to Frederick David De Hedervary, and
1999, when you changed your name to Rich Richard, on each
occasion that you went overseas you used a passport in the name
of Richard Lloyd Westbury, which was a false passport?'

'No. No, I never had a false passport', Blum replies.

Again, this is semantics. Blum was actually using a passport in a name he no longer legally held, making it a false passport.

Smith refocuses on Marion and what Blum may have told her when they were together. He denies telling her his name was Fernand Remakel. Or that he travelled to Europe a few days before Marion so that she wouldn't see that his passport was in the name Richard Lloyd Westbury.

> BLUM: I never went to Luxembourg with Marion Barter and I never married Marion Barter in Luxembourg. That's a lie!
> SMITH: Was this going to be the means by which you fulfil your infatuation with Monique Cornelius … that you were going to be the new Fernand Remakel and Marion was going to be your wife, the new Monique Cornelius, as Florabella Natalia Marion Remakel?
> BLUM: No, no.

Blum once again denies visiting England with Marion Barter, even though she was writing postcards from towns very close to where he used to live. Just another 'coincidence'.

> SMITH: You had obtained an international driver's licence in the name Fernand Nocolas Remakel. And it appears Marion Barter has used an international driver's licence to get a passport in the name Florabella Natalia Marion Remakel.
> BLUM: What can I say to that?
> SMITH: Coincidence?
> BLUM: I don't know.

And what about the dates of Marion's trip and Blum's trip? Her passport left Australia on 22 June 1997 and returned on 2 August. He left on 17 June and returned on 31 July. Again, a coincidence.

After highlighting these coincidences Smith drills down on his final questions.

SMITH: Now, in light of all the matters we've discussed in evidence. Firstly, you were asked by police, did you in any way harm Marion Barter? And your answer was no, I never harmed anyone. Do you maintain that answer now, on your sworn oath?

BLUM: That's right. I have never hurt anyone. I have never hurt an animal.

SMITH: You were asked by police if you know where Marion Barter is and you answered no.

BLUM: No.

SMITH: You maintain that evidence on your sworn oath?

BLUM: Yes.

SMITH: You're asked by police, did you have any interaction with Marion Barter, once she returned to Australia after the second of August 1997? And you answered no.

BLUM: No, no sir.

SMITH: And you maintain that answer on your sworn oath.

BLUM: Yes.

SMITH: And you're asked by police, in your recorded interview, "Mr Blum, did you murder Marion Barter?" Do you remember your answer to that question?

BLUM: Oh … No, I didn't … oh, murder.

Blum is shaking his head, looking incredulous.

SMITH: Do you remember your answer to that question?

BLUM: No.

SMITH: You answered, 'Are you kidding?'

BLUM: Yes.

SMITH: Do you maintain that answer now?

BLUM: Yes.

SMITH: On your sworn oath to Her Honour?

BLUM: YES!

SMITH: Mr Blum, do you know what happened to Marion Barter after she returned to Australia on the second of August 1997?

BLUM: I wouldn't have a clue.

SMITH: On your sworn oath to Her Honour, you have no idea?

BLUM: No idea.

SMITH: Mr Blum, if you do know anything, this is your chance to say it.

BLUM: Yes, I know. I would have said it a long time ago if I had anything to do. I wouldn't have a clue.

And just like that, the final day of the inquest concludes.

Now it's up to Coroner Teresa O'Sullivan to weigh all the evidence and hand down her findings, including possible recommendations for charges to be laid.

CHAPTER 25

Flipping Coins

It's hard to find the truth amid Ric Blum's fanciful and twisted tales. There are some facts, however, that even this man of many names cannot deny. From information garnered through existing records, one of his relatives, and Blum's often fanciful and unreliable recollections provided to police and the court, a patchwork of his identity is forming. However, as much of the information about his early life has come from him, TLV remains skeptical as to its veracity.

Blum's life began in Tournai, Belgium on 9 July 1939, when his 26-year-old mother, Maria Coppenolle, gave birth to a son she named Willy. Blum believes his biological father to be Désiré David, who, he claims, was arrested and executed by the Germans during World War II. But Désiré, born in 1905 in the Belgian village of Gelinden, died in 1943 of peritonitis.

It was also during World War II that Maria, who was pregnant with Willy's younger brother (also named Désiré), allegedly suffered serious injuries and lost a leg when a bomb landed on the family's home. As a result, Willy says he was placed in an orphanage at three-years-old, where he would remain until he was 12. In 1951, he reportedly returned to live with his mother Maria and her husband Abel Wouters. Thus, Willy Coppenolle became Willy Wouters.

Blum had two brothers, Fredy and Désiré, both of whom used the surname David. Apparently, the family moved to Allied-occupied Germany after the war because Abel Wouters was a military man and was based there. Five years later they returned to Belgium, where Blum claims he studied pre-Columbian civilisation at the 'Academy of Arts'. Occasionally, at night, he created patterns for wall tapestries.

In 1958, Blum joined the Gendarmerie. He claims to have been thrown and dragged by a horse in about 1960, an accident that left him with debilitating, lifelong injuries, as he told the inquest: 'I was crushed. I was pulverised.'*

He received a large compensation payout when he was discharged from the Gendarmerie in around 1964. After that, Blum worked sporadically as a sewing machine repairer, a security guard and a photographer. He also visited Switzerland several times over four years, first to convalesce after his accident and later to ski. He went to chalets and visited a number of cities, but mostly Lausanne.

Blum was married three times before he met his fourth and current wife Diane De Hedervary. He can't remember the date or year he wed his first wife, Janine LeRoy, but says it was in the early 1960s while he was still in plaster from his accident in the Gendarmerie. During questioning by Adam Casselden SC, Blum tells the inquest the couple had two children.

> BLUM: I had a son and a daughter, which I recognise. But I can't be sure it was my daughter and I think she [Janine LeRoy] had another one after.
> CASSELDEN: What was your son's name?
> BLUM: He was called Gaetan. That was my wife's choice. [Gaetan had the surname Wouters.]
> CASSELDEN: And the daughter who may have been yours, what was her name?

A long pause follows.

'It was … oh God, I can't remember,' Blum claims. 'Mainly because I didn't want to remember. It was a bad time of my life.'

Blum's second wife was Nicole Renaud. He does not have much to say about her: 'I was only with her for a few weeks – the second one. And I can't exactly remember when.'

---

* Transcript, NSW Coroner's Court, 16 February 2022.

As we saw, he claims to know nothing about a company called Renov Pubs, which was registered in Belgium on 1 October 1968, around the same time he was married to his second wife. He now also denies registering another business, C&L Constructs, in the name 'Willie David Coppenolle'.

Wife number three was Ilona Kinczell, who was born in Budapest, Hungary, in 1946. The pair married on 10 May 1969 in Brussels, Belgium, just before Blum sailed solo to Perth, Australia, on a passport in the name Willy Wouters. He arrived on a tourist visa on 24 May 1969, before heading to Sydney. He says he planned to stay for three months, yet Ilona flew to Sydney on a migrant visa at this time. It seems she planned to move here permanently.

It seems so strange for newlyweds to travel separately to the other side of the world, apparently with very different ideas about how long they will stay. Rather than just three months, records show Blum departed Sydney to return to Europe approximately nine months later, in February 1970. He left the country as Willy Wouters, but while living in Australia had been using a different name. Blum applied for Australian residency two days after his arrival on 26 May, on the basis he was married to Ilona, who had legally immigrated to Australia. It was granted in the name Frederick De Hedervary on 2 October 1976, although he would go on to use variations of the name and spelling.

Blum has a good recollection of the day.

BLUM: I was living then in Rose Bay [a suburb of Sydney] and I received a telegram from Canberra saying I had to go to Commonwealth House in Chifley Square [Sydney], to make an appointment. I did ring and they told me to come with an amount of money and two photographs, which I did. And then I went to an office. I had the deed poll with me when I went to Chifley Square. They filled out some paper, which I signed, and they told me to come back an hour later and gave me an Australian passport.

CASSELDEN: Why did you change your name?

BLUM: Didn't want to be ... memories of the past, that's all.
CASSELDEN: Did you not want to be found?
BLUM: No.
CASSELDEN: Did you want a fresh new life?
BLUM: In Australia, which I did.

While Blum was applying for residency in 1969, he says he was working as a photographer for Australian Associated Press on George Street in Sydney. On 17 October of that year, Willy Wouters was named in fraud charges in Belgium relating to bad cheques. Ilona was pregnant when Blum claims she ran away with another man to Melbourne.

Blum says he was not present at the birth of his daughter Evelyn on 18 January 1970, but he believes she was born at Camperdown in Sydney.

CASSELDEN: There is a New South Wales birth certificate, it identifies you as the informant.
BLUM: Yes, I see that.
CASSELDEN: When did you first become aware?
BLUM: Probably a few days before I went to register the birth.

Blum clearly states the only time he ever saw Evelyn was as a newborn, when Ilona came to see him off at the airport a few weeks after Evelyn's birth, but Evelyn can recount a number of occasions when she met her biological father as an adult.

Blum departed Sydney on 15 February 1970, and says he never saw his wife Ilona again.

Ilona died on 13 July 1977, at the age of 31. She was found slumped over the steering wheel of her car near the Melbourne hairdressing salon where she worked. She had not been in an accident and suffered no apparent physical injuries. She had recently returned from visiting her dying mother in Belgium, who passed away soon after her daughter.

Ilona's younger brother in Belgium, Attila, also died a short time later. Blum chose not to claim his seven-year-old daughter when Ilona died. Instead Evelyn lived with her stepfather, Michael Reid. Ilona had met Michael on a cruise ship from Sydney in May 1970. She filed for divorce from Willy Wouters sometime in mid-1970 and married Michael Reid in December 1971.

Blum admits that he has two, possibly three, children with previous wives, but has never disclosed that information to his present wife, Diane. When asked by Casselden if there was any reason why he didn't tell Diane, he responded, 'I always put the past in the past. When I met my present wife, we were on a ship for about three months and I never talked about my past.'

Blum doesn't want to talk about his past of course because of his criminal history. Willy Wouters has an extensive record dating back to 1965 in Belgium, where he was convicted of fraud and other crimes in Tournai, Brussels, Charleroi, Leuven and Bruges.

Diane Walker was 19 when she encountered 31-year-old Blum on the ship *Chusan* while sailing from England to Sydney in January 1971. She was accompanied by her parents. He was supposedly newly single, indicating he had recently divorced from Ilona, and was travelling under the name 'Freddy' David – the name of his brother, who never actually visited Australia. When he adopted his brother's name as an alias, Blum added another 'd' to the spelling.

Blum says he first spotted Diane at a hotel before they embarked on their voyage: 'I stayed at the Hilton in Southampton, and my wife and her parents were at the same hotel. I saw them at the top floor in the swimming pool before the departure.'

On board the ship, Blum introduced himself to Diane as Frederick De Hedervary. 'She called me Ric,' he says. 'She didn't want to call me Fred because in Australia, Fred is a frog, so she called me Ric.' Perhaps she was referring to chocolate Freddo Frogs, which are still popular in Australia today.

Upon arrival in Sydney, Blum stayed with Diane's family for five or six weeks before travelling to New Caledonia, Tahiti and on to Paris. Blum says he was planning to see family in Europe for a short time before coming back to Australia, but he did not return for three years because he went to jail instead.

On 23 June 1971, Willy Wouters was arrested in Rouen, France. On 9 December he was sentenced to four years' imprisonment for multiple offences committed in Rouen and Lille, including fraud, attempted fraud, breach of trust, use of false documents, false impersonation and concealment. While he was incarcerated, Blum and Diane wrote to each other. After his release on 21 May 1974, Willy Wouters flew to Sydney for a supposed 15-day stay at an address at Bondi Beach.

When questioned at the inquest about his long history of committing fraud, Blum speaks about obtaining fake identification cards and bank accounts, and using cheques in false names that bounced. 'I've gone through it,' he says. 'You know, I've been arrested in France and been arrested in Belgium.' When Casselden reads at least 30 of Blum's many aliases to the court one by one, Blum admits to using 13 but dismisses the others.

CASSELDEN: Roger Lauzoney.
BLUM: No.
CASSELDEN: You can't recall ever being arrested as Roger Lauzoney while carrying an Australian passport in the name of Frederick De Hedervary?

He cannot remember and offers no explanation.

Since 1976, when his first Australian passport was issued, Blum became adept at changing his name by deed poll, then changing his name on a driver's licence and on the electoral roll. But he has never told his family about his multiple identities and passports.

Diane De Hedervary was born in Australia in 1951, the youngest child of Robert and Margaret (Peggy) Walker. She has a sister, Penelope, who is two years older, and a half-brother, Robert, who's nine years her senior. At the time of her marriage to Blum on 20 February 1976, at Potts Point in Sydney, Diane was working as a secretary and living in the exclusive suburb of Vaucluse.

In July, the newlyweds travelled to Luxembourg for what was meant to be a nine-month stay, but Diane didn't return to Australia for more than two years.

In the months after the couple's arrival in Europe, there was a flurry of criminal activity committed by Blum under the name Roger Lauzoney in Bruges, Belgium. Offences included forged cheques and fraudulent car ownership. Records suggest Roger Lauzoney was arrested at Wiltz, Luxembourg, and found with an Australian passport in the name Frederick David De Hedervary. There are also records of false documentation used in relation to the lease of a flat in Middelkerke, Belgium, in October 1976 and January 1977, which can be traced to another of Blum's aliases, Bernard DuPont.

On 17 March 1977, Frederick De Hedervary arrived alone in Sydney on a flight originating in the United Kingdom, staying just four days before leaving again for Belgium. Blum's ex-wife died in Melbourne in July 1977.

In 1978, a three-year prison sentence was imposed on Roger Lauzoney in Tournai for offences of forgery, counterfeit sales, fraud and larcenies. The full term was not served. Blum, still known as Frederick David De Hedervary, arrived back in Australia with his wife Diane on 14 August 1978.

Blum and Diane have a son and a daughter: David, born on 2 April 1979 in Sydney, Australia, and Maite, born on 17 April 1981 in Luxembourg City, where the young family was then living. Both have the surname De Hedervary. This is when Blum worked for the family furniture business.

Blum's young family also resided for a time in Belgium and in East Sussex in southern England from around 1983 to 1986, before returning to Australia, where they lived across a number of states: New South Wales, Tasmania, Queensland and Victoria. For the most part in Australia, however, Blum has resided in various communities across northern New South Wales.

The De Hedervary family was based in Australia when Diane's parents both passed away. Her father, Robert died at the age of 74 from a heart attack in January 1987. Her mother, Peggy, died from cancer, aged 66, in September 1988. Diane received an inheritance around this time and the court hears the family used it to move to Tasmania.

In 1989, Fredy David died at the age of 48. He apparently fell to the ground after getting out of a car. The cause of death is believed to be an aneurysm or heart attack. Soon after, Blum's stepfather, Abel Wouters, and mother, Maria, also passed away. Blum is entitled to receive an inheritance, which apparently must be collected in instalments. He has no contact with his living brother Désiré.

Blum's constant trips between Australia and Europe continued throughout the 1980s, 1990s and 2000s. Over the years, he visited Belgium, France, England, the Netherlands, Germany and Luxembourg multiple times. Sometimes there would be stopovers in Asia too, including in Japan and Bali. Blum would often be away from his wife and children for months on end. They never travelled with him. Diane would stay home running the household on a carer's pension.

During this period, on different continents and in various Australian states, Blum's name changed frequently, as did his driver's licences and passports: from Chaim Frederick David De Hedervary in 1985, he became Richard Lloyd West in 1987, and then Frederick De Hedervary in 1988, the year when a Queensland driver's licence was also issued in the name Fernand Remakel. It was back to Richard Lloyd West in 1989 until Blum's brother and stepfather died, then the original Willy Wouters made a comeback just in time for the death of his mother in early 1990. Hello again to Richard Lloyd West in 1991, who morphed into Richard Lloyd Westbury in 1992.

The year 1994 was a particularly frantic one on the identity front. Frederick David De Hedervary registered the business Ballina Coin Investments, and 'F Remakel' placed a personal ad in *Le Courrier Australien*, while Richard Lloyd Westbury flew out to the Netherlands. That same year saw a legal name change and a licence issued for Frederick David De Hedervary, although the passport for Richard Lloyd Westbury continued to be used with great regularity.

Between 1995 and 1998, Richard Lloyd Westbury was very active flying back and forth between Australia and Europe; this includes the period when Marion Barter, or Florabella Remakel, disappeared while travelling to England.

In 1998, Frederick De Hedervary met Ginette Gaffney-Bowan, while in 1999, avid coin collector Richard West legally became Rich Richard before an overseas trip with Janet Oldenburg. Then it was back to Frederick David De Hedervary in 2000.

By 2010, the surname Coppenolle was being used to sell a large quantity of valuable coins. A legal name change in 2011 heralded the arrival of Willy David Coppenolle.

Finally, in 2014 Ric Blum introduced himself to the world.

Blum, who has received a disability support pension in Australia for decades, claims his numerous expensive international trips over the years were mostly to visit family. This seems strange for one glaring reason: Blum's closest family members, his mother Maria Coppenolle, his younger brother Fredy David, and his stepfather Abel Wouters, all died more than 30 years ago. He says there are a lot of cousins, but none with whom he is particularly close. His claims of visiting family don't seem to stack up.

Seymour takes a look at Blum's trips to Europe between 1991 and 2012. Some years he only made one trip: for 13 days in 1991; 28 days in 1992; 43 days in 1997, when Marion vanished; and 52 days in 1998. In 1995, he travelled abroad on three separate occasions for a total of 32 days. He often took two trips a year, spending 89 days away from home in 1993 and 103 days away in 2006.

In total, Ric Blum made 21 trips between 1991 and 2012, spending 524 days away from his home and family. That's 75 weeks, 17 months or nearly one and a half years. Taking into account the flights, transfers to and from airports, food and transport while abroad and very basic entertainment, Blum spent at least AU$81,000 on these trips, though it might have been much more.

Certainly, it's far more than he himself claims he could afford.

One thing is certain: Blum is an avid fan of collecting and trading rare, valuable coins. In fact, when talking about his pet topic in court, he presents himself as something of an expert, appearing disdainful of anyone without his apparently superior knowledge. He also does not seem enthused about the calibre of the Australian coin-collecting market.

In 1994, Blum registered Ballina Coin Investments in Australia, and in 2000 the Australian government's Centrelink welfare service launched an investigation into the business, which Blum denies ever turning a profit on.

There were short periods of time when he paid for safe deposit boxes at banks, to store valuable items or cash, though he remains vague about what was in them. Apart from the safe deposit envelope obtained shortly before $80,000 was withdrawn from Marion Barter's account, a safe deposit box was used in 1999, around the same time Blum worked for Status International, an auction company dealing in stamps and coins. Interestingly, Blum's stint with the business coincided with some customers' valuable coin collections being 'lost' in the mail.

There are also at least two instances, one in Amsterdam and the other on the Gold Coast, Queensland, when Blum claims to have been attacked and robbed of money or valuable possessions.

In his police interview and in his initial evidence at the inquest, Blum seems arrogant. He boasts of speaking several languages and flaunts his appreciation of European history and the arts, which fuels a clearly overinflated sense of importance. He conceitedly sprinkles irrelevant historic or cultural references into his testimony, and name-drops frequently. Whether he's trying to impress, condescend or distract with these intellectual flourishes is unclear.

A constant feature of his narrative is his casual attempts to dismiss and belittle the women to whom he has been linked. His ex-wife Ilona Kinczell was an adulteress, Janet Oldenburg had fanciful dreams of being an international belly dancer, Andrée Flamme 'had dementia and couldn't put two words together', and he claims his current wife Diane has a problematic memory issue.

BLUM: Well, she was born with craniosynostosis.

Mr Blum produces a document which explains the condition Mrs De Hedervary apparently has.

Craniosynostosis affects the growth of the skull and brain in infants; Mr Blum seems to be suggesting it affected his wife's memory.

> BLUM: I choose to tell you that my wife's got memory problems, that's all.
>
> CASSELDEN: I do not recall during any of your wife's evidence this week she claimed to have memory difficulties of the nature that's recorded in the document just marked for identification.
>
> BLUM: She doesn't want to talk about that.
>
> CASSELDEN: Have you provided that document and the purported reasons for its relevance to distract from my question as to why it was, it appears you have not disclosed to your wife all of the names or aliases you have used in your lifetime since 1976?
>
> BLUM: All I'm saying is that most of the time, she can't remember.

As for Marion Barter, the slur against her is particularly cruel. Blum implies that she was an oversexed man-eater, preying on hapless victims such as himself.

The look on Sally's face as Blum trashes her mother is heartbreaking.

CHAPTER 26

Dead or Alive

17 October 2022

Nothing with this case is ever straightforward.

The team is expecting to hear the closing submissions of each of the parties involved. After all, the Coroner is due to hand down her findings at the end of November, only weeks away. Instead, a surprise witness is called: Joan Hazlett.

Hazlett was the manager of the Byron Bay branch of the Colonial State Bank in 1997. She was interviewed by police before the inquest but has since remembered some new information. The evidence is being heard at the courthouse in Lismore, not far from Ballina and Byron Bay. Hazlett provided two statements to NSW Police, one on 26 August 2020, and her most recent on 21 September 2022. The content of the statements is markedly different. In the earlier one she can't remember Marion Barter at all.

The court hears Hazlett worked at the Colonial State Bank in Byron Bay from August 1995. After she describes the physical layout of the bank in detail, Adam Casselden SC directs her attention to Marion Barter.

'The name meant nothing to me,' Joan says. 'It was only when I was driving home from Grafton and I saw a missing persons ad, and saw her picture, that it actually then came back.' The billboards erected in northern New South Wales in early 2022 caught her eye.

Joan confirms to Casselden that the detective who interviewed her didn't show her a photograph of the missing person.

After her initial police interview in 2020, Hazlett denies having undertaken any internet searches in relation to Marion

Barter. 'I spoke to a few of the people that I thought might have been tellers or in the branch at the same time,' she says. 'But no. It didn't interest me at all.' She says back then she was never told the name Florabella Natalia Marion Remakel and she had no idea about *The Lady Vanishes*. Nor did she take any notice of any news bulletin or articles that made mention of Marion Barter.

'As I was driving at 100 kilometres per hour,' Joan says, 'I just saw the photo. I just remembered her. She's the lady that came in and did a transaction. She had a hibiscus behind her ear and that actually just came back. I just remembered.'

If it's true, it means Hazlett is the last known person to have seen Marion alive.

Once she got to her destination, Hazlett says she called Crime Stoppers and left a message. Casselden reads out excerpts of Joan Hazlett's second statement to police from September 2022.

CASSELDEN: You say in paragraph 10: 'I recall Marion coming to the branch of State Bank Byron Bay at the time that I was the manager.' Then, you say: 'She came into the branch a number of times.' Just pausing there, what time of the year or what month do you have a recollection of seeing Marion?

HAZLETT: I vaguely remember it's roundabout springtime, maybe September, October. I'm just not sure of the month. It was in the warmer months and there were quite a lot of tourists around.

CASSELDEN: And do you remember what sort of clothes she was wearing?

JOAN: Not the clothes. All I can remember is she had a hibiscus behind her ear.

CASSELDEN: Do you remember what colour the hibiscus was?

HAZLETT: White.

Hazlett also can't recall if the woman she remembers wore jewellery, or the colour of her hair.

CASSELDEN: What was it about this one occasion that enabled you 25 years later to recall having just recently seen a photograph on the side of the road of Marion Barter?

HAZLETT: The teller had got me to come out to do the transaction because it was to do with significant cash or suspicious cash transactions, which we'd have to fill out and supply to AUSTRAC [Australian Transaction Reports and Analysis Centre].

CASSELDEN: Was there an internal bank policy that if a particular sum of money was to be withdrawn or transferred, that you had to follow a particular procedure?

HAZLETT: Yeah, it was the procedure as per the government's regulation.

The court hears that Hazlett can't remember how much the transaction was for, but she is adamant that it was a withdrawal, not a transfer.

CASSELDEN: Withdrawal? And why do you say it was withdrawn as opposed to a transfer?

JOAN: We didn't do reporting on transfers.

CASSELDEN: What if it was a transfer to an overseas entity?

JOAN: That would actually go to the international transaction area. We would just fill out forms and it goes straight to the international. We never did it internally. From my recollection, I just took her aside into the inquiry area and completed the form and asked her a few questions. She was fully aware that I was doing a report.

CASSELDEN: Did you need to sight any identification to satisfy yourself that she was in fact the account holder?

HAZLETT: Yes. Yes.

CASSELDEN: And what identification did you sight?

HAZLETT: I'm not a hundred per cent. It would have had to be something with a photo on it and we'd make photocopies of them which would always be attached to the form.

CASSELDEN: Were you required to sight one or more than one photographic identification?

HAZLETT: Normally it only required one as long as it satisfied what we had on our records with the bank.

The court is told that the report and photocopy of the photographic identification would then be sent to a bank office in Sydney.

CASSELDEN: Were you also required to sight a State Bank card?

HAZLETT: Um, not with the actual transaction, because we had to verify her signature and identification with the actual withdrawal slip. But from my recollection, she had come and done a number of transactions over the counter due to the fact she didn't have her card.

CASSELDEN: Pausing there. How do you know that?

HAZLETT: Well, the teller had done the transactions at the counter.

CASSELDEN: The same teller or a different teller?

JOAN: I think there were various tellers.

CASSELDEN: And what were you told on this one occasion by the teller in relation to her withdrawal history, if anything.

HAZLETT: This was basically to ensure that they had verified her identification. And then they just said that we needed to if it was over a certain amount because they can also be classed as suspect if it's a lot of legal transactions which exceed the amount.

Casselden asks Hazlett to provide more detail about what would lead to her filling out a suspicious transaction form. 'You have to log into the bank system to verify the account details?'

'We actually had her details from the teller who had actually completed the transactions,' Hazlett replies, 'and he or she, I don't know, had contacted the branch to confirm her details previously.'

Hazlett says withdrawals above $5000 triggered an alert.

HAZLETT: So, for example, $500 withdrawals, normally you
wouldn't report. But ten $500 withdrawals, it would be over
$5000. So you would have reported it.
CASSELDEN: Any memory of the amount that was being
withdrawn being the order of $80,000?
HAZLETT: No sorry, I don't have any recollection of the amount.

Hazlett says the woman she believes was Marion Barter told her
that she was on holiday in Byron Bay but did not disclose whether
she was holidaying with anyone or where she was staying. She
didn't know if the woman was married, had children or had
recently returned from a trip overseas. But what about whether
she intended to go overseas?

HAZLETT: She mentioned that she was going to go to
Bali and find herself because she called herself a different,
something different, a different name. This is why I
remember the transaction … I can't remember the name.
Honestly, we thought she was a bit of a flip.
CASSELDEN: Right. By that do you mean, she was presenting
as perhaps an interesting or unusual person by Byron Bay
standards?
HAZLETT: Yeah.
CASSELDEN: Did that not raise in your mind a degree of
suspicion that she's presenting to you a driver's licence in one
name which is consistent with the account at the same time
as saying, 'I go by this name'?
HAZLETT: It didn't because of what she presented to me. She
said I just like to be named … I can't remember it, it was
airy-fairy sort of.

The Coroner interjects.

CORONER: Can I just seek some clarification. How did she
say she'd like to be known by a different name? Did she ask
you to call her that?

HAZLETT: No, no, no. She just said that, I can't remember it now.

CORONER: If you could remember how she said it to you?

HAZLETT: In a nice way, friendly, happy.

CORONER: If you could use the words that she used. What did she say?

HAZLETT: Just that, saying that 'I want to be called a flower because I'm free' and, like, she was happy.

CORONER: She might have used the name of a flower?

HAZLETT: Yeah.

CASSELDEN: Have you heard the name since?

HAZLETT: No.

The name of a flower. Something like Florabella perhaps?

Hazlett tells the Coroner she recalls meeting Marion because at the same time the band Silverchair was playing at a music festival in Byron Bay. Seymour quickly searches online and discovers that Silverchair played that festival in 1996, the year before Marion sold her house and had a large sum of money in her account.

It's now time for each of the parties to deliver their final submissions. Casselden concludes that Marion Barter is deceased, Ric Blum is a liar and NSW Police botched the investigation, at least in part. He also reveals that Blum has not made any submissions and will not be responding to the submissions of other parties.

He then summarises Marion's life leading up to her trip of a lifetime to the UK, then continues: 'In our submission, Your Honour is in a position to find that Marion deliberately travelled using her new name and took steps to ensure that no close family or friends were aware of her return to Australia.'

He details the anomalies between the two flight passenger cards Marion filled out: 'When Marion left Australia as Florabella, she was an Australian resident who was divorced and on her way to Luxembourg. Forty-one days later, when she returned to

Australia, she was married and apparently lived in Luxembourg and was staying in Australia for eight days as a visitor. These records suggest that Marion had met a man and married him overseas, or at least planned to do so, and considered Luxembourg to be her new home.'

The court hears that if Marion did intend to depart Australia again only eight days after her re-entry, there's no evidence that she did. Her passport was never used again.

Casselden tells the Coroner that the evidence suggests it was Marion herself who withdrew the money from her account, including the $80,000 on 15 October 1997: 'Marion's family have also made submissions that the court should find that Mr Blum had some involvement, whether direct or indirect, in the withdrawal or transfer of the $80,000. The family's position includes the statement that indirect involvement means that Ric Blum required or persuaded Marion Barter to make it.'

Casselden concludes Marion acted on her own behalf, which, he says, is supported by a notebook entry made by someone he describes as an 'experienced missing persons investigator'.

The fact is that no one gave evidence that they saw Marion and/or spoke to her. Not one single person.

'Finally, Your Honour,' Casselden says, 'as I submitted earlier, Joan Hazlett gave evidence that she identified Marion when she attended the Byron Bay branch for a large transaction. Although Joan Hazlett gave clear evidence that she herself spoke with Marion and identified her when she completed a suspicious transaction report, the timing of this incident is not clear and therefore in our submission, Your Honour cannot find that the interaction with Joan Hazlett occurred on October 15, 1997.'

Casselden then addresses whether Marion's disappearance was intentional: 'It is not known what Marion did or where Marion stayed on her return on August 2, 1997. Having regard to the totality of the evidence, we submit, Your Honour, that Marion was last seen in person at a branch of the Colonial State Bank on October 15, 1997, for the purpose of transferring a sum of $80,000 from her account.

'It is the position of those assisting Your Honour that between August 2 and October 15, 1997, her disappearance *was* intentional. The family does not support such a finding.'

He submits that Marion, after returning to Australia, planned to move to Luxembourg under her name Florabella.

'Your Honour, it is necessary to comment on some aspects of the submissions served by the family which, in our submission, are speculative about marriage intentions and the question of whether she sought to voluntarily start a new life.

'For example, it is simply not known how and why nearly $15,000 remained in Marion's bank account and why her superannuation was not withdrawn. This is one of the many puzzling and deeply troubling aspects of Marion's disappearance.

'Finally, on this point, it should be made clear that those assisting Your Honour do not make any submissions as to Marion's whereabouts or intentions after October 15, 1997. It is for this reason that the proposed findings are framed as such in the written submissions, that is that Florabella Natalia Marion Remakel, formerly known as Marion Barter, is deceased and died at some unknown time after October 15, 1997.'

Casselden moves on to Ric Blum's evidence: 'It has been necessary to explore the circumstances of Mr Blum's relationship with Marion and the connections between his use of the name Remakel and her change of name. Mr Blum agreed he has a long history of committing fraud. Between 1965 and 1973, he was convicted of offences of cheque without cover, false documents and usage thereof, larcenies, embezzlement, fraud, attempted fraud, breach of trust, use of false documents, false impersonation and concealment. Mr Blum has routinely changed his name and admitted to numerous, numerous aliases.

'Your Honour should make, in our respectful submission, a finding that the primary motivation for Mr Blum's name changes was in order to dishonestly represent himself to others.'

Casselden raises the similar travel itineraries of Marion and Blum in mid-1997 and also Marion's name change to Florabella Remakel: 'The international movement records of Mr Blum indicate that he travelled to Japan on June 17, 1997, with his outgoing passenger card simply stating he intended to spend 30 days in Belgium. His incoming passenger card demonstrates that he returned to Australia on July 31, 1997. Mr Blum travelled in and out of the country on his passport under the name of Richard Lloyd Westbury.

'Based on the close proximity of the dates of travel, and Mr Blum's admissions he travelled to England during that trip, it is likely, in our respectful submission, that Marion and Mr Blum made plans to travel together in England as a couple in a relationship.

'It is equally plausible, though speculative, that Mr Blum was involved in planning Marion's itinerary, but did not travel with her to any or all of these destinations, telling her he had business elsewhere, and making plans to meet up with her at some other place and some other time.

'Further we submit, Your Honour can find that Mr Blum and Marion spent at least some time together in England. While there is no objective evidence that Marion and Mr Blum married while overseas based on the incoming passenger card, in our submission you can find that Marion believed she was married to Mr Blum or at least sought to represent to others that she was married to him on her return to Australia.

'However, it is the position of those assisting that there is insufficient evidence to prove that Mr Blum had contact with Marion after she returned to Australia.'

Additionally, Casselden suggests there is not enough evidence to prove Blum fraudulently obtained money from Marion, although it is clear he is a shady character. 'Your Honour received evidence that Marion changed her name, travelled overseas, got married and intended to start a new life in Luxembourg in 1997. These facts are consistent with Mr Blum's tendency to pursue dishonest relationships with vulnerable middle-aged single women. He represented himself as Fernand Remakel when Marion was likely not aware of his real identity and the fact that he was married with children.

'We submit there is insufficient evidence that Mr Blum was either involved with or had knowledge of the series of withdrawals of money from Marion's bank account after her return to Australia or of the transfer of $80,000 to an unknown account, possibly overseas.'

Despite an extensive and ongoing police investigation into Marion's disappearance, Casselden points out that: 'It is not known when she died, and whether she died as a result of natural causes, misadventure, homicide or suicide. To make any submissions in this regard would amount to speculation. This includes any submissions as to whether or not Mr Blum is capable of committing any act of violence.'

After 90 minutes, Casselden concludes his submission with the following suggestion: 'That the formal finding should be that Florabella Natalia Marion Remakel, formerly known as Marion Barter, is deceased and died at some unknown time after August 2, 1997, having returned to Australia from overseas. There is, in our submission, an insufficient basis for the court to find that Marion died shortly after return.'

Sally's barrister Bradley Smith then steps up to deliver his submission. He argues the need for the Coroner to recommend that Ric Blum, whose evidence is full of contradictions, exaggerations and lies, be charged with perjury. Smith homes in on the fact that Blum used passports and licences in names other than his legal name: 'Not only was Ric Blum masquerading under a fake name using a Queensland driver's licence fraudulently obtained, but we say additionally, he was masquerading under a false passport.

'And if it is sufficiently relevant for Your Honour to make a finding about the driver's licence, we say the passport is in a similar camp. And we'll invite Your Honour to make that finding.'

Smith also argues that Blum was instrumental in Marion's decision to quit her job and sell her house: 'The obvious and compelling inference being that Mr Blum, representing himself to Marion as Fernand Nocolas Remakel, is the explanation for why Marion changed her name to Florabella Natalia Marion Remakel, and we support you in making a finding to that effect.

'Your Honour knows that that happened in the very same time period, a couple of months before she went overseas. And Your Honour knows that Marion selling her house and resigning for her employment also happened in the same period of time that Mr Blum first became acquainted with Marion in 1997 in February or at the latest, early March.

'We say it's very improbable, most unlikely, that her decision to sell her house and resign her employment were unconnected to her involvement with Mr Blum at that time.'

Smith asserts that Blum was with Marion Barter as she travelled around southern England, particularly given his familiarity with Sussex. He also claims Blum would likely have had contact with Marion upon her return to Australia in August 1997.

'We say, Your Honour,' he continues, 'taking everything together, Mr Blum and Marion re-entered Australia within two days of each other … Marion indicated on her incoming passenger card that she was married and that she was a resident of Luxembourg.

'Your Honour knows that only two years later, Mr Blum went to the UK with Janet Oldenburg on a trip which had many similar characteristics to what the evidence bears out about Marion's trip to the UK.

'And Your Honour knows that when Janet Oldenburg returned to Australia, separately from Mr Blum, there was further contact between them after that time, and it is not a short leap to find on the balance of probabilities that Mr Blum did have contact with Marion after she returned to Australia.'

Smith highlights the significance of Blum purchasing a car two days before Marion Barter's Medicare card was used at a Grafton optometrist, and selling this car only months later. 'It is difficult to rationalise why Marion came back to Byron Bay, having had her life on the Gold Coast. And apart from two bank withdrawals of Burleigh Heads, there's no evidence that she went near the Gold Coast. All the evidence suggests that she was in the Byron Bay, Grafton, Northern Rivers region of New South Wales, precisely where Mr Blum was living at that time.

'And we think that's particularly significant when one bears in mind the absence of any particular connection between Marion and Byron Bay and the very close temporal relationship between Marion, what we know about what Marion was doing at that time, and what Mr Blum was doing at that time.'

Smith also claims Blum was likely involved in the withdrawal of $80,000 from Marion Barter's bank account on 15 October 1997: 'Sally found out that money had been withdrawn from her mother's account, very, very proximate to the time at which it occurred, i.e. the 22nd of October, which is a week after the large transaction on the 15th of October 1997. She went to police.

'Now of course, there's every reason to think that if an investigation had been opened at that time, and if it had been a proper investigation, then there's every reason to think that the documents would have been available. Marion's bank records would have been available. 'The person who saw her, if someone did see her in the bank, would have been there, could have been interviewed, would have had a recollection of what happened.

'It is very possible, and indeed likely, if an investigation had been opened at that time, that Marion would have been located or that Sally would have found out more about what happened to her mother than she knows sitting here 25 years later.

'All that can be said,' Smith concludes, 'is that between when she came back into the country on the 2nd of August, and when the large sum of money was withdrawn on the 15th of October, we of course accept that Marion did not contact any of her family or friends. One can only infer that that was a conscious act on her part.

'But certainly beyond that, we embrace the position that the court simply can't say what happened to Marion after the 15th of October 1997, other than to unfortunately conclude, as the family accepts, that a finding that Marion is deceased is appropriate.'

When Kim Burke makes her submission on behalf of NSW Police, she rejects any criticism of any of the officers involved: 'The evidence regarding Senior Constable Childs' actions in recording the incident as an "occurrence only" needs to be viewed in the context of his experience, what it was that he knew, what it was that he was told. The amount of training he had with respect to a person reported missing … He had never dealt with a missing persons case before.'

Next Burke tells the Coroner that the police investigation wasn't treated as a priority because of the way Sally reported it. 'The impression formed by former Senior Constable Childs,' she says, 'was that Sally was not reporting the mother missing, rather it was more in relation to the transactions. He did not get a sense of urgency and it was more along the lines that Sally wanted some information being recorded.'

Burke then questions Sally's memory of events: 'Sally's evidence in terms of various issues with respect to her memory show the fragility of her memory, and I'm not criticising her for that. But my point in relation to accepting the evidence from Sally that she in fact got a phone call from New South Wales Police from the Byron Bay Police Station unsupported by any objective evidence, in my submission Your Honour, does not meet the desired probability standard.

'It's apparent from the evidence given by Detective Senior Constable Sheehan that he understood that Sally understood her mother had estranged herself from the family and she wanted to know why. And one can understand that as the daughter, you'd want to know why your mother would ever do that to you. That is different to understanding in terms of reporting somebody missing and concern for safety and welfare. New South Wales Police don't investigate the reasons why, that's a personal matter that needs to be done elsewhere, not by New South Wales Police.'

This seems a strange statement. When police investigate crimes, they are required to investigate the why as much as the what. After all, it is difficult to get a murder conviction without a motive.

'In relation to Detective Senior Constable Sheehan, Your Honour,' Burke continues, 'his evidence needs to be viewed in the context of taking over an investigation that was opened by the Missing Persons Unit in 2007. His evidence also needs to be viewed in the context that he was not part of a strike force. He did not have the degree of resources available to the very dedicated investigating officers in this particular inquest.'

Casselden's junior, Tracey Stevens, concludes the submissions with a strongly worded criticism of Burke's argument that NSW Police did nothing wrong: 'There should be, in our view, Your Honour, no criticism of Sally's actions at the time in 1997 or in 2007 or any time thereafter. There should be no suggestion that she has in any way delayed any investigation by New South Wales Police or behaved in a manner that in our submission can be described as nothing less than totally understandable and consistent with a daughter very confused and anxious at finding out about her mother's circumstances at that time.

'I do feel compelled to say that it is unfortunate that there has been this resistance to accepting the inadequacies of the police investigation, which are clear on the face of the documentary records from 1997 and the years following.

'There has, from our understanding, Your Honour, been an attempt by New South Wales Police to perhaps try to reconcile the actions taken by the Officer Childs and Officer Sheehan with the approach that's been commented upon by Detective Inspector [Glen] Browne. Detective Browne gave very clear and useful evidence to the court about what he expected should have happened in 1997.'

State Coroner Teresa O'Sullivan then wraps up proceedings: 'I'd just like to thank the legal representatives. I would like to thank Sally and her family for your participation. I know it hasn't been easy, but it's much appreciated, your participation and involvement. I'd like to thank the investigating officers again for the incredible professionalism and an enormous amount of work put into this case. And my counsel assisting team – for their enormous assistance to me.

'We will adjourn for findings, which will be delivered at 10 am on the 30th of November here at Lidcombe.'

CHAPTER 27

The Price of Love

Monday, 10 October 2022

The inquest sittings are over, but Sandy is still receiving daily tips and theories about what happened to Marion. One particular message in French from a lady in Belgium makes her sit up and take notice. The English translation is worth quoting in full:

Last week I did a search on Frederic De Hedervary.

By chance I came across an article in a Luxembourg newspaper published on 10 July 2022 about the disappearance of Marion Barter whose story I was totally unaware of.

I am terribly shocked reading this story because I realise that my mother-in-law has had a similar story in 2006 with the same scammer.

The modus operandi that Frederic De Hedervary (aka Ric Blum and other pseudonyms) used to defraud my mother-in-law was identical to that used for Marion Barter: meeting via an announcement, selling her house, withdrawing cash, leaving for Australia without saying goodbye to her children. The scammer disappeared before the scheduled departure for this trip to Australia.

My mother-in-law (Ghislaine Dubois-Danlois) filed a complaint in September 2006 with the Tervuren police. A few years later my mother-in-law was contacted by the Tournai police about another victim of Frederic De Hedervary who narrowly escaped and who it happened to exactly the same.

I would like to describe to you the memory that I have
of Frederic De Hedervary because this individual seemed
to me extremely dangerous. I had the opportunity to meet
Frederic De Hedervary on August 9, 2006: the memory of
this evening makes my blood run cold!

A few days before, my mother-in-law announced to her
three children living in Belgium that she would like to bring
the whole family together to announce important news (we
don't know, absolutely not, what it is about). Her son living
in France cannot move, for this reason she is organising a
trip to France where we are also invited. On the scheduled
day I go to my mother-in-law in Tervuren with my
companion Gabriel Dubois and our two-year-old son. The
rest of the family is there too.

As I enter the house, I see a man I don't know and greet
him quickly thinking it was a neighbour who dropped by
unexpectedly, because we are not introduced.

When the whole family arrived, my mother-in-law
poured us a glass of champagne and announces, 'Here is
Frederic, we love each other, we are going to get married
and we are going to live in Australia'.

We are all shocked by such a brutal announcement.
I remember that we felt the emotion in my mother-in-law,
on the other hand Frederic remained frozen, as if he was not
concerned by this announcement. Some family members
try to lighten the mood by asking a few questions to this
Frederic De Hedervary.

For this 'party' meal, Frederic prepared a spaghetti
bolognese with star anise.

We sit down to eat. In front of everyone, he tells various
elements of his life. He explains that he was first a policeman
in Belgium then, following an accident, he went to Australia.
His accident left traces because he limps (we all noticed it).

During the meal he keeps telling morbid and unhealthy
stories. He says he participated in the Vietnam War (as an
Australian army volunteer?), he recounts a sordid episode

about it: he was taken prisoner and put in a hole in the ground
so narrow that he could only stand, next to him another hole
with a captive Vietnamese woman. He gave sordid details
about the agony and death of this woman. I was very disturbed
by what he was explaining. I found it quite inappropriate to
tell these kinds of details to people you are seeing for the first
time. During the evening, he also talked about poisons.

He tells us that he is a numismatist,* he travels all over the
world looking for old and rare coins, this is what justifies his
many trips.

The next day, we learn that my mother-in-law is going
to sell her house and all its contents, as well as her car,
before leaving for Australia. We also learn that Frederic
De Hedervary strongly advised to leave without telling her
children but that she refused this condition.

We learn that Frederic De Hedervary travels a lot
between Europe and Australia. My mother-in-law tells us
not to worry because she will come back often.

On our return from vacation (end of August), we help my
mother-in-law to empty her house since she really decided
to put it on sale and go to Australia very quickly. My
companion and I put books in cases ourselves (we do this for
several days in a row).

During this period, we see Frederic De Hedervary at
least twice at my mother-in-law's. He is quite cold and
distant. We see him burning documents of his own in the
fireplace. He asks my mother-in-law to do all kinds of
medical examinations before she leaves. While I put books
away, I witness a disturbing scene: my mother-in-law is
on the phone with her doctor and explains that she wants
to do medical examinations before leaving for Australia.
Frederic De Hedervary is nearby and he listens carefully to
everything she says on the phone.

Suddenly he said, 'Ask for an ultrasound of the liver!' My
mother-in-law is very healthy, everything seems weird to

---

* A numismatist is someone who studies or collects rare coins and notes.

me. She keeps talking to the doctor, disregarding the remark
of Frederic. Then he shouts insistently 'REQUEST AN
ULTRASOUND OF THE LIVER!'

My mother-in-law then talks to the doctor about it. The
behaviour of Frederic De Hedervary at this moment seemed
completely abnormal to me. He became aggressive for no
apparent reason.

Another day (the second day we see Frederic
De Hedervary at my mother-in-law's house then emptying
the house), we learn that certain objects are going to be sent
directly to Australia in a steel trunk he brought.

My mother-in-law would like to put some books in it
and photos she cares about, but he finds excuses to choose
for himself what will go in this trunk: basically he takes all
the valuables (including a cutlery set and money). He tells
her in front of us that it is stupid to send books there, it will
cost him less to buy them on the spot. He is in a hurry for
this trunk to be shipped as soon as possible because it is his
accountant who will receive it on site and the accountant
will not be there if he does not send the trunk right away.

Arranging the many books, my companion finds a book
on 'poisons that kill without leaving a trace'. Recalling that
Frederic De Hedervary had spoken of poisons during our
first meeting, he asks if this book interests him. He greedily
seizes the book. We are surprised by his strong reaction.

During these days of tidying up the house, my companion
insists that Frederic De Hedervary and my mother-in-
law come to eat with us before they leave. Frederic does
not want to because he has too many things to do but my
mother-in-law insists that she cannot refuse this. Frederic
ends up accepting and a day of appointment is fixed.

The day of the appointment (I do not have the date
in memory but it is the day when my mother-in-law
complained to the police at the beginning of September), my
mother-in-law arrives at our house. We wait a long time,
my mother-in-law worries more and more, she tries to reach

him on his cell phone which does not answer. She tells us that she is worried about the fact that he had a huge amount of cash on him and is afraid that he has been assaulted.

I accompany my mother-in-law to the police. She is told that she must go to the police station in Tervuren because she lives there. It was only a few days later that my mother-in-law admitted to us that she had been the victim of a scammer who disappeared with all her savings.

We learn that she met him a few weeks earlier via a dating ad she had herself published in a newspaper. My mother-in-law learns from the police that Frederic De Hedervary has been in prison for several years for various scams.

A few years later she was contacted by the Tournai police following the complaint of another victim of Frederic De Hedervary.

We haven't heard about him since, until I read these articles on the internet.

Alexandra Peereboom

Le 10 Octobre 2022

Sandy immediately organises to interview Alexandra on the phone with the help of her French assistant, Estelle Sanchez. Sandy hadn't realised Estelle was French when she hired her, but it proves an unexpected bonus.

Alexandra talks about the heartbreaking moment Ghislaine shared with them she'd been duped. 'She definitely tried to hide it from us because she felt very ashamed to have fallen for his show, to have lost all of her savings. So it was a feeling of shame, so she didn't want to talk about it. She didn't explain everything in detail, she isolated herself. It was quite terrible because it perturbed family ties a lot. So we were ready to help, but she didn't want us to because she felt guilty about what happened.

'When we went to the police, she was a bit embarrassed, she didn't know how to explain the situation to the police. She said, "Well, I haven't known him for a long time, what am I going to say, I'm not his wife, I'm not … They'll make fun of me."

'The same night she called us and told us, "He's a swindler, he took all of my money."'

Having only allowed for the cash, Alexandra says €70,000 was stolen, but Sandy later learns that including the value of stolen goods, the total losses are more than €300,000. It could have been much more, as Ghislaine changed her mind about giving Frederic the money to buy a house in Australia, instead using it to purchase a new home for one of her sons living in France, who'd been left homeless after a house fire. Ghislaine can no longer afford to live in Brussels, and instead lives in Lille.

'What we thought was, we imagined Frederic would grab the money she got from selling her house and because she didn't have that money any more maybe he told himself, "Well, that situation isn't interesting any more." That's what we thought.'

Alexandra says she feared for her mother-in-law's life. 'He told her, "You don't breathe correctly during the night, you need to do a check-up to find out whether you have sleep apnoea," which she did have. Afterwards, we thought he was looking for a weak spot to say, "Well, she died but it's normal, it's her liver or she had sleep apnoea." What I told myself at that point was how lucky we were that she was still here, because she wouldn't have survived.'

Alexandra hopes, 'That he would be found guilty and that he would finish his days in prison. That would be a big relief that we would all feel, of course, and that's why we've contacted you. That's what I hope is, thanks to the media, maybe we can change things.'

Alexandra expands on the story of the other victim: 'Yes, the police contacted [Ghislaine] a few years after because a woman from Tournai, a town in Belgium an hour away from here, followed Frederic on a trip. 'She found herself in Bali, on her own. I don't know the details but I know she was abandoned there and she filed a complaint to the police.

'I strongly encourage all the victims to talk about it, because, well of course they would be ashamed to have fallen for his show, I can imagine that it would be very difficult to talk about it, but it would be worth it. And it's important to understand that in this case, he's a professional swindler. There's no shame in talking about it. He knows how to manipulate, it could happen to anyone. There's no reason not to talk about it. By talking about it, it will help the victims, it will help the investigation to progress. The benefit justifies the cost.'

Ghislaine shows Sandy a copy of her engagement invitation in which his name was spelt 'Frederick de Hedervary'. He would often mix up the spelling of his fake names.

Sandy and the team have to move fast. Ghislaine's story is so similar to Marion's that they need to publish it before the Coroner delivers her findings on 30 November.

8 November 2022

Episode 43, 'Wild Claims', is released and quickly downloaded hundreds of thousands of times. It recounts how a 2019 article in the *Luxembourg Times* by Tom Rüdell and Yannick Lambert prompted Alexandra to reach out to TLV.

Along with Ghislaine, Sandy interviews others who've contributed to the podcast, who argue this account should be put before the Coroner. She also speaks about the victim from Tournai. This lady doesn't want to be identified, so is given the pseudonym 'Charlotte' by the Luxembourg newspaper. She was married to Blum's now deceased cousin. Tom and Yannick have discovered she reported Frederic De Hedervary to Belgian police after he allegedly stole €100,000 from her.

Her story is alarmingly familiar. After she met Blum and engaged in a whirlwind romance in 2012, he convinced her to join him to start a new life. They would go to Bali to get married as soon as she had gathered together the cash to buy their new home there. Instead, 'Charlotte' found herself stranded, her money gone and no return ticket. When she finally did return home, she discovered Blum had also taken valuable jewellery and a stamp collection.

One other person Sandy thinks can help convince the Coroner and NSW Police more action is needed is Monique Cornelius, who is now 74 and retired from teaching. The sticking point is that the last time Sandy called Monique, a year ago from Byron

Bay during the inquest, Monique told her in no uncertain terms not to call again.

But Sandy could tell that Monique knew much more than she was saying. Perhaps she knows Blum better than any other woman they are aware of, apart from his current wife, Diane. Blum still seemed to be infatuated with Monique during the inquest, so perhaps he truly loved her.

'Hi Monique. It's Alison Sandy from *The Lady Vanishes*. How are you?'

'I don't know you.'

'We've spoken before. I'm a journalist in Australia. And I'm doing the podcast *The Lady Vanishes*. I just thought you might have seen all the publicity recently in Belgium and Luxembourg with all these other people speaking about —'

Monique interjects, 'Hmm hmmm, I work together with the Australian police, you know. Give me a moment. I am not thinking in English, but it will come.'

'I am so sorry I don't speak French,' Sandy says.

'Oh no. But who are you, madam?'

'Alison. I spoke to you about the podcast we're doing, *The Lady Vanishes*. I wondered whether you've seen all the publicity in the *Luxemburger Wort*? … I just wanted to see whether you'd read about Ghislaine and "Charlotte" in Belgium who have spoken out about their dealings with Frederick De Hedervary, aka Ric Blum, aka a lot of aliases.'

'Mmm, I have them,' Monique says slowly.

'And I just wanted to thank you, because your testimony, what you provided in your letters and correspondence that you'd received was just so important, so I just wanted to thank you.'

'Of course, madam, of course, that's why I did it. So that no other women will be … he is just someone very, very, very dangerous. That's also why I am working together with Luxembourgish Police, the highest one we have here in Luxembourg, because I was afraid he would come and make … He is capable of anything. I cannot prove it. But I feel.'

Monique seems genuinely fearful.

'You seem to know him more than anyone else that we've spoken to,' Sandy says.

'I know him. I know him. Oh yes, I know him very good. His character, his reactions. And that's why I say he is very, for woman, especially for a woman, a very, very dangerous man. '

'Which was bizarre, because he seemed to love you,' Sandy notes.

'Oh no, he loves money, nothing else,' Monique says adamantly. 'I immediately left him when I saw that he had a wife. No, no, no, no, no. No, I didn't know. He was a friend, just a friend. Someone with whom I could discuss very good, he could tell stories. I didn't believe anything anymore. And I worked and I had my house. I had my work. I have my money. I didn't depend on him for nothing, for nothing,' Monique says fervently. 'And I was free, free, free, I know.'

Sandy is surprised she's being so candid. Monique is so engrossed in her memories that Sandy has to wait until she pauses.

'One day he told me, "Look, these hands have already killed," and he showed me his hands like that.'

'Why did he tell you that?'

'I don't know. He told me very, very much. He's very strong. He's also a master of manipulation. He never, ever says the truth. Perhaps in a moment of weakness. But he manipulates everybody. He tells stories, stories, stories. He did not manipulate me, I saw his manipulation. I saw when he lied or manipulated.'

Monique recalls discovering Blum was married with children when she overheard him talking to his wife at the airport. 'He talked to a woman and I knew they were a team, very intimate. Very close. After the phone call, we went to bring in a coffee and I asked him who the lady was.'

Monique says she also overheard Blum and his fourth wife, Diane, discussing a child. That was David, who was a toddler at the time. 'I didn't know this. He hasn't told me. I told him no, no, leave me alone.'

Monique then details all the other lies he told. 'He's very good at storytelling. He told me he was a secret agent of the English

Embassy here in Luxembourg. I believed it! I cannot say that I'm very intelligent, but I am not an idiot. He is focused on getting money and therefore, he is playing with the emotions of women. In the beginning, I trusted him too. He is a very good speaker. He knows the emotions of women. I was young and I was alone. I was divorcing. For me, he was interesting.'

Sandy seizes on the opening and jumps back in with her next question. 'I guess women who are divorcing or widows, it seems to be his MO [modus operandi] but you were the one who got away. Did he ever try to take money?' Sandy asks.

'I got away. I could.' Monique then refers to what she's read about Marion Barter. 'The lady who has two children, you know, the mother?'

'Marion Barter?' Sandy clarifies.

'*Oui*, it's Barter. Marion Barter, she had money. *Ja*. The women he manipulates until they are depending on him. And he only is playing with emotions. And if you are playing with the emotions of others you have possibilities to enslave them. He can do that. Oh, my God.'

'You are extraordinary, Monique, and an inspiration to all of us that you have the courage to speak out about him,' Sandy tells her.

'Oh yes, I have the courage, I have it. That it is not a talent. I'm proud to say you cannot do that to me.'

Sandy tells Monique that, possibly, the inquest isn't over yet and asks if she'd reconsider her decision not to appear.

'I cannot tell more because 40 years is a very long time,' Monique says. 'I speak to the police of New South Wales. I have written emails and emails to Australia. They know everything I can say. But I cannot face it, I'm too old for that. And I'm living alone here and in peace. I have forgotten this man.

'For me, he is just dirt. He doesn't have the right to live. He has taken so many. He's fundamentally, I don't know … Don't touch him, you will burn your hands. I can say to you and everyone should be very afraid. He should be in prison for the rest of his life. I hope so. Even in the tomb when he's buried, he will try to manipulate to get out of it, I tell you. He lies when he opens his mouth.'

'He's out of my mind. He cannot touch me any more. He's a bad man. Nothing is true. Every word, every breath is manipulation. The Coroner must be very strong and not believe him. He has no regrets. He must have money.'

'He stole your [ex-]husband's identity too, that was one of the many aliases,' Sandy says, referring of course to Fernand Remakel.

'I know that. My [ex-]husband can defend himself, very good,' Monique says.

'You've been amazing and so helpful, and this is to get justice for all his victims, including you, because you were his victim even though you didn't give him money. He tried to manipulate you and he's affected you,' Sandy says.

'Yes, of course, I know that now. I had a very long time to understand his character but now I am so sure of what I want. I had a chance, an unspeakable chance, to get out of that without any harm. And I know, I can tell you why. Because I could not give him millions, I have none. I worked at my job. I had a good class, but not enough to satisfy that gangster. No, I think he loved me a little bit, I think so.'

'I just want you to know that I'm grateful you're speaking to me … We will use this on the podcast,' Sandy says, then tells her about the other women who have shared their story.

'Oh *voilà*. I think we women, we must stick together. We are very strong. We are stronger than men if we stick together. We are more sensitive. We are more intelligent. One day you come to Luxembourg, you will enjoy it. For one week, two weeks, I will show you the place.'

Podcast Episodes 44 and 45, 'Tainted Love' parts one and two, are released, the latter just 12 days before the Coroner is due to release her findings.

Meanwhile, the team is unearthing more about 'Charlotte', the eighth woman Blum is known to have preyed upon. A tipster from Europe, with a great knowledge of accurate details of Blum's early life, has come forward with information that cannot be shared with listeners of the podcast, but it's passed on to detectives.

Then Seymour calls Ric Blum.

BLUM: Hello?

SEYMOUR: Hello Ric, it's Bryan Seymour from the *Lady Vanishes* podcast. I am recording this conversation. I'm calling to ask about Alexandra Peereboom and her mother-in-law Ghislaine. They claim you stole money and valuables from Ghislaine in 2006, and I'm offering you the chance to respond.

BLUM: That's a lie.

SEYMOUR: When did you meet, and how did you meet Ghislaine?

BLUM: Oh … please don't worry about that, thanks.

SEYMOUR: No, I have to worry about it, because they claim you've stolen money and valuables and that you were aggressive and threatening.

BLUM: Oh Jesus … yes, yes … ohhh.

SEYMOUR: How much did you take from them, Ric?

BLUM: I never took anything, just don't worry about it.

SEYMOUR: Did you ask her to start a new life with you in Australia?

BLUM: And what else? What else? Just, just leave me alone.

SEYMOUR: No, no, I can't do that, because more and more women are coming forward … how many women have you —*

Blum abruptly hangs up and the conversation is published in the podcast.

Then, on 29 November, the Coroner suddenly cancels the 30 November court listing in Lidcombe to deliver her findings. This must mean that she is sufficiently interested in the patterns of Blum's behaviour to include in her deliberations the victims profiled in the last podcast episode.

It demonstrates the powerful influence and resonance of *The Lady Vanishes*.

---

* Telephone call to Ric Blum from Bryan Seymour, 7 November 2022.

CHAPTER 28

Spotlight

As the team's investigation unfolds and new evidence is uncovered, other media outlets increasingly show an interest in the story, some claiming 'exclusives' for stories that were featured in detail in the podcast months, even years earlier.

There are now nearly 50 episodes covering hundreds of leads and interviews, thousands of details and a multitude of breakthroughs. That's the beauty of a podcast. Unlike traditional media, there's no editor or news director telling you it won't fit in the paper or bulletin or that it's running out of steam. The creators are in control.

Seven's flagship current affairs program *Spotlight* will do a series on Marion, much to Sandy's relief. She's been beating the drum about the network doing something other than news stories for a long time. Renewed enthusiasm for this is sparked when national newspaper *The Australian* runs a series of articles on the case three years into the investigation (barely acknowledging the podcast and the role it played in breaking the story).

One of *Spotlight*'s producers texts Sandy asking if the podcast triggered the inquest. 'Absolutely it did,' she replies. 'I have the documentation to prove it.'

Sandy catches up with the show's executive producer, Mark Llewellyn, who's clear he wants new information to take the story forward. Llewellyn is old school, with a very dry, black sense of humour and an impressive ability to compress a very complicated story into must-watch TV. He tells Sandy the key to bringing this forward is convincing Blum's estranged daughter Evelyn to become involved. Sandy feels her stomach drop, having already pursued this line of inquiry with no success.

She initially heard about Evelyn, Blum's daughter with his third wife, Ilona Kinczell, in 2021 when Blum was on the stand.

In 2021, Sandy made many calls to Evelyn that went straight to voicemail. She left several messages and texts. She was subsequently advised to back off because NSW Police would be interviewing Evelyn and she may impede an ongoing investigation. Then suddenly, Evelyn is quoted in *The Australian*. She doesn't say much in relation to Marion, but does claim she thought her father, Ric Blum, tried to poison her.

Realising Evelyn is willing to speak to media and there's no police gag in place, Sandy asks Seymour to call to see if she'll be on the podcast. Evelyn speaks to him but doesn't want to go on the record.

Sandy follows up with another call to Evelyn to see if she'll change her mind given some of her story has already been published. Evelyn is suspicious, but Sandy tells her about the podcast and how they've been doing it for almost five years now. She emphasises the importance of telling the whole story and how it could also bring Blum to justice and help solve the mystery of what happened to Marion. The issue with Blum is authorities seem reluctant to explore the potential that he is more than just a Casanova conman.

Sandy explains to Evelyn that much of what she has told Seymour on the phone was already alluded to in *The Australian*. Very reluctantly, Evelyn agrees to allow her conversation with Seymour to be used in the next episode, but says she feels she's being manipulated. Sandy understands, there's always a fine line in marrying privacy with the pursuit of critical truth.

March 2023

Sandy organises a meeting with Evelyn at a restaurant in Brisbane.

Evelyn exudes a kindness and warmth that becomes even more powerful as you learn what she's been through.

Evelyn was only seven years old when her mother died. The strange circumstances surrounding Ilona's death are important in establishing what Ric Blum is capable of. The team know he's a conman, but is he also a murderer? There's a clear pattern of behaviour that fits with what happened to Marion, but could he actually have killed her?

Evelyn is enthusiastic about appearing on *Spotlight*, but Sandy doesn't want to put pressure on her to commit to anything. It can be a daunting prospect to appear on national TV. Sandy comes up with an idea. Evelyn wants to know about her own history, as several mysteries in her life need solving. So why doesn't she travel with the *Spotlight* crew to Belgium and Luxembourg? It's an offer not made lightly. It's a lot of pressure to put on someone who isn't a public figure and has zero experience with the media and what it involves. There's also the issue of what can and can't be covered.

Evelyn agrees to come to Belgium and says she's also happy to meet with Sally Leydon and film a joint interview with her. Sandy lets newly appointed *Spotlight* producer Duane Hatherly know and he comes to Brisbane to go through all the footage the team has collected over the past four years.

18 April 2023

Sally is keen to meet Evelyn and participate in the *Spotlight* story, so Hatherly scouts an old-style club/cafe in Brisbane. Their interviewer will be *Spotlight*'s newest recruit, former *60 Minutes* reporter and respected investigative journalist Liam Bartlett.

Evelyn is excited and nervous as Sandy ushers her and her husband, Mario, up the stairs. They walk into the area they've set up as a makeshift studio and Sally greets Evelyn.

'I'm very sad about your mum,' Sally says. 'I've been sad about your mum for a long time, and I knew something wasn't right and I just needed to find you and I just needed to … that's what I felt like. Anyway, I'm glad I found you.'*

'Thank you so much for acknowledging that. I've always been so, I don't know, I just felt a bit crazy for thinking anything terrible had happened to my mum.'

---

* Interview with Evelyn Reid by Sally Leydon and Liam Bartlett, 18 April 2023.

'I'm sure. I'm the same. Like it's hard to sort of put it in a clear perspective,' Sally agrees.

Evelyn looks over to where Sandy is sitting with her husband Mario, seeking reassurance. They give her a thumbs-up. It is nerve-racking for both women, especially Evelyn, who has never spoken publicly about her difficult and very traumatic upbringing. Evelyn and Sally are united by one basic fact: their mothers were involved with the same man before they died, a man using different names.

Bartlett lets them gets acquainted with the cameras rolling, then puts to Evelyn: 'Thirty-one is just such a young age.'

'I think just the fact that I felt that something had happened to her, and I had an instinct that whatever it was, was nefarious and dark, that alone is what made all the people in my realm treat me like I was pretty crazy. So that was, that was really my experience growing up with it,' Evelyn says.

'But you still have those thoughts? You still think that?' Bartlett asks.

'I still have those thoughts now, but it's different, because it caused so much pain to me to be treated that way by everyone around me that eventually I had to go through a process where I had to let it go, so that I could live my life, because otherwise I was probably going to die myself. There's no way to live with that amount of trauma, and the dysfunction of relating to people from a place of that much trauma. So that was sort of my journey and it was a long journey and a challenging journey.'

Bartlett then asks how Evelyn feels having Blum as her biological father and him denying they ever met as adults. 'I don't see him as my father. I mean, in my 30s, the last time that I met with him, I was left in a way that was very scarring to me where, again, I thought something terrible was happening. I thought that maybe this person was trying to hurt me in a bad way. Again, anyone I spoke to really didn't buy in too much into what I was thinking was going on. So it was really that on one hand, and I've got this man that's meant to be something to me, like a father, that's meant to care about me. So the combination of those two things just left me scarred. And I have completely disassociated myself from him as a relative of mine.'

'It's very sad,' Bartlett agrees, 'but ... Sally, it's fair, isn't it, to say from your position that you think Evelyn's biological father has had something to do with your mum's disappearance?'

Sally is careful in her reply. 'It's hard because I can't, I can't say that he definitely has. But if I look at all the facts, and I'm a pretty level-headed human, it's pretty fair to say that he probably knows something that he's not telling me.'

'You haven't reached a definitive conclusion because you can't?' Bartlett probes.

'I can't yet, and it's hard for people to understand. Like everyone who looks at the facts and goes, "Oh, you know, we think ..." [but] I can't say that yet.'

Bartlett presses the point. 'But you think on the balance of probability that he's had something to do with your mum?'

'I have to consider that my mum changed her name to his name. She went overseas at the same time as him. She came back the same time as him, and all of her known whereabouts and money came out of her bank account and being in that location where he was living and he's still living today. So I cannot *not* think that there is some connection somehow. Ric Blum admits to having an affair with my mum and a relationship with her, and if you look at all the other ladies that have come forward ... and said, "Hey, this happened to me, as well."'

'So, Evelyn, how do you process that connection with Sally? You've lost your mum, tragically at a very young age, there's that connection. You both lost your mothers but your father may or may not have been involved. How do you work that out in your mind now, in front of Sally?' Bartlett asks.

'Well, I personally feel that my connection to Sally is based on the fact that both of us lost our mother.'

'Yeah, I feel that way too,' Sally says.

'Nothing to do with any connection to Ric Blum the man, but rather what we both went through for losing our mums,' Evelyn continues. 'And even though it seems to me that he is guilty of something, I still have to pinch myself to realise that he potentially did these terrible things, but what terrible things did he do? Well, none of us really know. We have to hopefully find out. Maybe he'll tell us.'

'Have you been thinking about this meeting for a while?' Bartlett asks.

'I didn't know I was ever gonna get to meet Sally. And I didn't know if Sally would want to meet me. I didn't know whether people would in some way try to put me in some context, you know, with him as a relative, which I was very frightened of, but after only recently becoming aware of Sally's story, long story, I just wanted to give you a hug, really.'

'Me too,' Sally says. 'I mean, you were obviously a lot younger than me, but I think even if you take all that away, you still have things in life that you have to try and cope [with] as a daughter of someone who's no longer there to help you and, and not knowing what's actually happened to your mum like that, you're in the same position as me. I mean, I know you were young. How old, seven?'

'Seven,' Evelyn confirms.

'And I was 24. So there is that age difference between the two of us and I feel lucky that I got to see my mum, you know, and grow up with her through my teenage years, but I just had this overwhelming want to meet Evelyn and just give her a hug and just tell her I'm here for her and I'm someone who understands and is grappling with the enormity of what this is and the craziness of what it is.'

Bartlett suggests that some of Sally's research may help Evelyn.

'Yeah, amazing,' Evelyn says. 'It's so encouraging after what I've been through that there's people out there that believe that yes, something's gone on. And discovering what that something is, is something important as well. If I can get a few answers, then that would be amazing. But at the same time, my mother is dead and it would be good to know what happened to Sally's mum.'

'It's tragically sad, your mum at 31 years old. What does the death certificate say?' Bartlett asks.

'I actually can't remember the medical word for her heart stopped. I did look it up in a medical book. It said that it was, you know, an overload of toxins, but it's actually the heart's inability to sort of like deal with toxins in the blood as it pumps it around, but it's a very common cause of death. It's up there with cardiac arrest. It's the environmental toxins, a lot of people, their hearts can't cope.'

'But at 31, she must have had a lot of toxins in her body?' Liam presses.

'Yeah, well, when I grew up, I got told things like she had scarlet fever when she was a child and had a weak heart or she died of a broken heart. There were some welfare papers where my stepfather had reported that she died from suicide on those documents. So I didn't really ever get a clear answer about it, and I think that maybe I wouldn't have accepted it if it wasn't for the fact that my grandmother died the same year.'

Evelyn says her uncle Attila, Ilona's brother, was also very young when he died, soon after her mother. 'My uncle being only somewhere in his twenties, so much younger than my mother, apparently had a stroke. I mean, it's unheard of. The first time when I was in my twenties and I thought, maybe this really happened. Maybe I'm just, you know, have invented all this stuff in my head because I can't deal with the trauma of losing my mother. I thought, if that's the case, I better go and get checked out, so I went to the doctor and told him the history and the doctor was horrified enough to run heaps of tests on me. They came back and everything was normal so, you know, it was just confusing growing up trying to get answers.'

Sally takes the opportunity to tell Evelyn about Ilona's autopsy report. The anomalies around Ilona's death have been discussed in the podcast, but Evelyn is unaware of a document Joni found in PROV (Public Records Office Victoria) that raises more questions about the nature of Ilona's death.* 'I hope it's okay to tell you that we actually have her autopsy report and her heart is normal, well, they say the heart was functioning normally and there was no

---

*   1977/2388 Ilona Reid: Body card. Public Records Office Victoria.

damage to the heart. So on her death certificate, it said she'd had a heart attack and then the autopsy report came back that the heart is normal.'

Sandy didn't realise Sally was going to raise this during the interview. Evelyn is clearly shaken by this turn of events. 'Why would a hospital say one thing on a certificate and an autopsy say something different?' Evelyn asks.

'Another question in the abyss that we're trying to grapple with,' Sally says.

'That's amazing,' Bartlett says. 'You didn't know this?'

'No, how could I know?' Evelyn shakes her head.

'Have police interviewed you, Evelyn?' Bartlett asks.

'They did call me, I had a phone call.'

'Surely they've taken a statement?'

'No, nothing.'

'Nothing at all? They haven't asked you to turn up as a witness to say something? Nothing? Oh, that's extraordinary. Do you find that unusual?'

'I have goosebumps,' Sally says.

'I mean all this is,' Bartlett continues, 'you know, these circumstances surrounding the death of Evelyn's mum, surely are completely pertinent to the overall case, the whole story, would you agree?'

'Well, I think it's very important,' Sally says. 'I was so sad to hear what happened to your mum and shocked at the same time and just my gut feeling told me something wasn't right ... And sometimes that leads me down rabbit holes that are a dead end but sometimes I end up sitting next to the person that we've been looking for. And it wasn't like we were on a mission to find you either, but I'm glad we found you ... People think I'm crazy if I say something. "Strength in numbers," is what I say to my girls ... Everyone needs to be looked after and cared for and treated with sensitivity and care, right?'

Evelyn is still stunned by the autopsy report. 'Yeah, it's a bit of a process,' she says, looking a bit dazed. 'I'm sorry. I'm not trying to take away from what you just said, I'm just struggling to understand how professionals can deliver something on one report and then people in a similar profession put a different cause of death onto a death certificate ... How does something like that even happen?'

'It paints a very different picture, potentially, of what happened,' Bartlett says.

'Yeah, potentially, if I can find out what happened,' Sally says.

Bartlett is winding up his interview. 'Can I ask you both individually, what's your hope for each other?'

'Well, I hope we can become friends and we can actually be there as a support for each other,' Sally says. 'And it's kind of weird because we've just met, but I feel like I know you and I feel like I have a really deep love for you as a person and, you know, you've been through a lot and I have a lot of empathy for you for what's happened to you and what you've had to deal with. I would just like you to know that I'm here as someone if you ever want to have a coffee, or catch up, or go out for lunch or something, because at the end of the day, that's what life is about.'

'I've lived a life where what I've been told hasn't been reliable, but I do remember what I was told,' Evelyn says. 'So there was my grandmother who was in Brussels, she lived with her second husband, and Atilla her son was staying there. He had a partner and they had a child, I think a girl, but I don't have any of those details. And my mother had been to Brussels to visit then she came back to Australia and passed away. And then my grandmother, who was over there, passed away and then her son who lived in the house with her, passed away.'

'They all had been together in the same home in Brussels and just happened to all die within how many months of each other?' Bartlett asks.

'I'm not 100 per cent sure. I was seven. It's very difficult to put the time around it, but it was a condensed sort of a timeframe.'

Evelyn says she doesn't even know if her younger brother Chris is her half-brother or full brother, as his birth certificate shows they share the same father. 'It says on there very clearly that Willy Wouters is his father, which is the current Ric Blum,' Evelyn says. 'However, when I confronted Blum with that document, he denied that Chris was his son. And when I confronted Michael [her stepfather] with that document, he said, "No, Chris is absolutely my son." So both men agree, but here's the birth certificate saying something completely different.'

'You know, Evelyn, if Sally can solve the mystery of her mum, that will surely help you solve your mystery,' Bartlett suggests.

'I mean, I hope so, but the reason that I've come out is because I want to help you whether I find answers or not,' Evelyn explains. 'I've got a story and my story might help get answers for what you're going through, that's what I hope for. I have, for want of better words, a duty of care, to help in any way that I can. It's really important. I may not get the answers, but we can do things and the things that I've been through might somehow help. I don't know how, but hopefully they'll help uncover more.'

CHAPTER 29

Kiss of Death

It's surprising and heartening how resilient Evelyn is given everything she's been through.

'The pictures of you as a child and your mum, knowing what was ahead of you, it's heartbreaking,' Sandy says.

'Yeah. I guess I don't look at those photos very often, but when I do, I see a little girl as well, and I always feel in my heart I want to talk to her. I just think, "That poor little thing, she had no idea what was coming down the road in front of her." So often I just want to grab her and give her a little hug.' That little girl in her time of innocence, before it was stripped away so savagely, is a pointer to a life that could have been.

Included in Evelyn's stash of old photos are quite intimate shots of her mother and father, including their wedding. Ilona was still a teenager in some of the photos and Ric Blum was in his twenties. Both are grinning broadly and sharing longing looks. They are, by all appearances, madly in love.

'They look incredibly happy,' Evelyn muses.

'They do. And there, the way they're looking at each other, it's just true love.'

'Yeah, you can imagine when I was quite young ... and thought that I would find this man out there that would be a father to me – that would love me and look after me and care for me, because they do look so incredibly in love. I never imagined for a second, after seeing these photos, there'd be someone out there who was more like a monster that I don't want to have anything to do with.'

'He looks nice,' Sandy agrees before moving to the next photo, from their wedding. 'So that's their wedding day. She looks beautiful.'

'Look how happy he looks on his wedding day,' Evelyn agrees.

'Yeah, it looks like a genuine marriage.'

Evelyn has the couple's travel records from when they arrived separately in Australia. 'It was the 11th of September '69 and here's the 18th of September '69 and they've both referred to each other as each other's spouses. She would have been pregnant with me when she travelled out in September '69. I was born in January 1970.'

'Yeah, and this one is of?' Sandy asks, looking at a photo of three jovial people.

'That's my grandmother [Erzsébet], that's her [Ilona's] stepfather, Joseph Biro, and my mother.'

Also in the photos is Evelyn's uncle Attila. Along with Joseph Biro, Ilona and Attila were joint heirs of Erzsébet's estate. When Ilona died and Erzsébet passed away months later, Ilona's share was meant to go to Evelyn and her brother Chris.

'So we've got that situation that we want to resolve, to try and find out what happened to your grandmother's estate – because Ric Blum was involved?' Sandy asks.

'Yes … We've got documents saying that he made a private arrangement with a lawyer in around 1978. I didn't find out that my stepfather wasn't my own natural father until I was around the age of 15, 16 … It appears as though he's … made some sort of a private arrangement … in relation to what the documents say are both his children, myself and my brother Chris, in 1978. It would be great to find out what his private arrangements were.'

Sandy says they can also do searches in Belgium, and adds it to the growing list of tasks for the upcoming trip.

In the meantime, Evelyn explains how she came to know her father in the mid-1990s after getting his details from the Belgian consulate. He was using the name Frederick at the time. 'They were familiar with who he was because he was regularly getting his international or Belgian passport updated with them for travel. So they contacted him and asked him if he was agreeable to meeting me. And he said yes.'

The first time they met was for dinner in Melbourne, where Evelyn lived at the time. 'We didn't really talk too much about anything. I was just so excited. I couldn't believe it. I found my father, so I was just giddy with excitement about that. We had dinner. He had a briefcase with him. And he told me over dinner that it was full of cash because he just got back from overseas where he sold coins. He told me he was a coin collector and dealer. I guess I was sort of excited about that too. Being a single mother at the time, I thought, "Oh, that's great. He might help me pay the electricity bill." But that was it. We just had a nice dinner, smiling at each other a lot. I've never had the experience before of looking at somebody else's face and being able to see some of the characteristics of my own face in their face ...

'He sounded like a big traveller ... like he was constantly back and forth and selling coins and collecting coins. The next time he came to the house, that's when he gave me the picture of his children [David and Maite], born here in Australia, and said to me, "You've also got more family, you've got another brother and sister. And here they are." He was very proud of them ... I was a little bit jealous.'

'Did he say anything about your mum?' Sandy asks.

'Well, yes. He said terrible things about my mother. First of all, my main question for him was, "Why didn't you come and find me?" I was out here in the world on my own. He told me that he didn't know I existed, and that he didn't even know that my mother had died. And only when the consulate contacted him, that was the first time he'd ever heard of me and ever knew that my mother had passed away.'

'So that's a lie. We already know that,' Sandy says.

'Well, but I didn't know that straight away when he said that to me. I mean, I was obviously perplexed by the answer, but I was really young and ... I hadn't unpacked all that trauma at that stage. So I didn't really have the common sense or the ability to unpack the things that he said that made me feel uncomfortable, or to even necessarily question them further, because I was so fearful of rejection. I really wanted a family.

So yeah, I didn't question him too much, but he said … my mother was a slut.'

'What justification did he have for saying that?'

'She would go out to nightclubs. She enjoyed partying too often. Really, she was just a slut. I mean, it's not like we were having any conversation that I recall that would lead a person to say something like that. I was just a young woman wanting to know about his relationship with my mother, which I thought was a person that he loved. So it wasn't something I expected to hear. I remember thinking, "I'm a pretty mixed-up person, but even I wouldn't speak about somebody that's not there to defend themselves in that way." I thought it was really inappropriate.'

Evelyn says she told Blum that she and her brother didn't know the particulars of their inheritance from their grandmother, and whether they'd received it in full. 'He said that he was going to Belgium again sometime soon and that while he was there, he may know a relative or a friend of a relative of my mother's who he can get in contact with and that he should be able to find something out for me and then when he comes back, he would let me know. And then, when he returned, he gave me the news.

'That's when I decided that I never wanted to speak to him again. He said to me, the rumour people had heard was that a private arrangement had been made between Joseph Biro my grandmother's second husband, whereby Joseph Biro would have the rights to keep the majority of the finances from my grandmother's estate, and Michael could keep the daughter.' By this, they meant her stepfather could keep Evelyn.

'That's what he came back and said to me. So yeah, he left my house. And my boyfriend at the time came home and sort of found me sitting on the floor … trying to … I couldn't actually repeat what had been said to me, like my brain was unable to accept that I had heard what I had just heard.'

Evelyn says a lot of time went by before she contacted him again, at the urging of a partner who wanted her to work out her past trauma and thought it would help. 'I contacted the consulate and got an updated number. I don't remember how it all went down, but I found him, called him and he was really cold on the phone. And the thing is, I decided never to speak to him again. But I never heard from him again either after he had said those things to me. So there was ... I guess some sort of a mutual feeling of not wanting to have anything to do with each other. So he was cold on the telephone. And I asked him, "I haven't heard from you. And it's been a long time." And he responded, saying something like, "Why would I speak to you? I put $10,000 in your bank account to help you. And you never even called me to say thank you."

'Excuse me?' Evelyn recalls laughing in response. She had no idea what he was talking about, because she had never received any money.

'He said, "Well, I'm going to go to the bank and check what happened to that, and find out from my end, because I definitely paid you $10,000." And then he called back and he said, somehow there was a mistake and that the transaction had been lost. And now he was sort of a bit friendlier towards me,' Evelyn says.

Despite her serious misgivings, Evelyn continued to meet with her father. 'He was at my home, my children were there. He met my children. And he and I were sitting on the couch chatting. He wanted to know the contact details of my stepfather and said that I should provide them to him so that he can rightfully seek revenge as my father. I just said: "I don't really, I don't really do that." Something like that.

'And then he said, "Well, the least I can do for you then is teach you how you can poison people. So you can protect yourself if anyone tries to hurt you." And so then he went through a ... I guess, procedure for poisoning people. I'm not comfortable repeating it. But I remember the details of it vividly. It's etched in, like in Hindi when they say *samskara* it's like a scar on your psyche. I can remember every single word of that procedure. He said if I was ever in need of doing that, that the person would develop flu-like symptoms, maybe a cold and then within a week or two they would be dead and that there wouldn't be a trace of what had been done to them.'

'It was obviously through food,' Evelyn continues. 'A mechanism for turning food into poison. He seemed quite proud, boastful even, that he used to bury people alive when he was growing up – that's one of the things that he liked to do in the village, him and some of his friends ... Someone had harmed one of the girls in their village so they got the guy and they buried him alive with hungry cats. And that this is, you know, how they used to take care of people. Yeah, he was, he was ...'

'Terrible,' Sandy finishes

Evelyn wonders if his 'recipe' for killing someone may have been designed just to scare her, which it definitely did. 'I've had a pretty colourful life myself, and have managed to always surround myself with some pretty dubious characters. And I was very conscious of never hearing anything that I thought would put me in danger or seeing anything that I thought would put me in danger. I always had that self-protective sort of streetwise. I grew up on the streets. I was 13 on the streets. So I guess I had that streetwiseness and I think that when he started sharing things like that with me, inside my brain I was just thinking: "Oh no, stop, stop. Stop talking. Stop talking." Because I felt like, by him sharing those things with me, it was putting me in danger.

'So yeah. I felt like I was in danger just from hearing those confessions. But I was unsure whether they were real or whether he was just trying to brag and that was his way of impressing me or impressing people. I couldn't tell. I couldn't tell whether he was real or not real with what he was saying. But yeah, I was scared.

'After that meeting at my house, I mean, he told me so many things. He told me that he was a survivor – at five years old that he lost his mother and father and brothers and sisters all in Auschwitz. That he was Jewish but didn't believe in God any more. Because you know, how could God do that? To his family? I raised my children with his story and their whole identity is wrapped up in this idea that we're sort of generationally from victims of a holocaust. And it's probably not even true. In fact, I don't think it is true.

'You know, so there's a lot of things – just lie upon lie, upon lie. How do you ever get to the bottom of any of it to find out if there's truth there? And then the next visit, he contacted me and said he was going to be in town and asked me to meet him in the city. And so I did that. I went to meet him.

'He said that he had a proposition for me. He pre-warned me that he had a proposition so I was pretty scared. I didn't know, because I'd had this one meeting and he was telling me about burying people alive and how to poison people. And then I have this next meeting with a proposition so … I went to this meeting.

'We were in a cafe and he was … started to explain to me that … in a very philosophical sort of a framework that in life, we don't have a lot of options, and that if you don't have creativity, which he said clearly I don't and that therefore, I can't produce anything from my mind to be self-supporting as a single mum, that then the only other way was to sell my body.'

Evelyn says she thinks he wanted to manipulate her into helping him commit fraud. 'He had an idea for me that might help and it involved drawing up a contract regarding life insurance policies that would be effective on people in another country. And that I didn't need to worry about what was going to happen to the people. That was going to be something that he was going to take care of.

'This was just a more terrifying experience than the one in the last meeting when he was explaining to me how to poison people. This was, to me, it had just gotten, you know, dialled up a notch. And it was and I was scared, because I didn't know what that meant, what he was saying to me. It could have been stitched together to be something absolutely diabolical, which I'm starting to think it might have been.

'Like, I just, it's so unbelievable. To think that someone could say something like that. And that it was as bad as it sounded. So I was unable to process that. I left that meeting. I told him I would think about what he was saying. I thought I was in grave danger and I went out to my car. I barely made it to the car. I got a really sharp pain in my head and I started vomiting. And I don't know how I drove home. I had the worst migraine. I couldn't get out of bed for a day or so. I was unable to mentally unpack what had been said to me. I didn't know whether I had lost my mind.'

Seymour approaches Dr Anne Chappelle, a toxicologist based in Philadelphia who has 25 years' experience with toxin verification, to see if the poisoning method Blum told Evelyn is plausible.

'It's possible, but you've really got to make sure you've got that bacteria in the system,' Dr Chappelle says. 'The method you described was, it reads well on paper, let's put it that way, would be really great in an Agatha Christie–type scenario,' Chappelle says. 'And it strikes me as curious, as they thought it might work on that person. So I think that there must have been some kind of trial and error. So were there any similar types of deaths? … It wouldn't surprise me if there was some other evidence of a cat or dog or some other kind of animal, horse, whatever that may have passed under suspicious circumstances as they perfected and tried this method.'

The last time Evelyn saw her father he gave her a gift that she now believes may have been laced with poison. 'I went to the airport, picked him up, he opened the boot of the car, pulled out a Bollinger and said to me to take off. I said, "Oh, no, no, that's okay. I'll just wait for you to come back." And he said, "No, no, take it, take it home, put it on ice and just wait for me. You drop me off and then I'll be back for dinner, which we'll get together."

'And so I drove him to … it was around Kew, Hawthorne, that area. He got out of the car. He was bragging that someone was giving him 40 or 50 thousand dollars and all they had was a telephone number that he could just change, they'll never be able to find him. He jumped out of the car.

'I went home, put the champagne in the fridge, set the table, sat there and waited, waited, and I've never heard from him again. That was the last time and I did try to call a few days later. Not because I wanted to speak to him but just because I was just … I thought that I was losing my mind. My intuition is that there's been an attempt on my life made. That's my intuition …'

'Was [the champagne] tampered with?'

'There were little holes in the foil, but it was the combination of everything: him telling me how to poison people; him bragging about how he had killed people, buried them alive; him trying to involve me in some scam that sounded like it involved …'

'Deceit?' Sandy suggests.

'More than that. It sounded, it was a scam that involved life insurance policies. And he said he was going to take care of the people, so I didn't know what that meant. So it was a combination of all those things. I thought I was losing my mind. I thought that's what the bottle of champagne was. I thought it was poison. So I tried to call him a few days later because I was trying to really just ascertain for myself how crazy I was, and his mobile had been cut off.'

Evelyn says she went to police about it, who dismissed her fears as crazy. The champagne was never tested.

After the interviews with Evelyn, it's clear TLV also needs to interview her stepfather, Michael Reid. Both Evelyn and her younger brother Chris were made wards of the state after their mother died, and they struggled during their developmental years.

At first, Reid is hostile, telling Seymour he has nothing to say. Sandy then sends him a list of questions. Shortly after, he calls back saying he'll do an interview, which he will also record.

Reid has an English accent and tries to sound at ease, but it's clear he's not. He recalls how the year before her death, Ilona had been to visit her mother Erzsébet in Belgium for three months, in October 1976. 'We moved into the house in February of '77. She died of a heart attack on the 13th of July six months later, five months later,' Reid says.*

'Ilona had thrown this birthday party for Chris and me, and … one of my friends turned around and said, "Now you're gonna get the biggest birthday present, Mike," and Ilona looked at me and she said, "No, you're not, no you're not," and she didn't. I looked back on that moment and I said, "Well, it's very unusual for Ilona because she never knocked me back." Without being too smart, she never knocked me back.'

---

* Interview with Michael Reid by Brian Seymour, 13 June 2023.

Reid says they went to bed and in the morning Ilona told him she wasn't feeling well. 'I said, "Well, you better go to the doctor and get yourself checked out." She said, "I will." Now when I kissed her goodbye in the morning of the day she died, her lips were very cold.

'And I said, "Oh, that's a kiss of death!" You wouldn't believe this. And I said, "That's a kiss of death, that is terrible, Ilona." And she was cold.'

Reid says he gave her a hug and asked her if she was right to go to work. She replied she was. They planned to meet for lunch but he never made it and she died later that day.

Reid says it was a tragedy, 'Ilona dying the way that she did, her mother died three months later in September and then Attila died.' He says he tried to look after Evelyn and Chris but it became too much for him and both went into care. Seymour moves on to questions about Evelyn and Chris's inheritance from their grandmother's estate.

'When "Erzey" died, sorry, Ilona's mother [Erzsébet] died there was a percentage of the property that was left to Ilona, but because Ilona had passed on, it was to go, equally divided, to both the two siblings [Evelyn and Chris].' Reid says. 'Now I had no information or dealings with that money. That money was directed to both the children. I never knew how much they got and I was told nothing. Now going further, Joseph Kinczell, Ilona's father, died in Hungary and also left money to both the children that I know nothing of either. I know nothing of how it was sorted and how they were paid.' He denies ever being part of any private agreement with Blum and Ilona's stepfather, Joseph Biro.

As for a workers' compensation claim lodged in Ilona's name after her death, Reid says it was organised by her employer, celebrity Melbourne hairdresser Edward Beale. 'He called me up and he said, "Come in, we might be able to get some workers' compensation here for you or the children. I have the forms here. Come and fill them in."' He says this compensation amounted to about $18,000 and Chris and Evelyn received the full amount in its entirety.

Sandy asks him about when he told Evelyn that she wasn't his daughter and he corroborates what Evelyn told her.

'Yes, I remember it very clearly. We'd had a big row. She was just off the rails and I just said to her, "Look, I never wanted to tell you this, but I'm just going to tell you that the life you've given me and what you've put me through, and I'm not even your fucking father!" It's exactly what I said to her.'

They also discuss Ric Blum. He tells Sandy and Seymour he has no relationship with Blum, recalling very little contact, except at a ferry terminal as he and Ilona left for England in the early 1970s. They'd only been together a short time after meeting on a cruise ship where he was a maitre d'. He says Ilona told him Blum was a gambler and would buy her 'nice rings' but they always disappeared.

And what does he think caused Ilona's death? 'Now, I've never known that they said there was nothing wrong with her heart, but she had the autopsy comments that you sent me. It's blown me away, because she had heart pills to take because when she was young she had scarlet fever and it left a mark on her heart, I believe.

'This is what I was told by Ilona and obviously, when she died, you know I just said, well, everybody said, "How was her heart?" I know she had a weak heart. But I never, ever thought about the possibility that something untoward had happened to her. Never.'

Despite his professed love for his 'dear wife', Michael Reid had her buried in an unmarked grave. 'Well, you have really hit a very sore point. Mea culpa, mea culpa, mea culpa. I basically never wanted to go back there. I didn't accept that she'd gone. And that's basically it. I can say no more,' he confesses.

Seymour tracks down Evelyn's brother, Chris Reid, who agrees to speak with him on the record. His story is also harrowing. He was just five when his mother died.

'Oh, I was told that she had a stroke at the wheel apparently and that was it so, yeah, by the time they got to the car, she was dead,' he says by phone. Ilona had apparently driven almost all the way home when she died.[*]

---

[*]   Interview with Chris Reid by Brian Seymour, 12 June 2023.

'Two weeks later I went into a home. So my dad didn't cope at all, you know, and put me and my sister into a home. My life pretty much turned to shit after that. Sorry to use those words.'

Seymour tells Chris he too was a ward of the state and understands the feelings of abandonment and hopelessness children in out-of-home care have to deal with throughout their lives. Now aged 50, Chris is a father of five and runs his own successful business, but indicates the demons of his past are ever-present.

'I still have very little memory, like, I remember everything kind of before going [to the home] and then coming out. But there's kind of a lot of parts my mind, I think, blocked out. I don't remember my dad having a funeral for my mum. In fact, my dad didn't even give my mum a proper burial.'

Seymour wonders aloud how different Chris and Evelyn's lives might have been had Ilona lived. Finding religion helped Chris through a lot of his trauma, but it never truly goes away. He says he often wondered if Blum is also his biological father, as was claimed on his birth certificate and his first passport.

'So I grew up for so many years believing that I actually was this guy's son. And in fact, I wasn't.' (There remains a lingering doubt over Chris's paternity.)

Chris asks to be kept informed about what TLV finds out, but he doesn't want to get bogged down in doing his own investigation. 'For me, I didn't want to go on the journey of having to go through all that again, like, I always say, you can't change your past, but you can change the future. I wasted 20 years of my life dragging the ball and chain of the past with me and trying to drag it into the future and blaming everyone around me because of circumstances that I had no control of.'

As the call ends, Chris says something surprising: a relative told him Ilona remained in love with Willy even after they separated and she met Michael.

He was the love of her life right up to the day she died.

CHAPTER 30

Brussels

26 April 2023

It's the day of the departure for Brussels. Sandy and Evelyn will take four flights: Brisbane to Sydney (one hour), Sydney to Singapore (seven hours), Singapore to London (14 hours) and London to Brussels (1 hour). They are leaving Wednesday and will arrive Thursday evening.

They're seated together on the first leg and both are buoyant. Evelyn has sent through as many details as she knows about her family, and they discuss several questions about the inheritance of her grandmother's estate and whether Ric Blum swindled it from the family.

Ghislaine Dubois-Danlois's daughter-in-law Alexandra Peereboom is eager to assist. She's helped organise the *Spotlight* interview with Ghislaine, arranged an interpreter, and offered to host the interview at her home. She's also undertaken a bit of her own detective work using the details Evelyn has shared.

She visited the Kinczell/Biro family home, even taking a photo of the names out front listing the current residents in case they are familiar. She tracked down the law firm that helped with the settlement of Erzsébet's estate. And she's even made a start on finding Attila's former partner and their child, and has come up with a surname.

It never ceases to amaze Sandy how generous people are in helping and supporting them in their investigation. Alexandra has taken most of Friday off, telling Sandy she has a van and can provide transport.

Since *The Lady Vanishes* began in 2019, many brave women have come forward telling their stories of how Blum scammed, threatened and humiliated them. And those are only the victims who are still alive. There could be others who, like Marion, can't speak out because they're dead.

As well as admitting to a sexual relationship with Marion at the time she disappeared, it's clear Blum travelled overseas at the same time as her and that she seems to have thought herself married to him. Yet police haven't raided his property or confiscated his computer. Perhaps they think it's too hard. That he's too old and no longer a threat.

That's not to blame the officers assigned to work on Operation Jurunga, Detectives Pinazza and Pessotto, who did a great job. It seems likely that there's a case against Blum, but maybe a prosecution is another story.

This is bigger than the police think it is. Not just because it's in the public eye and the media spotlight is finally starting to shine brighter and broader than it did after the initial news storm died down. But it's the public driving the call to action. Without the sustained audience interest in the podcast, it would likely just have fizzled out, like so many other stories.

And thankfully Seven has never lost interest either, thanks, in part, to the network head of legal, Bruce McWilliam, who has committed the company's lawyers – Richard Keegan, Rico Jedrzejczyk and Bradley Smith – to seeing this all the way through. The team has never seen a media company do that, especially for a daughter 'just' searching for her mum. These commitments were all made before they even knew about Ric Blum. The inquest went on a lot longer than anyone thought, and Sandy and Keegan have had to justify why the investment should continue. The legal bill is enormous.

Yet for all the kicks in the teeth taken in this four-year battle, and there have been many, the support from the listeners, colleagues, network and random people who just want to help continues to astound them.

*

On their first day in Brussels, Evelyn and Sandy meet with Alexandra Peereboom at a nearby cafe.

Alexandra recognises Sandy first. '*Bonjour!*' she calls out. She says her English isn't very good, but of course it's terrific.

After they order brunch, Evelyn brings out a document written in French for Alexandra to translate. It relates to the inheritance of Blum's late brother, Fredy David, who died in 1989 aged 48. Alexandra explains that Blum, under the name Frederick De Hedervary, has renounced the estate on behalf of his wife, Diane, and kids, David and Maite, because it constitutes a debt of four million francs.

This seems strange to Evelyn, because in Australia you cannot inherit debt. Alexandra says she must renounce the debt too. The confusion here is whether the debt is that of Fredy David or of Blum himself, who'd used his brother's name, with the extra 'd', as an alias.

'I better get on with renouncing that,' Evelyn says. They opt not to do it while in Belgium though, in case it causes Evelyn problems.

Alexandra has contacted Jérôme Otto, whose mother was a party to the personal agreement between Willy Wouters – apparently organised and signed while Wouters was in Tournai prison – Joseph Biro and Michael Reid, although the latter denies ever entering such an agreement. She will drop them off after she takes them to see Evelyn's childhood home. Sandy sits in the back of Alexandra's purple van and Evelyn is with Alexandra in the front.

They park very close to a large, three-storey grey building with a basement. Evelyn's grandmother owned the entire apartment block and it was all part of her estate when she died. Evelyn recalls living there with her kind grandmother, who had enormous patience with her. 'It had a lot more life back then,' she says.

Two people, a man and women, are standing outside the neighbouring property, and Alexandra asks them questions, learning who the new owner of the building is. They tell her it was purchased from Biro and his new wife when they moved to the country.

Evelyn laments the sale, as even if Blum had somehow ripped off the inheritance, there is nothing left to be recouped. 'But that's not why I'm doing this,' she says. 'I just want to know what happened.'

Alexandra next drives them to the student accommodation where Blum stayed while he was courting Ghislaine. Nearby is Jérôme Otto's office. She drops Sandy and Evelyn off, as she has to pick up her 12-year-old daughter from school.

'*Parlez-vous anglais?*' Sandy asks the receptionist.

'No, I'll get our student.'

A young woman comes out and says with an English accent, 'Hello, how can I help you?'

Evelyn explains she has documents arranged by a notary from this firm and she's hoping to get a copy of the personal arrangement. The young woman, whose name is Abi, is incredibly helpful, asking questions in French of the receptionist, who starts to do some searches.

'Are you English?' Sandy asks.

'No, I'm Belgian,' she replies.

'Your English is very good.'

She smiles, flattered.

Abi spots the notary and asks if he has a minute. He has meetings scheduled until 5 pm, but thankfully he makes time to talk. Evelyn explains everything and he asks them to wait in a room nearby while they do some searches.

Evelyn and Sandy are pleasantly surprised at how helpful they're being, especially without an appointment.

When the notary returns, he says he only has one document relating to Evelyn's uncle Attila, who transferred his claim to the inheritance to his stepfather, Joseph Biro, on the basis that he, his partner and their child could stay in the building free of charge. Although it's not in the documents, Evelyn advises Sandy that when Attila died, Biro kicked out his partner and child.

Evelyn isn't allowed a copy of the document because she isn't one of Attila's heirs, but the notary knows someone who can track down the heirs and maybe put them in touch. Sandy asks if they can look for other documents, such as Evelyn's grandmother's will, or anything to do with Willy Wouters and her mother

Ilona. She offers to pay any costs associated with the search and they accept.

The next day they go to Alexandra's home to meet Ghislaine. Born 14 August 1934, at 89 Ghislaine is five years older than Blum. She is very spirited and greets them warmly. The *Spotlight* crew is set up and accompanied by an interpreter, Larry, so Ghislaine can relax and speak in her native tongue.

Ghislaine knew Blum as Frederic De Hedervary (which is how he spelt it at the time) and thought they were engaged to be married. She shows the engagement announcement to Sandy, who takes a photo. In 2006, Ghislaine was lonely, having lost her husband years earlier, so she placed an advertisement in the local newspaper looking for companionship.

'He wrote a letter to me in perfect French – a very nice letter,' she says. 'And I thought Frederic would be able to cheer me up, to console me, to give me some relief. If he had loved me, he would've helped me. But he didn't love me.'

De Hedervary later took the letter back, claiming he'd frame it and put it above their bed in their house in Australia – bought at Ghislaine's expense, of course.

She recalls him having a keen interest in old coins, cooking for her, and staying at her home. They did not have sex, though, as he told her he was impotent from the war. 'He was so intelligent and so smart … because he understood that I was not going to ask anything,' she says. 'I believed, stupidly, I believed all that he said.

'The first time I went to the police to file a report, I went there because I was afraid that something had happened to him,' she says. 'I was scared that he would have been attacked, because he said that he was running a risk of being attacked, because, first of all, he was over there with my money. But then the police told me that he was okay, that there was nothing to worry about, because he had been sighted at customs between, I guess, Belgium and Holland, and he was leaving to catch a plane. 'Then, of course, I understood at that moment that he was actually leaving me.'

Ghislaine does not cry. She's a proud, strong woman, but she's visibly distressed by the memory of the deception. 'On top of everything else, then I had to find a place to stay when I visited my family in Belgium. But I didn't have enough money any more to buy an apartment directly, so I bought a per life annuity. And I'm still paying today after all these years. Nowadays I pay €918 every month for a place where I cannot stay,' she says.

'The way he operates is very similar, very similar to all these different women across so many different years. He's very calculating and conniving, despicable. He's a bad person to the inside of his bones. Sometime after he left, he called me on the phone and he said, "If I ever hear from you again, you'll see what will happen."

'At that moment, I replied, "Give me back everything you took from me." And he said: "I did not take anything."'

Much later, Ghislaine visited police again to make a complaint, and they told her of another victim who later made a statement to NSW Police. 'I filed a complaint, because I wanted to prevent him from harming other people.'

Ghislaine recalls Blum asking her to undergo a liver test, and medical records show that Marion, a teetotaller, also had a liver test not long before she disappeared.

Bartlett asks Ghislaine what was wrong with her liver.

'Nothing. And I knew that,' she says. 'I went to the hospital, they gave me an ultrasound for my liver, and there was no problem.'

The fact that Blum knew about her sleep apnoea did, however, make her uneasy. 'It's difficult to be very clear about it, but he made me feel that he would not want people to believe that he would have suffocated me with a pillow. And so he was kind of relieved that I was suffering from apnoea, if you see what I mean. From the beginning, his one and only idea was to take as much money as possible from me. But of course, he never loved me. That's clear.

'Never.'

Later, TLV will promote a GoFundMe set up by Alexandra for Ghislaine to help her recoup some of her losses. Podcast listeners prove to be very generous.

CHAPTER 31

Master Manipulator

Evelyn, Sandy and the *Spotlight* crew leave Brussels and cross the border into Luxembourg, arriving in Luxembourg City in the afternoon. Sandy and Evelyn find a cafe in the middle of the public square. As they sip their drinks and watch the world go by, Evelyn discusses her stepfather, Michael.

Sandy listens sympathetically; this trip is bound to trigger a lot of emotions. Evelyn and Chris not only lost their mother and grandmother in 1977, but their childhoods. Evelyn recollects how everything they owned was placed into little boxes. Sandy understands that both would have been instinctively aware their lives were changing forever, but unable to comprehend the true horrors that lay before them as a result.

Evelyn vents for a while before declaring: 'That's it, I'm done! Where's our ham and cheese?'

The trip is arduous, and on their second day in Luxembourg Sandy really starts to feel the pressure. Precisely at midday she rings Monique Cornelius, who doesn't answer, even though Sandy had arranged to call her. She keeps trying. About 3.30 pm Monique finally picks up. She's run her car into someone. There's some debate about a place and time for them to meet, but Monique is hesitant. 'I don't want to talk about De Hedervary,' she says.

'No, no, we'll just have coffee.' Sandy hopes to be able to tell Monique all they've done while they've been here, show her a clip of the interview with Ghislaine and try to persuade her to talk on camera without being identified – just feature her voice without showing her face.

So far, no photographs of Monique have been published with the podcast. Sandy has asked her for a photo but Monique isn't interested. She explains to Sandy that Luxembourg is a small place and everyone knows everybody. She's worried people will gossip about her.

Eventually, Sandy convinces Monique to do the interview with *Spotlight* and they arrange to meet at her home at 11 am. It's one thing to invite Sandy to come and visit, but it's quite another for her to actually turn up three months later. It must be daunting for Monique. But Sandy has promised the *Spotlight* crew the interview and they are already grumbling that it will be a major problem if it doesn't happen.

When Sandy arrives the next day at Monique's home, an apartment in a three-storey building in the suburbs, she finds her in a jubilant mood.

'AL–I-S-ON!' she calls out in her melodic voice. 'Oh mamma mia, look at those long legs,' she says as Sandy, wearing high-heeled boots, climbs from her cab.

Monique rushes over, the front door slamming shut and locking behind her. Sandy gives Monique, who is tiny in comparison, a big hug. Before inviting Sandy in she proudly introduces her to her neighbour, a middle-aged man tinkering in his garage. He greets Sandy warmly.

'She's all the way from Australia,' Monique explains excitedly.

After some small talk, Monique retrieves her spare key from a hiding place to unlock her apartment. She talks about her cats, two British blues, who have the run of the house. In many places, there are food bowls overflowing with cat food. She offers Sandy coffee and they head upstairs as the cats hide.

Upstairs is Monique's main living area and it's decorated with artworks and antique furniture. Dust specks dance in sunbeams streaming through the curtains as Monique points out loved ones and friends in photographs. One is of her former partner, the love of her life, an engineer from Germany who sadly took his own life. Monique recalls finding his body. 'He was a good man,' she says. Monique also shows Sandy photos and newspaper clippings of her favourite students over the years.

For a long time, they don't talk about Blum. But when Sandy shows Monique a video clip of her recent interview with Ghislaine, the floodgates open. Much of what she says now is very similar to their earlier conversation over the phone, but there are a few new insights.

She, like Ghislaine, knew him as Frederic De Hedervary, although she encountered him 25 years earlier, in the 1980s.

'He paid for me, I never give money to him,' she says.

When Monique was involved with Blum, she was 31 and going through her divorce from the real Fernand Remakel. Sandy revisits the letter from Blum to Monique that was read at the inquest, which mentions 'a song in his testicles'. Sandy asserts again that he appeared to genuinely be in love with her.

'Oh no, he loves money, nothing else,' Monique repeats. 'Oh yes, I got away, I got away. I could. But because I was always, always a free woman. I don't let someone else think for me and that's what saved me.'

Monique also repeats the assertion that, in her view, Blum is a killer, and adds that she believes he is responsible for Marion Barter's disappearance. '*Oui*, Marion Barter, *oui, oui, voilà*. I'm sure, I'm sure. She had money. *Ja*. He manipulates until they are depending on him. I can understand Marion Barter because he is a master of manipulation.

'When he opens his mouth, that is a lie. That is manipulation. He doesn't forget anything. He cannot hurt me any more. But every single thing he says, every word, every breath is manipulation. He has no regrets. He knows how to manipulate, with his body, with his brain. You cannot imagine, so profoundly and he can speak like an angel or devil, depending on the situation. He has a very big talent to manipulate, never seen that in all my whole life.

'I know the direction he is going,' Monique says. 'In the end I could feel it and I was disgusted, and that's why I went to our police in Luxembourg, and I said I don't know exactly what he's doing … I don't know, some bad things.'

Monique outlines a general impression of Blum working with gangsters as part of a dodgy furniture dealing operation in which he tried to involve her before police stepped in. She says he was stealing beautiful furniture from old castles in England and restoring it to sell in Belgium. She recalls a time at a restaurant in Tournai where he met up with other criminals. 'One day we were eating outside, there were only men but not educated,' she says, before clarifying they were gangsters. 'We sit with those men, [they ask] "Who is she?" [He replies] "She belongs to me. Yeah, she belongs to me."'

Monique tells Sandy she almost got arrested as an accomplice because he used her address, and she was taken to the police station and interviewed. '"You're a member there, in this circle?" [the police asked]. "Oh no," I said. The police arrested him and I knew it now. He was not the man he pretended to be.'

'This was at the end of your relationship?' Sandy asks.

'Yeah, and then school began.'

Eventually Monique agrees to an interview with the *Spotlight* crew on the basis that her face not be shown. She remains fearful but goes on the record because it may help others. 'I think we women must stick together.'

The interview is filmed without a hitch. On the way back to Brussels the crew stops in Tournai, Ric Blum's home town, which resembles Brussels on a smaller scale. Many of the historic structures in this once prosperous, fortified medieval city are crumbling into disrepair. Even in the busy tourism district, shops are boarded up and abandoned.

The city suffered heavy bombing during World War II, and today 70,000 mostly working-class residents enjoy a modest life there. In an unassuming street, the crew visits the house of Blum's brother, Fredy David, which is listed on a document Evelyn has. It's a neat three-storey brick building within walking distance of Tournai's Grand Place, the pride of the city featuring the famous belfry and Gothic cathedral, both listed as World Heritage sites. Tournai is only 15 minutes from the French border, and many citizens consider themselves more French than Belgian.

Blum's mother, Maria, had 12 siblings by her Dutch father, Charles, and his wife, Julie, who was a local. A distant cousin has told TLV that Maria was rejected by her family because of 'Willy's misdeeds'.

Sandy tries again to reach out to local Blum victim 'Charlotte', but she continues to reject requests for an interview. The crew also pays a brief visit to the police station where Ghislaine reported her encounter in 2006, but nobody is available to talk to them.

There's nothing more they can do right now but drive back to Brussels and begin the long journey home ... hopefully to a breakthrough in the final days of the coronial inquest.

CHAPTER 32

The Last Stand

30 May 2023

The last three days of public hearings in the coronial inquest are due to begin in Lismore. Sandy makes the two-and-a-half-hour trip from Brisbane, stopping by the airport to pick up Kristina Panter. She records their reunion for the podcast, and catches Kristina up on all the recent goings-on. They reach Lismore around 3 pm, in time to catch up with the camera crew – Andrew Currie and Michael Brown – who film their arrival.

31 May 2023

It's a crisp, blue-sky morning – the last day of autumn. The inquest is beginning 90 minutes earlier than the usual 10 am because a witness on the other side of the world has stayed up very late at night to tell her story.

A handful of journalists joins Sandy in the public gallery. Seymour is watching the livestream from Sydney. Eeles is at work in Brisbane and will have to review the day's proceedings and make a start on scripts later that night.

As Sandy speaks with some of the people there, she notices a man who stands out because his phone unexpectedly goes off in court. She later discovers it's Marion's former brother-in-law, and Deirdre's ex-husband, John.

There's no sign of Ric Blum, although this time he has a lawyer, Matthew White SC. A senior counsel is one of the most expensive barristers you can hire, charging up to $8000 a day, but White is representing Blum pro bono as he is obliged to under the 'cab rank' rule. In Australia, a barrister has to take a case unless they have a compelling reason not to, assuring everyone can get appropriate legal representation.

Adam Casselden SC opens proceedings: 'This is the fifth tranche of hearings of the inquest into the disappearance of Marion Barter, also known as Florabella Natalia Marion Remakel ... Those assisting Your Honour have become aware of two other women who allegedly had interactions with Mr Blum in Europe in the years following the disappearance of Marion Barter.'

He mentions Ghislaine Dubois-Danlois and 'Charlotte'. 'Charlotte's' 2012 statement to Belgian police will be tendered to the court and Ghislaine will be giving evidence via audio-visual link about her interactions with Frederic De Hedervary in 2006. The court also hears that 92-year-old Andrée Flamme, who encountered Frederic De Hedervary in 2010, will also be ensuring her story is heard. Afterwards, Ric Blum will again be called to the stand.

The face of Ghislaine Dubois-Danlois pops up on the screen from Brussels, where it is 12.30 am. Both she and the interpreter in Lismore give an affirmation. At times, Ghislaine trembles and her eyes water. This is hard for her. When Coroner Teresa O'Sullivan thanks her for staying awake so late, Ghislaine replies that it's very important for her to bear witness.

Through the interpreter, she tells the court everything she and her daughter-in-law Alexandra Peereboom have already told *The Lady Vanishes*.

'So he asked me to sell my house and then he asked me to give him the money so that he could open bank accounts in his bank for my children. I had four children and that would be four separate accounts, so that when they visited me they could find their very own money in their own account. He took advantage of the love I had for my children to steal my money.'

The court hears she took money from her shares, investments and savings and gave €72,000 in cash to De Hedervary to set up the bank accounts. But she decided not to hand over the proceeds from the sale of her house: 'No, because my son, who lives in France, told me that there was a house for sale near him and I was thinking of giving him money to buy the house. And Frederic understood at that point that he was not going to get the money. That's when he left.'

After De Hedervary didn't show up for the family dinner, she spotted him one day on the streets of Brussels. 'We were walking on each side of the street, and I think he saw me first and he dove into a chocolate store – probably to avoid me making a scene.'

She tells the court that De Hedervary never returned Ghislaine's money, but a few days after he left, 'One day he called me from Brussels ... And he said, "I took nothing from you, but if I hear from you again" – and I think he meant he was worried that I might lodge a complaint – "You will have to deal with me." I think he was hinting at some form of revenge.'

And the only reason he gave her for ending the relationship?

'In some ways, it is quite laughable,' she says. 'He said – "because you're noisy when you drink". Eventually I understood that he never loved me and all he wanted was my money.'

She also tells the court that De Hedervary had an unusual obsession with poison, and would speak about it often. 'In the end, what I was really worried about his interest in poison, because on two occasions I was afraid of him.'

After identifying the man she knew as Frederic De Hedervary in photographs, Ghislaine asks a heartfelt question of the Coroner. 'I would like to know whether you have any hope of finding the lady who disappeared. I'm very keen to know that, especially for her daughter.'

The Coroner replies on behalf of Sally Leydon: 'Thank you. I'm sure she appreciates your assistance.'

At 3 pm local time the inquest resumes, once again allowing for the time difference between Australia and Europe. The next witness is Andrée Flamme. She appears via video link from Portugal, where it's 6 am. She has a supporter with her and only the top half of her face is visible on the screen. While she seems a little tired, it's clear that she has a sharp memory.

The court hears she encountered a man from Australia named Frederic De Hedervary in May 2010, through her son-in-law

Pierre. Back then, Pierre worked at a Brussels library, which is where he met De Hedervary. When Andrée heard De Hedervary needed a place to stay, she offered him a bedroom at her home and he resided there from 10 May to 4 June 2010.

While it's the first time Andrée Flamme has given evidence in these proceedings, TLV has known about her for some time, thanks to a letter she wrote to the Queensland Governor about De Hedervary's behaviour. That letter, now on file in the Queensland State Archives, has been referred to throughout the inquest. It's dated 26 July 2010 – not too long after Andrée's interactions with De Hedervary. In it, she claims he stole her late husband's coin collection worth €20,000, and that he's a liar who is wanted by Belgian police.

When Blum first appeared at the inquest in February 2022, he was quizzed by Adam Casselden about Andrée Flamme and her allegations. Blum didn't hold back. His attacks were personal. He told the court that Andrée could not put two words together, had Alzheimer's and dementia, and sat in a wheelchair in her room all day. Casselden now puts those assertions to Andrée directly:

CASSELDEN: While Mr De Hedervary was staying with you in 2010 – were you confined to a wheelchair?
FLAMME: No, not at all.
CASSELDEN: While Frederick De Hedervary stayed with you, did you need to use a wheelchair from time to time?
FLAMME: No! No, never.
CASSELDEN: At that time that he stayed with you, had you been diagnosed with Alzheimer's or dementia?
FLAMME: [laughs] No, no. Never.
CASSELDEN: During the time that he stayed with you, were you able to put more than two words together?
FLAMME: [laughs] Yes!

Casselden then examines her claim that De Hedervary offered to value her husband's coin collection.

CASSELDEN: What became of your husband's coin collection?
FLAMME: I don't have it any more. It was him who took it.
CASSELDEN: How do you know that it was Frederic
De Hedervary that took it?
FLAMME: He was viewing the coins and I went out for an
errand and when I came back, everything was gone.

The statement 'Charlotte' made to Belgian police on 10 April 2012 is now tendered to the court. 'Charlotte' was born in Tournai in 1951. While her original statement is written in French, it has been translated for the court into more than three pages of English.

The team is allowed a copy of the statement and includes it in the podcast, removing her husband's name to protect her identity and trimming out some of the administrative sections.

Statement of 'Charlotte'

I am aware of the brief communication of facts for which I will be heard, that being a complaint for a scam against my distant cousin being Frederic David De Hedervary, alias Willy Wouters, alias Willy Coppenolle, alias Willy David Coppenolle.

My husband and I received, every year, a card from a first cousin living in Australia. These cards were signed 'Willy' and my husband told me that he had a cousin called 'Willy Wouters' who had been in the army in Brussels, in the cavalry in the 1960s, but without a doubt had committed actions that caused him to no longer be able to return to Belgium, the country which he left at the end of the 1960s. He moved to Australia in the mid-1970s.

I had only ever seen him once in 20 years in France at the funeral of an aunt.

Shortly after the death of my husband, the accused contacted me by telephone. He sent assorted cards and bit by bit he started to contact me by telephone every week to give me news.

As I had a wish to discover new horizons, he returned to Belgium on the 24th of February 2012. I went to meet him at the train station off a train coming from London. He stayed with me during this period, and in the meantime, we took a holiday in France.

For the entire duration of his stay, he explained to me that he had a house in Australia on the Gold Coast and he also owned a house in Bali, Indonesia. He offered for us to live together.

Knowing that I wasn't short of money and that I owned real estate, he proposed that we invest in equal parts in the purchase of a property on the coast in Bali for us to live in. He estimated the purchase at about €200,000 and he proposed that I invest €100,000 and I accepted.

We had decided to leave for Bali to finalise the project and Willy had reserved two plane tickets – return, leaving from Amsterdam Schiphol, destination Bali. Our departure was scheduled for the 23rd of March 2012 and the return trip remained 'open'. I was the one who went and paid and collected the tickets at the agency in Tournai. I paid with my Visa card the amount of about €2500 plus an extra €300 for an upgrade to comfort class.

The tickets were registered in my name and that of Willy David Coppenolle. I remember the Australian passport of Willy was in the name of 'Willy David Coppenolle'. I made a remark concerning his name and he told me that the name came from the names of both his parents. I didn't ask anything further.

I found it surprising that the day of the trip Willy left before me on the first train from Tournai to Brussels and then Amsterdam because he didn't want to run into anyone in Belgium. We found ourselves at the airport and had boarded for Bali via Singapore on a KLM plane. After we arrived in Bali, Willy drove me to a hotel in Seminyak.

I asked Willy why we were not staying in his house in Bali, but he responded that it was currently being rented out for a few weeks. During the following days, we just walked along the roads of Bali and did some shopping. Willy told me that he was waiting for a meeting with his businessman on the 29th of March 2012.

I must tell you that I had given the money I had – in cash – to Willy before he left. Looking back, with Willy wanting to arrive at the Schiphol airport first and by himself, I ask myself now the question that he may have deposited my cash in a Dutch bank account because according to a Bali guide, it is very difficult to enter the country with that amount of cash because customs checking is very common.

I had given him the sum of €100,000 in €500 and €200 notes, an amount that I withdrew in two lots.

Willy told me that he was leaving for his business meeting, but he never came back to the hotel. I didn't know where he was because he didn't want to tell me and it wasn't until the first of April that I received a message at my hotel.

I will give you this email where Willy explains in a few words that he took the money as compensation for an amount that he had loaned my husband in a previous investment deal. He spoke of a copy of a receipt that he sent to an address in Tournai. However, I never received the receipt.

Curiously, Willy never spoke of this previous investment – nor did my husband, who was a man of integrity. I then understood that I had been scammed and abused by this individual and with the help of my interpreter I was able to get my return ticket and return to Belgium on Saturday the 7th of April.

What surprised me was that upon my return, I discovered that Willy had also taken my jewellery which was in a box inside the office of my husband. I had, in particular, a ring of white gold set with 13 diamonds in a circle – a ring estimated at about €6000, assorted earrings in white gold, each set with a diamond, estimated value about €3000. I also had my engagement and wedding rings, a chevalier ring in yellow gold. I must add at this point that Willy also took a collection of Belgian stamps dating from 1972 as well as a collection of euro coins. All in all, I estimate the theft to be about €25,000.

Bit by bit, I rebuilt my spirits and came to the realisation that I had no means of contacting Willy. I know that during his stay from the 24th of February to the 23rd of March he made at least one phone call to Australia – in any case, that's what he told me. This phone call was made on my private number. As far as I know, Willy has no address in Belgium, but I think he still returns from time to time.

Sometime before my husband's death, he spoke about problems Willy had with the law.

I must also tell you that he requested that I buy for him, but in my name, Ancient Greek and Roman coins. He ordered by postal courier and I went to collect the coins. He gave me cash for the purchase, but I suppose now that that was part of the money that I had already given him, because he gave it to me the day before we left for Bali.

The statement continues, with 'Charlotte' saying she can provide a recent photo of the accused as well as an email address from which he sent an email. She explains how 'Willy' does not have a precise mode of communication, and how he had taken the SIM card she had given him with her old phone number.

Matthew White SC fails in his bid to have Blum testify via video link from the aged-care facility where he now lives, unable to convince the Coroner that he is too infirm to appear in person. He arrives early in White's car, which pulls straight into the private driveway of the courthouse to evade the waiting media. There's a flurry of activity and a frenzy of cameras clicking. Through the gate Sandy catches a glimpse of Blum. He appears to have lost weight and his white beard is noticeably longer.

Seven women have now given accounts claiming that Ric Blum targeted and exploited them.

Adam Casselden wastes no time quizzing Blum about Andrée Flamme's allegations that he stole her late husband's valuable coin collection in 2010. Blum denies taking anything and maintains he stayed at the widow's house as a guest of her son-in-law Pierre.

CASSELDEN: Do you understand that Madame Flamme alleges against you that you stole from her a valuable coin collection that belonged to her husband?*
BLUM: No, because the collection was given to me by Pierre.
CASSELDEN: If it was given to you by Pierre, why did you send some of the collection back to Pierre in June of 2010?
BLUM: I sent the whole collection that he gave me … it was about 2000 …?
CASSELDEN: Madame Flamme says that you stole the coins and that the coins that you stole were valued in the order of perhaps €15,000.

Blum shakes his head.

'On the 18th of February last year,' Casselden says, 'you said on your oath that Andrée Flamme was in a wheelchair with Alzheimer's disease and she couldn't put two words together. You said, "She was … she had Alzheimer's disease and dementia. And she was sitting in a wheelchair in her room all day. You know, worse, probably in a worse state than I am now." Do you remember giving that evidence last year?'

Blum tries to explain himself.

BLUM: I saw it that way. I was, I spent most of the time with Pierre at the library. And I only saw her when I left the library in the morning and when I came back to my room.
CASSELDEN: Mr Blum, I want to suggest to you, when you gave your evidence on oath on the 18th of February 2022, when you said Andrée Flamme was in a wheelchair with Alzheimer's disease and she couldn't put two words together … That was a lie. Do you accept that?
BLUM: No, that's the way I saw it.
CASSELDEN: And I want to suggest to you that you invented

---

that lie to undermine what Andrée Flamme had written in a letter that was shown to you in February of last year. You accept that?

BLUM: No.

The questions turn to Ghislaine Dubois-Danlois and why, in 2006, Blum was again answering a personal ad from a woman seeking companionship. 'In 2006 you lived in Australia, did you not, with your wife of many years, Diane,' Casselden says, 'and you had two children also living in Australia at that time? Why did you answer the ad placed by Madame Danlois in 2006 in a Belgian newspaper?'

Blum responds in a fashion: 'Can't explain that.'

CASSELDEN: When you first met her were you lodging at a university accommodation?

BLUM: I was in Brussels. I was, I was ... I had a month there. And I spent most of my time there and at the library, because to the library I had a direct tram from the uni, whereas where she was living was far away.

CASSELDEN: Madam Danlois has given evidence on oath that you moved into her place in Brussels.

BLUM: As a service. I stayed there for four or five days.

CASSELDEN: And she says that you stayed there for some weeks.

BLUM: No. No.

CASSELDEN: And that you were in a romantic relationship?

BLUM: What? That I was in a romantic relationship? No, no sir.

CASSELDEN: And that you shared a bed together in her place in Brussels in Belgium. And she says that she quickly fell in love with you. Did you read that in her statement to police?

BLUM: Yes. That statement is lies.

Casselden fires off questions and every single one Blum rejects.

CASSELDEN: Did you tell her you worked for a bank in Australia?

BLUM: Never.

CASSELDEN: Did you ask her to marry you in Bali in Indonesia?

BLUM: No, no.

CASSELDEN: Did you suggest to Madame Danlois that you should marry in Bali but for her not to tell her children?

BLUM: This is lie after lie. What do you want me to say?

CASSELDEN: On Madame Danlois' account, Mr Blum, it could be said that you are lying. Do you accept that?

BLUM: I don't accept it.

And so it continues. He also denies suggesting that he would open bank accounts for each of Ghislaine's children in Australia.

BLUM: It's just lies! What do you … it's all elaborate. I don't know.

CASSELDEN: You say today, on your oath, that Ghislaine Danlois is telling lies.

BLUM: Hate to say it, yes.

Listening to this, Sandy remembers the photo she took of the engagement announcement Ghislaine showed her in Brussels and texts it to Seven's lawyer Richard Keegan who is representing Sally and her family. He then forwards it to counsel assisting the Coroner.

Casselden then brings up *all* of the other women who've made allegations about Blum.

CASSELDEN: Just like you said about Janet Oldenburg, correct? She too was lying?

BLUM: Janet Oldenburg is lying, yes.

CASSELDEN: And just like you said about Ginette Gaffney-Bowan, correct, that she also lied?

BLUM: Well, yes.

CASSELDEN: And just like you said about Monique
Cornelius, that she also lied?
BLUM: That's why she never signed her ... She never
signed ... she refused to sign the deposition she made.
CASSELDEN: And just like you said, just now about Andrée
Flamme, that she also has lied.

Blum claims other people made Andrée Flamme make
allegations. He then blames *The Lady Vanishes* for inspiring so
many women to come forward. He clearly hasn't thought that
one through.

CASSELDEN: Do you say that Ginette Gaffney-Bowan, when
she goes to police in 1998 to complain about you, was in
response to a podcast, do you?
BLUM: I can't see any other way.
CASSELDEN: I want to suggest to you that any podcast
relating to Marion Barter was not in existence, Mr Blum, in
1998. Would you accept that?
BLUM: Possible. You know, it's just what I ...
CASSELDEN: And I want to suggest to you or say, Mr Blum,
that there was no podcast in relation to Marion Barter in
1999 or early 2000 when Janet Oldenburg went to police to
complain about you. Do you accept that?
BLUM: If you say so.
CASSELDEN: And I want to suggest to you that when
Madame Danlois went to the Belgian police to complain
about you there was no podcast in existence concerning
Marion Barter. Do you accept that?
BLUM: Yeah, if you say.
CASSELDEN: And I want to suggest to you, Mr Blum, when
Madame Flamme wrote a letter complaining about you
in July 2010, having also lodged a complaint with Belgian
police that year, there was no podcast in relation to Marion
Barter's existence. Do you accept that?
BLUM: Yeah, if you say.

CASSELDEN: I want to suggest to you, Mr. Blum, that it is in
fact you who is lying about what took place with the women
I've just mentioned. Do you accept that?
BLUM: No, sir.

During the lunch break, Sandy is approached by one of the police
detectives investigating the disappearance of Marion Barter. They
ask if she's willing to go with them right now to make a statement.
This is highly unusual, but Sandy quickly agrees.

They want to know about the engagement announcement
Ghislaine showed her from when she thought she and Frederic
De Hedervary were going to get married in 2006. (At this stage,
he was spelling Frederic without the 'k'.) The photo Sandy has of
the engagement notice is now part of evidence.

For the rest of the day, and most of the next morning, Blum is
peppered with the allegations made by 'Charlotte' and the other
women. When he starts giving evidence, he has a pronounced
stutter, but as time wears on it drops in and out, sometimes
disappearing altogether. He simply replies no to detailed questions
about the €100,000 in cash and €25,000 worth of jewellery
'Charlotte' says he took from her in 2012.

Then Casselden circles back to Ghislaine.

CASSELDEN: Did you have any discussions with Ghislaine
Dubois-Danlois of getting engaged or getting married,
Mr Blum?*
BLUM: No.
CASSELDEN: No discussions whatsoever of being engaged to
marry?
BLUM: No.
CASSELDEN: And you're quite certain of that today, that you
never discussed the engagement with Ghislaine Danlois?
BLUM: I don't remember this, no.
CASSELDEN: I want to suggest to you that you would
remember that, wouldn't you … because you were married

---

* Transcript, NSW Coroner's Court, 2 June 2023.

to Diane at the time. I want to show you a document please, Mr Blum. You can read French?

BLUM: Yes.

CASSELDEN: Take a moment to read quietly to yourself the document I have open for you.

It is, of course, the engagement notice.

CASSELDEN: And do you see there it's a document that says 'Ghislaine Danlois'. You see that at the top? And do you see the next line … 'is very happy to announce her engagement to Frederic De Hedervary'. Do you see that? Do you see that, Mr Blum?

BLUM: Ahh. *Oui* … yes, yes.

CASSELDEN: Rather suggests, does it not, that Ghislaine Danlois thought she was engaged to Frederic De Hedervary, correct?

BLUM: According to this, yes but I never seen that.

CASSELDEN: I want to suggest to you that Ghislaine Danlois provided that document recently and then it has been provided to those assisting Her Honour today.

BLUM: Yes.

CASSELDEN: Were you engaged to be married to Ghislaine Danlois in 2006?

BLUM: No.

CASSELDEN: I want to suggest to you, you were, Mr Blum, and that your denials are a lie.

BLUM: No, I've never seen that notice.

CASSELDEN: Did you have discussions in May and June of 2006 with Ghislaine Danlois as to where you may hold an engagement party?

BLUM: No.

CASSELDEN: So you're very clear, Mr Blum, I'm suggesting that your evidence today on oath denying having any discussions with Ghislaine Danlois about engagements to marry are false?

BLUM: Yes.

CASSELDEN: You agree with me, do you?

BLUM: Never seen that. I've never participated or anything of that. That's all. That's all I know. I, I don't remember such a thing, never seen it, never.

CASSELDEN: Could you have been caught out in a lie, Mr Blum, about your denials of being engaged to marry Ghislaine Danlois?

BLUM: I was never engaged. How could I be engaged? I was never, never engaged.

CASSELDEN: Were you engaged to Florabella Remakel in 1997, Mr Blum?

BLUM: No. No.

CASSELDEN: Now is the time for you to be full and frank about your interactions with Marion Barter in 1997. Is there anything you wish to say that you have not already said in relation to the disappearance of Marion Barter?

BLUM: What, what could I?

CASSELDEN: You don't know what became of Marion Barter?

BLUM: I myself believe that she's still alive. But I don't know anything about where she is or abouts, or nothing at all.

CASSELDEN: Your Honour, that concludes my examination.

Coroner Teresa O'Sullivan is clearly intrigued enough as she asks her own questions.

CORONER: Thank you, Mr Casselden. Mr Blum, why do you believe Marion is still alive?

BLUM: Because she, I can't tell you exactly when, but in a conversation before she went to England she said that she wanted to separate from her family. She didn't want anything to do with any member of her family. She was a bit of a strange person.

CORONER: All right. Can I just ask you, where were you when she said that to you?

BLUM: When she said that to me it was in her place.

CORONER: In her house?

BLUM: In her house, yes.

CORONER: Whereabouts was that?

BLUM: In Queensland. I can't remember the name of the
suburb. She said she's had enough of her family. And she
didn't want … She was, I explained to Mr White before,
that she was strange in a way that whatever she did, she was
strange in the way she dressed, she was strange …

CORONER: I'll cut you off there, Mr Blum. It's not really
assisting in what I need to find out.

Sally's barrister Bradley Smith begins his questioning via audio-
visual link from his office in Sydney. His attention turns to
Marion's name change in 1997.

SMITH: But at the time she did that in 1997, you had a
Queensland driver's licence in the name Fernand Nocolos
Remakel, correct?

BLUM: Yes, I had for a certain time until it disappeared. It
was stolen from me or I lost it. I don't know. Because in the
previous time, I can't remember if it's in Ballina or Byron
Bay, I … I … repeat the question, please.

The team, in their separate locations, feel their jaws drop. He
just said Byron Bay! Ric Blum lives in Ballina. When he was in
a relationship with Marion in 1997, he lived at Wollongbar and
Marion lived at Southport. He claims they met up on the Gold
Coast. The TLV team has identified 15 different places Blum has
lived in Australia, in four states. He has *not* lived in, nor ever
mentioned visiting, Byron Bay.

Marion was of course reported missing in Byron Bay. Was Ric
Blum in Byron Bay then? Was what he just said a misstep? Did he
simply make a mistake or did he just inadvertently reveal a crucial
piece of evidence?

SMITH: Arising from the evidence of Ghislaine Danlois
that you persuaded her to withdraw money from her bank
account, and the evidence of 'Charlotte' that you persuaded
her to withdraw money from her bank account … Did you
persuade Marion Barter to withdraw funds from her bank
account between August and October 1997?

BLUM: No, sir, never had a penny from Marion Barter, never!

SMITH: Did you persuade her to withdraw $80,000 from
her bank account? On or about the 15th of October 1997, in
Byron Bay?

BLUM: No sir.

SMITH: And when you gave evidence earlier, that Marion
told you she wanted to separate from her family? That was a
lie, wasn't it?

BLUM: No, sir.

SMITH: And you agree with me you've been asked on a
number of occasions previously in this inquest if you know
what happened to Marion Barter?

BLUM: I don't know.

SMITH: And you never before today said anything to the
effect that she wanted to separate from her family in answer
to any of those questions, did you?

BLUM: Because that's the conversation she had.

SMITH: Thank you, Your Honour. No further questions.

Blum's final day of giving evidence arrives. It's a cool winter
morning in Lismore and people are packing the public gallery of
the courtroom. This time, Blum is allowed to appear remotely via
video. While he looks tired, he appears more comfortable than he
did the day before.

'I want to come now to some evidence you gave yesterday in
answer to a question from Her Honour,' Casselden begins.

Suddenly, the reporters and people in the public gallery are
attentive.

'At the conclusion of my examination of you yesterday,'
Casselden continues, 'I asked you this question, Mr Blum: "Would

you like to say anything further in relation to the disappearance of Marion Barter?" And you answered, "No, what could I say?" I then asked you, "You don't know what became of Marion Barter?" And you answered, "I myself believe that she's still alive. That's what I believe." Do you remember giving that evidence yesterday? Mr Blum?'

Blum does remember giving that evidence, so Casselden prods further.

CASSELDEN: Can I ask you, are you able to give more detail about which visit you had with Marion in 1997 when she said those matters to you? Was it the first occasion you met with her in Southport, the second occasion you were there in Southport or the third occasion that you met with her?
BLUM: I can't remember.
CASSELDEN: And are you sure that she said those words to you in Queensland, or could it have been said to you here in New South Wales?
BLUM: No, no, no, it was in Queensland.
CASSELDEN: And how did that conversation come about, Mr Blum?
BLUM: It was a general discussion but I can't remember.
CASSELDEN: You can't give any more context as to how it was she came to say those matters about abandoning the family.
BLUM: No, no, no. No.
CASSELDEN: Would you agree with me, throughout the course of your evidence in this inquest, you have rarely descended into that level of detail in relation to your interactions with Marion Barter?
BLUM: What do you want me to say?
CASSELDEN: Well, do you agree or disagree with what I've just suggested to you, Mr Blum?
BLUM: I just said I remember that particular thing that she said but that was all. I wasn't, you know, I wasn't particularly interested in anything of that kind. So I found I can't

remember. She made that point that I thought was probably
a bit strange.

Blum denies suggestions the 'new evidence' he has suddenly
remembered about a conversation with Marion Barter is a lie.
He becomes befuddled and again stutters and stumbles repeatedly
when Casselden asks whether he realises how important such
information is.

> BLUM: I can understand that. But I can't ... so many years
> ago, I don't remember.
> CASSELDEN: I have to ask why you did not volunteer that
> information to New South Wales Police when you first
> spoke to them about Marion's disappearance in June of 2021?
> BLUM: Because, because they never asked anything about it.
> And I just don't remember.
> CASSELDEN: Mr Blum you knew in June of 2021 that the
> police wished to question you in relation to your interaction
> with Marion Barter because she was a missing person, is that
> correct?
> BLUM: Yeah. Yeah.
> CASSELDEN: And if I can return to my earlier question,
> in those circumstances, why did you not volunteer the
> information, which you disclosed here, to the New South
> Wales Police?

Blum doesn't have a definitive answer as to why he suddenly
announced yesterday, for the very first time, that Marion Barter
told him in 1997 she wanted to separate herself from her family.
Yet he denies he's making it up.

Casselden pointedly asks why such a conversation was not
mentioned during Blum's interview with police on 14 September
2021. Why did he not mention it when prompted during court
proceedings on 16 February 2022? And why did he again fail to
reveal the information when asked in April 2022 whether he had
any more information about Marion Barter?

As he struggles to explain, Ric Blum appears to highlight his claimed cognitive decline by stuttering.

BLUM: I, I, I don't remember. That's how things work in my head. I do things now that I won't remember this afternoon. I don't remember and sometimes I remember.

CASSELDEN: Could the reason you disclosed that information only yesterday be because you know more about the disappearance of Marion Barter than you have previously let on and you let down your guard yesterday?

BLUM: No.

CASSELDEN: I suggest that you do know more than you are letting on about the whereabouts of Marion Barter.

BLUM: No sir, no.

CASSELDEN: I want to suggest to you, Mr Blum, that you know more about the whereabouts of Marion Barter than you have been letting on to Her Honour throughout the course of Her Honour's inquest. Do you accept that?

BLUM: No, sir. No, I don't. I don't know. Anything. Anything about Marion Barter.

CASSELDEN: I have no further questions.

The Coroner adjourns the court. The public hearings are completed. Now begins the agonising wait for her to release her findings.

CHAPTER 33

Resurrection

21 June 1997

'You can think of me when you look at this,' Marion says as she lingers, looking at a picture of Norfolk pines at Sally and Chris's home. Marion had previously gifted the artwork to her daughter.

Sally and Chris are hosting a 'bon voyage' dinner, because it's Marion's last night on the Gold Coast before her great overseas adventure. At her mum's request, Sally has cooked a roast. She has also invited Lesley Loveday for the occasion, to say thanks for opening her home to Marion in recent weeks.

The evening is full of jovial banter – about the upcoming trip, about the young couple's wedding plans. Sally offers to drive her mum to the airport, but Marion declines, saying she'd 'get all teary'.

Before they say goodbye, a snapshot is taken of the mother and daughter. Marion hugs Sally tight, before climbing into the car beside Lesley and driving away. When the photo is processed, Sally notices that she's the only one smiling. Her mother appears wistful, sad.

29 April 2022

The glass doors slide open and the hulking frame of Ric Blum looms over his walker as he exits the Byron Bay courthouse. Blum has completed three days of answering questions during the second round of inquest evidence, and he is keen to escape any further scrutiny. At this stage the end of the inquest is still almost a year away.

'Hi there Ric, how are you feeling, mate?' Seymour says as he moves in beside Blum for the walk to the road, where he expects a car will be waiting. 'Okay, so, I'm gonna put to you the prevailing theory that we have about what happened. You feel free to jump in at any time.

'So you met Marion Barter sometime in the first half of 1997 at the Performing Arts Centre on the Gold Coast. You then convinced her to sell her house, quit her job, knowing that she was a divorced woman who owned a house.'

Ric smiles and looks into the camera lens on Seymour's phone.

'This is something you'd done before and would do again; preying on middle-aged, single women with adult children and assets.'

A TV news reporter appears and nestles in on the other side of Blum, holding a microphone outstretched.

'And then, once you'd done that, she went overseas. You went on a different passport because you were using the names Frederick De Hedervary and Fernand Remakel, as she knew you, which is why she changed her name to Remakel. And you had a passport, I think, in the name of Richard Lloyd Westbury.

'So then she comes back. Over the next two months she withdraws all the money from her account. And finally, on October the 15th, 80 grand comes out a day after you opened an envelope at the bank so that you could put cash in it.

Seymour then outlines a theory that Marion was killed, possibly by strangulation, and her body was driven to a remote location and disposed of.

The other reporter chimes in, pushing her microphone towards Blum as she asks the question already posed by police and lawyers. 'Can you tell us, did you kill Marion Barter? Do you have anything to say to Marion's family? Can you tell us, did you kill Marion Barter?'

He ignores her.

'Can you tell us why you are here? How has this happened? '

'I never say anything,' Blum says, breaking his silence. He leans in, eyes wide, to engage Seymour face to face. 'I never saw her again!' Blum says.

'No, no, I know you're saying that, but you've lied about everything, you've lied about everything. Look what you did to

Janet Oldenburg! You almost got away with that one. You had the power of attorney, you had the title deed, you had the house keys. You came back early, she was stuck over there, you'd arranged and paid for the trip so you'd come back early, it was brilliant. You get back and there she is! Oh no! Damn, so close! That would have been the biggest score since Marion.'

Blum raises his eyebrows, still smiling.

'There's no one else around, mate. Man to man, what have you got to hide? I know you won't tell the Coroner or the world and the police. Tell me, yeah?'

'You're wasting your time and mine,' Blum says.

'Is that because you're too clever? Come on, mate, what do you do with the cash?'

Blum scoffs and shakes his head.

'I mean, it's a lot of money, and how many other women were there? I know you want to tell, mate, just you and me. I know you want to tell me, I know you're dying to. What's the point in getting away with it if no one ever knows? At least let me know, yeah?'

Blum smiles and shakes his head.

'You got away with it, mate!'

'I'm tired of hearing you,' says Blum.

He looks more annoyed than tired. They cross the street and walk on the footpath beside a lengthy strip mall. There is no car waiting to collect him and it seems Blum is heading for a taxi stand a couple of hundred metres away. That gives Seymour the opportunity to keep grilling him.

'Are you? Well, you'll be unsurprised that I don't really care what you're tired of, because I know what you are. And I'm not some divorced, middle-aged woman you can just lure in with your crappy schtick and your lame stories and those letters. To me you're just a pathetic loser who preys on middle-aged women who are vulnerable. I mean, man to man, you're deeply unimpressive to me. You're not half the man I am, or any other man is. I mean, you're way down here. You know that, don't you? I mean, where's Evelyn, your first daughter? What kind of person are you, seriously? So you think you got away with it?'

Blum stares at Seymour over his glasses.

'Give me something to tell Sally, Marion's daughter. Are you sorry for Sally?'

'I feel sorry for me,' Blum says.

Seymour is incredulous. 'Why are you sorry for you?'

'Because ... you ...' his voice trails off.

'Why are you sorry for you? There's no reason to feel sorry for yourself. After all, I mean, you're a convicted fraudster. After all the women you've tried to seduce and defraud, don't feel sorry for you, feel sorry for the women. You don't feel sorry for the women? The only person you feel sorry for is yourself. You know, they have a word for that, it's called sociopath. Do you know what that is?'

Blum arrives at the taxi stand and sits down. He takes out his phone to arrange a lift as he tries resolutely to ignore the barrage of questions.

'It's funny, though, because I grew up in an orphanage, I had a really hard childhood. And I'm nothing like you. So there's no excuse for the way you behave and who you are. So that's not the excuse.'

Blum raises his eyebrows dismissively.

'What about your own children? What does Maite think about this? You know this isn't going away. This doesn't end here. This is only the start for you. You know that, don't you?'

Blum smiles into the distance and gently nods his head.

'I just want to get a handle on the state of mind that can just smile through and think you've won something, you've achieved something. Was it the domination of the women or the obtaining of the money? Was it the getting away with it? What was the best part?'

Blum shakes his head.

'The other question, of course, is how many other women have you done this to? I mean, I know you guys always keep a tally. You know the number.'

Blum shrugs and smiles under his mask.

'Who taught you how to initially, you know, try to cash in fraudulent cheques and steal identities, the stuff you went to jail for in France? Who taught you that? Was that stuff you learnt yourself? Or did someone teach you that?

'When did it start? When you were a boy, or as a young man with no prospects, no qualifications, no real education, no real idea of what he was going to do? You decide to take the easy way out, no particular moral empathy for other people. You thought, "If it's there, I'll take it. I'll be one of the sharks. Most people play by the rules. I'm not going to"?'

Blum is avoiding eye contact, shifting his head left to right and clearly annoyed at the continuing questions.

'Your poor wife. What have you done to her? I mean people are wondering if she's complicit in all of this. Has she just been very submissive, never asking questions, accepting what you say, you're in total control? You're the alpha, you just control, she just goes along with whatever you say?

'With all the name changes, all the trips away for months at a time with young children at home, with no money, no job. Any other woman would have walked out on you, you know. Why didn't she? Why did she stay, your fourth wife?

'You can't look at me, can you?'

Blum scoffs again, shaking his head and giving a dismissive flick of his hand.

'Well, I wish I could say this was goodbye, but we both know that it's not goodbye. We both know that you've got a lot more to tell and we're going to find it out. So I'll say so long until we meet again, Ric, Willy, Frederick, Richard, Chusan, Freddy, Bernard … until we meet again. Okay?'

August 2023

Sandy, Seymour and Eeles are talking in a group chat about possible future episodes of the podcast. They will, of course, cover the Coroner's findings and any developments flowing from them.

There are still questions to be answered about Marion, but there's now a second story that may prove to be even bigger. To date, the TLV team has found eight alleged victims of Ric Blum and it seems certain there are many, many more.

One of the key clues is the paper with the 'Hotel Nikko, Narita [Japan]' letterhead Marion used to write to Sally.'

It's clear to the TLV team that more investigation is required there, which is what Sally and Joni plan to do after the findings are delivered.

Inquiries will be helped as, at the very least, Sally will finally be able to obtain a death certificate for her mum, now that the Coroner has officially ruled she is dead. No longer will Sally be hindered by privacy restrictions on the basis Marion could still be alive.

The TLV team feels the analysis of Ric Blum given by criminal behavioural analyst Laura Richards is very insightful. Richards, formerly of New Scotland Yard and host of the *Crime Analyst* podcast, details Blum's techniques in convincing intelligent, vulnerable women they can trust him and explains how he's more than just a 'Casanova Conman'.

'Some of them, he tried to get them to sell their homes, the lure of something better, and marrying and moving abroad,' Richards says. 'The ruses that he'd use, there's similarities there.

Then when the women don't do what he wants, he then, in some cases, turns nasty. So we know there's another side to him.

And when I say nasty, the threats, the things Ginette went through where he's trying to damage her professionally.'

Richards explains Blum's behaviour is very telling.

'It tells us that [he] doesn't value women very much.

And he doesn't like women very much, but more so, it's everybody else's fault. It's all of them, not him. And the fact that he called them all liars, I think that was very interesting. And saying that all the women got together through *The Lady Vanishes* podcast.

But of course, each woman, bar Monique I think it was, of course reported him to various authorities and police.

So we know that they weren't liars. But we know that he is. And really, it just shows us again that he's a misogynist. And he leans into these sexist tropes about women and stereotypes about women. If you say a woman's drunk or crazy, therefore, you devalue them – you discredit them, they don't matter anymore.

But what's interesting about Marion is when listening to Sally and others who knew her, talk about victimology, Sally was very clear that she would have confronted Ric Blum.

'Let's say, they did get married … let's take what he said with a grain of salt but he said that they broke up.

Now, he didn't say what happened after they broke up but Marion was the only one who changed everything.

She had changed her name, she'd given everything up, she'd gone overseas.

She was in a very vulnerable state by doing that, everything was in secret.

'There is a scenario and one that I believe occurred, which is that they did break up and Marion possibly found out he was married, most likely challenged him and been angry about leading her on a merry dance because that's what it was.

So what's he like when things don't go his way?

We've seen some flashes of that, haven't we? Through what Ginette said, she even took out the equivalent of a restraining order she was so scared of him. Evelyn said [she] was really scared of him that she just had this physical sense and that, in her view, he may have tried to poison her.

We can just be in the physical presence of a man who gives a look or behaves in a certain way and we get the message. We know what the microaggression means.

'What happened with Marion and Ric Blum? Did she challenge him? Did she say she was going to out him, she was going to tell everybody what happened? It's possible that she wouldn't have stood for, "You've taken my money, you've taken everything from me, and you've made a fool of me."'

The biggest obstacles to pursuing this story are the ravages of time and, in some cases, the unwillingness of victims, and their families, to come forward.

Regardless of the Coroner's findings, there is plenty still to discover about this man of many names.

29 February 2024

Seymour pulls into the carpark of the Coroner's Court at Lidcombe, about a thirty-minute drive from Sydney's CBD. Sally's supporters, about forty people, mostly women, are milling around the entrance wearing a splash of green to honour Marion at Sally's request.Sandy is there too, having flown from Brisbane the previous morning on the same flight as Sally and her husband, Chris. Sandy is recording interviews with some of Sally's supporters and lingers there until just before the inquest is due to begin. As Sandy makes her way in, she sees the head of the NSW Homicide Squad, Detective Inspector Nigel Warren, who tells her Sergeant Pinazza won't be there she's just spent two weeks on a double homicide investigation. A couple of days prior, Sandy watched Pinazza head a press conference after arresting the accused killer, a police officer.

The court is delayed for several minutes but as soon as the door opens, lawyers and supporters spill into the large, hexagonal courtroom. Everyone stands and bows as Coroner Teresa O'Sullivan enters, also bowing before she sits down. Sally sits with Chris, her best friend Rae and sleuth Joni in the middle of the public gallery. This time, Sally and Chris's children have stayed in Brisbane.

Seymour is at the end of the front row, where he can see both the Coroner and Sally. Sandy is in the nearby media room, while Eeles and Wrighty are in Brisbane watching the livestream and taking notes to get a head start on writing the last podcast episode that will inform listeners of the findings.

Fifteen thousand people join the livestream on YouTube as the lawyers announce their appearances. Mr Blum's lawyer, Matthew White, is appearing via audio/video link but technical difficulties plague him. His dog barking sparks laughter, before Mr White's voice is heard. He informs the Coroner he is not in a 'condition' to appear on camera.

There is no sign of Ric Blum.

Coroner O'Sullivan looks directly at Sally and Chris and acknowledges them. 'My thoughts are with you today,' she says.

O'Sullivan announces she will only be reading a short summary of her findings as they are very long, 168 pages. The full findings will be made available once the inquest is closed.

First, she revisits the facts before making clear the parameters in which she works. The witnesses and agencies involved are not on trial and it is not her role to attribute blame, punish anyone, or make findings of civil liability and award compensation or damages.

Now it is time to hear her findings.

I find that Marion, under the name of Florabella Natalia Marion Remakel travelled overseas on the 22nd of June 1997.

I find that consistent with Sally's opinion the handwriting on the outgoing passenger card was Marion's except for the words Europe, Luxembourg, and 'S Korea', which were not written by Marion.

I find that Marion deliberately travelled overseas using her new name and took steps to ensure that no family or close friend was aware of the change of her identity.

I find that Marion returned to Australia under the name of Florabella Natalia Marion Remakel on the second of August 1997 and took steps to ensure that no one was aware of her return to the country.

I find that Marion did not leave Australia again after the second of August 1997.

The Counsel Assisting submitted that the coroner should find Marion withdrew a series of sums of $500 in August 1997, and attended the Byron Bay branch of the Colonial State Bank and facilitated a transfer of $80,000 on 15 October 1997.

The TLV team is initially confused by this, given Sally's recollection from her conversation with a staff member from the bank back in October 1997 was that daily withdrawals of $5000 were being made.

However, it's understood the Coroner made this finding based on: the memo to the Salvation Army made by Marion's father,

John Wilson, outlining a series of $500 withdrawals; as well as evidence provided by bank staff that the ATM limit was $500.

O'Sullivan finds it was Marion herself who attended the bank and requested the transaction that day, and told the bank teller that she did not want her whereabouts disclosed. But she says there is insufficient evidence to determine what Marion's intentions were.

Just three days later, on 18 October, Sally's suspicions were raised when Marion failed to contact her son Owen for his birthday. On 22 October, a missing persons report was made at Byron Bay.

The Coroner makes a lot of findings in regard to Blum, but only reveals the pertinent ones in court.

> I find that the primary motivation for Mr Blum's name
> changes was in order to dishonourably represent himself to
> others... and that Mr Blum's weak explanation and denials in
> this regard should be wholly rejected.

Sally looks impassive and resolute as the findings are delivered. Seymour and Chris Leydon often catch each other's eyes, nod and smile as Sally is vindicated by the Coroner on many fronts.

The Coroner finds that Blum placed the ad in *Le Courrier Australien* and kept it secret from his family. She says there is a sufficient basis to find that Blum met Marion at least three times, but beyond that, his evidence is too unreliable.

Coroner O'Sullivan says she believes Marion and Blum travelled together in England, because of the close proximity of the dates that each travelled to Britain, and due to the coincidental evidence of other women. It is not clear if Blum travelled with Marion to Rye, Hastings, Alfriston and Tunbridge Wells.

O'Sullivan also discusses the note paper that Marion used to write a letter to Sally between 22 and 30 June 1997 with the letterhead of the Nikko Narita Hotel in Japan: 'I find that Mr Blum travelled to Japan at the relevant time and stayed at the hotel, obtained the note paper and gave it to Marion in England.'

She says the reference to Luxembourg as Marion's purported address on the passenger card, combined with Blum's connection to Luxembourg, indicates that Blum, while representing himself as Fernand Remakel, suggested to Marion that they start a new life together in Luxembourg.

She also says there is a strong link between Blum's application for a safety deposit envelope and the transfer of $80,000 from Marion's bank account a day later: 'I find that there is a sufficient factual basis to make a finding that Marion withdrew the sums of money in August 1997, and transferred $80,000 to an unknown account in October 1997 ... on the encouragement of Mr Blum, and in circumstances where Marion believed she was in a relationship with him.'

However, based on the evidence, the Coroner could not determine whether or when Blum received some or all of Marion's money.

Significantly, O'Sullivan announces that she accepts the evidence of *all* of the other women who have come forward with their own traumatic accounts of their time with Ric Blum.

While she does not read those findings to the court, the Coroner says the evidence of Ginette Gaffney-Bowan, Janet Oldenburg, Ghislaine Dubois-Danlois, Andrée Flamme and the woman referred to as 'Charlotte' in the podcast, demonstrates Blum's tendency to misrepresent himself to single, vulnerable women for financial gain.

I also find that Mr Blum exploited Marion in 1997, in the manner in which he later exploited other women who gave evidence in these proceedings. I make this finding despite Mr Blum's denials in this regard, and notwithstanding that the women involved in his later relationships remained alive and well.

Coroner O'Sullivan says Blum encouraged Marion to start a new life with him in Luxembourg and that Marion, on returning to Australia, represented herself as his wife. It is clear, the Coroner finds, that Blum did not intend to pursue the relationship with Marion because he was married with children, and lived in Wollongbar, New South Wales.

O'Sullivan raises a giant red flag over Blum's credibility:

> In short, I do not accept as accurate anything that Mr Blum has said in evidence … in the absence of independent corroborating evidence.
>
> I find that Mr Blum, whilst in an intimate relationship with Marion, persuaded or otherwise encouraged her to sell her house in 1997.

Coroner O'Sullivan finds that Blum encouraged Marion to sell her house and took possession of several tea chests containing her belongings, just as he had taken a chest filled the possessions of Ghislaine Dubois-Danlois. The mystery man in a uniform Blum claims to have seen with Marion was 'implausible'.

The Coroner says that Blum was in communication with Marion after she returned to Australia and noted that he purchased a Mitsubishi Magna two days prior to her visit to the optometrist. And, she determines that Blum's evidence in the final days of the inquest hearings 'was extraordinary'.

On the eve of the last day of giving evidence, Blum suddenly volunteered a conversation he claims he had with Marion the last time he saw her, before she travelled overseas. He said she told him she no longer wanted anything to do with her family and was cutting off all contact. It was the first time he made that claim, never once telling police, lawyers or the coroner previously. It was a stunning turn of events and one that clearly impacted on O'Sullivan. 'This evidence, along with his lies and deception throughout the inquest, has convinced me that he does indeed know more than he is saying,' she says.

Coroner O'Sullivan sums up her key findings: Blum has further knowledge of Marion's travel overseas, of his relationship with her before and after she travelled abroad; he has knowledge of the withdrawals and transfers from Marion's account; and he is deliberately unwilling to divulge this knowledge to the court.

She then focuses on the New South Wales Police, and does not mince words. She finds the nature of their investigation into the disappearance of Marion Barter in 1997 up until 2019 'was not adequate'. Very little was done after Sally's first report on 22 October 1997 until a decade later.

It wasn't until *The Lady Vanishes* team contacted NSW Police at the start of 2019 that the investigation in Marion Barter's disappearance was reopened by Detective Senior Constable Gary Sheehan.

The Coroner notes that on 16 January 2019 the status of the case was changed from 'suspended' to 'current'. Sheehan also requested a review of the investigation. She adds that Sheehan only asked Australian Border Force to check entry and exit movements for a Fernand Remakel after he was contacted by the TLV team. There were no records in that name.

Finally, on 17 July 2019, police made the decision to place Marion on the Missing Person's Database. Several months later Sheehan was taken off the case and it was transferred to the Unsolved Homicide Unit headed and assigned to then Detective Senior Constable Sasha Pinazza and Detective Senior Constable Leza Pessotto. The detectives quickly discovered there was someone else using the name Fernand Remakel – and that man was an international convicted fraudster who had many aliases, lived in Ballina in northern NSW, and now called himself Ric Blum.

The coroner lists specific findings in regards to the police investigation, including 6 of the 11 proposed by Sally and her legal team.

1. That Senior Constable Graham Childs should not have classified Sally's report made on 22 October 1997 of her mother being missing as an occurrence only event.

2. That Graham Childs was unaware of the definition of a missing person in the Commissioner's instruction, and

that he classified the report based on his own subjective view of the sense of urgency.

3. That it was unsatisfactory and inappropriate for Graham Childs *not* to have reclassified the event from an occurrence only to an active investigation.

4. That as a result of failures at the first reporting of Marion Barter's disappearance, her case was not investigated for almost 10 years until 2007 … and that led to the unavailability of crucial evidence.

5. That Marion Barter was listed as a missing person for the first time on 6 July 2007 by Senior Constable Joanne Williams as a result of being contacted by Rebecca Kotz of the Australian Federal Police.

6. That Detective Senior Constable Gary Sheehan's decision to recommend that Marion Barter be removed from the missing persons register on 22 September 2011 was incorrect and Marion should not have been classified as located.

Coroner O'Sullivan agrees that there should be no suggestion that Sally in any way delayed the investigation by police or behaved in a manner that can be described as anything other than what one would expect from a daughter who was confused and anxious about finding out what had happened to her mother.

O'Sullivan also notes that the resistance by NSW Police to accept the inadequacies of the initial police investigation is difficult to understand, especially given the clear evidence of Detective Chief Inspector Brown about what should have happened in 1997.

However, she is complimentary of the subsequent investigation by the Unsolved Homicide Unit.

Finally, the moment that everything has led to, all the heartache and all the searching: the Coroner's formal findings. From their various locations, each member of the TLV team holds their breath. In the courtroom, Seymour watches Sally, whose focus is transfixed on the Coroner. After almost 27 years of not knowing, she is about to find out whether her mother is alive or dead.

> Having considered all of the documentary evidence, the oral
> evidence given at the inquest, and submissions, I find on the
> balance of probabilities … that Florabella Natalia Marion
> Remakel formerly known as Marion Barter … is deceased.

It's what they expected, but hearing the words formally spoken at last is like a punch to the heart. Sally's face does not give away what she is feeling. However, a wave of barely-contained emotion washes over her supporters. Every member of the TLV team feels it too.

The Coroner is unable to find when, where or how Marion died. However, she finds the circumstances around Marion's disappearance are troubling.

She recommends that the New South Wales Commissioner of Police ensure the case remains with the Unsolved Homicide team, 'for ongoing investigation, review and monitoring'.

Not missing. A possible unsolved homicide.

While Sally and her legal team submitted that Blum be formally referred to the Director of Public Prosecutions or the Attorney-General to consider charges of either perjury or making a false statement, the Coroner stops short.

'I am of the view that any referral … is a matter best left for the police investigators, particularly considering the investigation has not concluded.'

She emphasises that the $500,000 reward for information leading to the arrest and conviction of anyone responsible for Marion's disappearance still stands, and encourages people with information to contact police.

She also confirms that Sally Leydon's DNA profile has been uploaded to the New South Wales and national DNA databases for continuous searching against any unidentified human remains.

In closing, Coroner O'Sullivan commends the legal representatives, especially the counsel assisting team – Adam Casselden, Tracy Stevens and Clara Potocki. She expresses gratitude to the work carried out by New South Wales Police Detectives, Inspector Nigel Warren, Sergeant Sasha Pinazza and Senior Constable Leza Pessotto.

Then, there's a special message for Sally.

I'd like to acknowledge and commend Sally on her
unwavering commitment and participation in the coronial
investigation and inquest to find out what happened to her
mother. She has shown fortitude, dignity, resilience and
grace throughout these proceedings.

She expresses sympathy for Marion's family, friends and loved
ones and the many people whose lives Marion touched.

It is fitting to end with the words shared by Sally to the
court, reading from the family statement, in which she
described Marion as 'a kind, caring soul with a wicked
laugh. She was intelligent. She was cultured. She had so
many friends who love and miss her still. She would always
bring you flowers or a cake. She was a very generous
human.'

With that, and a final nod to Sally, Coroner Teresa O'Sullivan
closes the inquest and exits the courtroom.

As Sally confers with Channel Seven lawyers Richard Keegan
of Addisons and barrister Bradley Smith, who have been with her
throughout this inquest, her supporters move outside to digest
what has happened.

'Glad with what we heard,' says a Sydney woman named Terry.
'Obviously could have been a bit more, but I think Sally's really
been vindicated … I just hope that the police pursue to their full
capabilities and someone gets charged with something.'

Sally is asked by a TV news reporter about the crowd of
supporters around her.

'I didn't bring them; they came!' Sally says with a smile. 'I
put out the call and said, "Would you come and wear green in
support of my mum?" It's been amazing. These humans and the
many millions that are following who can't be here today are
really passionate about me finding out what's happened to Mum

and I'm really grateful for that because without their support I don't think I'd be able to do what we've achieved. Thank you.'

The reporter asks Sally if she now has a better understanding of what happened to her mum.

'I definitely have a better understanding. Obviously even the coroner can't tell us where, when, how or why, but I know she's deceased,' she says.

'The coroner has firmly suggested that Mr Blum was with my mum when she came back to Australia. I think that was a pretty big call … so I hope that police want to look into that a little bit further.'

Seymour and Sally steal away from the crowd to talk about the findings and he tells her, 'I was watching you when the coroner was giving her findings. You were pretty stoic. You didn't share much emotion, but I'm guessing it was boiling away inside.'

'It was boiling!' Sally says. 'There were a few tears welling, but I just wanted to try and keep it together.'

'I cried,' Seymour admits.

'Did you? I looked at you once and then I got distracted. I was, like, I need to look back at the Coroner.'

They talk about the journey they've had since he first interviewed Sally at her Brisbane home in November 2018. He then asks about the key findings, beginning with the coroner asserting that Blum lured Marion away from her family with the promise of a new life.

'Well, we knew that right? We put it all together. You and I got on a plane and went to Luxembourg together to go and source the answers before any of that even happened. So you know, I think just hearing it from someone at an official level is important,' Sally says.

She is angry as they discuss the findings against the police, who bungled the early investigations into Marion's disappearance. They're both frustrated that police claimed they had searched all available records for the surname 'Remakel', but had failed to find the drivers licence that was registered in Queensland in 1988.

'You know I still haven't – from the police – had any apology,' Sally says.

She is adamant that there remains a lot of work to do. 'I just would have liked her [the coroner] to refer it to the DPP for further investigation. I think there's more to see, more to find, more to look at, more to investigate.'

Seymour reminds her just how much has been achieved already. 'You're an absolute hero, not just for all the followers around the world, but to me as well, and everyone involved in the case … Good on you for hanging in there,' he tells her and they hug.

'I'm grateful for the opportunity to be able to get to a coroner's inquest,' she responds. 'I said to you guys at best I would like just a proper investigation done because I just really felt for so long it wasn't being done properly. And I feel like I've got to that point. I don't know if we're at the end. Joni [Condos] and I have a few more things that we have to do and we'll share with you what we find and what we do moving forward.'

After chatting a bit more with supporters, taking photos and sharing a hug with Sally, Sandy returns to the court and contacts Criminal Behavioural Analyst Laura Richards, formerly of New Scotland Yard, who tuned in to the findings from her base in Los Angeles. Richards believes the coroner could have referred the case to the DPP to consider laying charges. 'I think the significant things were that she acknowledged that Ric Blum was in a relationship with Marion … and that they were in England together. She acknowledged the other women and … she found them credible … that Ric Blum exploited them and that they were credible.

'And I think it's significant that she's saying that he knows more. And yes, it's disappointing not to hear a referral to the Director of Public Prosecutions. But I sense that she believes that there's still lines of inquiry to follow, and there's still evidence to find.'

Richards makes the argument for referring the case in her Crime Analyst podcast, outlining 41 facts in evidence that, she claims, make a strong circumstantial case for charges to be laid. 'There are still stones that need to be unturned like, for example, did they get married in Japan? ... Maybe there are other witnesses.'

As Sandy is leaving court to meet with the main protagonist in an investigation she's undertaking for a new podcast, she sees the Coroner's Counsel Assisting, Adam Casselden, coming out of the cafe and he gives her a wave. They've rarely spoken during inquest proceedings, but Sandy is impressed by his calm, intelligent and articulate probing of Ric Blum. Casselden had Blum's measure and certainly caused him to drop his doddering grandfather guise a few times, especially when reading the salacious letter he wrote to Monique. Sandy smiles. It was her favourite part of the inquest.

The TLV team throws their energy into producing their final podcast episode. It features the voices of each key team member – Sandy and Seymour as hosts, Eeles as the Coroner and Wrighty as a media spokesman of the court. They're so attuned to collaborating together, they work remotely yet in tandem, like clockwork. Within two days, Episode 57 'The Findings' is written, voiced and edited, awaiting final legal approval.

Over the next few days, news of the findings has been reported by all Australian mainstream media along with many other countries including the USA and UK, Canada, France, Belgium, Luxembourg and Korea.

Until we meet again

It's so long, not goodbye, for TLV. They have forged strong friendships that will endure long after the podcast ends, and may all yet unite for another project down the track. Sandy, Seymour and Wrighty have already produced another podcast titled *Shot in the Dark*, about another woman, who was found dead, apparently after shooting herself in the head with a rifle. It seems increasingly likely that this podcast, too, will trigger another coronial inquest.

Eeles has taken on a senior role with the Australian Broadcasting Corporation, Australia's national public broadcaster.

The Lady Vanishes has been a watershed moment in their working lives. They're proud and grateful to have been involved in such a meaningful and momentous story, and being able to help Sally when seemingly all avenues available to her, had shut down.

None of them expected that the proposed eight-episode podcast they'd convinced their bosses to support would become a five-year quest. It's been as much about the journey as the destination, and the emergence of podcasts as a popular medium has allowed them to chronicle an investigation in real time, in a way never possible before.

Sally's determination to find answers, as well as the fortitude of the other women who came forward with their stories about Blum, drove the TLV team forward.

While there remain questions about what happened to Marion, the TLV team wonders how many other women may have fallen prey to Ric Blum. They already know of several, but there could be more.

Seymour reflects back to the first day he met Sally. 'I promised her that I would do everything possible to find out what happened to her mum and I'm satisfied we've done that,' he says. 'But the bottom line is we wanted to find Marion and bring her home. I don't think we'll ever consider this over until that happens.'

He thinks back five years earlier, to the very first interview with Sally and the last questions he asked: 'What would you say to your mum if you saw her?'

Sally's response echoes still: 'I'd just give her a hug. I think there's too many words, too much to say, so I'd just give her a hug, tell her that she's loved and that we've missed her.'

Marion Barter Timeline

1945

3 October: Marion is born to parents Jack and Colleen Wilson. She is the eldest of four girls, which include Deirdre, Bronwen and Lee.

1963–4

Marion attends Balmain Teachers College where she qualifies as a teacher.

Early 1966

Marion travels overseas for 23 days on holiday.

1967

December: Marion Wilson marries Johnny Warren and they set up their home in Mortdale, Sydney. Marion continues working as a teacher.

1968

10 September: Marion takes six months leave without pay from NSW Board of Education and shortly after travels with Johnny Warren to the UK. During this time, she works briefly in an Anglican school.

1969

2 February: Marion arrives back from overseas under the name Marion Warren, ticking the box 'married'. Marion and Johnny divorce shortly after

1973

12 May: Sally is born to Marion and Stuart Brown.

1974

18 November: Owen is born to Marion and Stuart.

1977

29 October: Marion marries Stuart.

1979

Marion and Stuart divorce.

1985

9 June: Marion marries Ray Barter at Lapstone in the New South
Wales Blue Mountains. At the time, Marion is working at
Springwood Public School. They honeymoon in Switzerland,
Germany, Austria, Italy and France.

1990

Marion and Ray divorce.

1994

January: Marion moves to the Gold Coast after getting a job heading
up the reception class at The Southport School.

27 January: Marion withdraws $57,480 from her State Superannuation
Fund for a house. She rolls over what was left in her superannuation
($500) into her new TSS Superannuation Fund.

February: Marion purchases a house at 15 Merinda Court, Southport,
for $180,000 with a mortgage registered at the State Bank of NSW
(later renamed as the Colonial State Bank).

10 December: A lonely hearts ad from a M(onsieur) F Remakel appears
in the Australian French-language newspaper *Le Courrier Australien*.

1995

December: Marion (under the name Marion Barter) travels
to Norfolk Island with Greg Edwards who worked as a
groundskeeper at The Southport School. The couple were in a
relationship for a couple of years.

1996

6 July: Marion cancels her passport and obtains a new passport under
the same name. (She never travels using this passport.) Marion's

friend Barb Mathie later gave evidence that Marion said her handbag or purse containing her ID had been stolen around this time.

November: Marion wins Queensland Teaching Excellence Award.

13 November: Marion changes her last will and testament, leaving Owen three pieces of furniture of his choosing, and everything else to Sally.

December: Marion spends Christmas with her family at Moffat Beach on the Sunshine Coast where she told them of her plans to take an overseas trip.

1997

1 April: Marion has a day procedure at Pindara Private Hospital, in Benowa, Gold Coast.

13 April: Marion writes the first of two resignation letters to The Southport School. She nominates her resignation date as 14 June.

25 April: Marion sells her home in three weeks for $165,000, a loss of $15,000.

7 May: Marion has two blood tests at the Queensland Medical Laboratory pathology centre.

15 May: Marion changes her name via deed poll to Florabella Natalia Marion Remakel.

16 May: Marion applies for a new passport in Queensland in the name Remakel. It is signed by Marion's dentist.

20 May: Marion is issued with her new passport under the name of Florabella Natalia Marion Remakel.

About 21 May: Marion moves in with her friend Lesley Loveday.

8 June: Marion attends Sally and Chris's engagement party at their home in Tallai on the Gold Coast.

16 June: Marion writes her second resignation letter to The Southport School advising she'll be travelling overseas for an indefinite period and confirming she will leave four days later (20 June). She also sought approval for her teaching registration for 1998 in advance and provided a forwarding address c/ Lesley Loveday.

17 June: Ric Blum, in the name Richard Lloyd Westbury (aka Fernand Remakel, Richard Lloyd Westbury, Richard West, Frederick De Hedervary) leaves Brisbane, Australia, via Japan.

21 June: Marion goes to Chris and Sally's home (with Lesley) for a
    roast dinner.
22 June: Lesley drives Marion to the bus station in Southport so she
    can get a bus to the airport, and is the last known person to see
    her. Marion leaves Brisbane, Australia, for the UK via South Korea
    on Korean Air, leaving 9.38pm.
30 June: Marion sends Sally a letter dated 22 June 1997, postmarked
    Tonbridge, Kent, England, on paper with the letterhead 'Hotel
    Nikko, Narita'.
July: Sally receives two postcards from Marion, postmarked Sussex
    Coast and London.
7 July: Date on a postcard sent to Marion's elderly relative from
    Brighton, Sussex.
31 July: Ric Blum, in the name Richard Lloyd Westbury arrives
    back in Brisbane, Australia. Marion leaves a voicemail message on
    Sally's answering machine.
1 August: Marion phones Sally, allegedly from Tunbridge Wells,
    England, late afternoon/early evening AEST.
2 August: Marion arrives back in Australia at Brisbane Airport.
7 August: The date on the postcard from Marion received by her
    sister Lee.
13 August: Marion's Medicare card is used at the optometrist in
    Grafton, New South Wales.
18 August: Two withdrawals of $500 each from Byron Bay, NSW.
21 August: One withdrawal of $500 from Burleigh Heads, Gold
    Coast.
22 August: One withdrawal from Burleigh Heads, Gold Coast.
23–28 August: A withdrawal of $500 each day from Byron Bay.
14 October: Ric Blum opens a safe custody envelope at the
    Commonwealth Bank.
15 October: Final transaction from Marion's bank account –
    reportedly a withdrawal of $80,000. (The Coroner later finds that
    this transaction was made by Marion at Colonial State Bank in
    Byron Bay.)
21 October: Sally calls Owen to see if Marion contacted him
    for his birthday on the 18th – she hadn't. Sally then calls the

Commonwealth Bank and is told $5000 is being withdrawn daily from Marion's account in Byron Bay.

22 October: Sally travels to Byron Bay to canvas locals with a photo of Marion. Sally is suspicious the teller at the bank knows something they're not saying after seeing Marion's picture and making a copy of it. Sally reports Marion missing with Byron Bay police.

October: Sally receives a call from Byron Bay police, who inform her Marion has been located and says she doesn't want her whereabouts known.

1998

February: Marion's Father Jack (John) Wilson asks the Salvation Army Family Tracing Service for help finding Marion.

18 March: The Family Tracing Service writes to Jack Wilson claiming they spoke to a police Missing Persons officer, who in turn spoke with a security officer at the Colonial State Bank who claimed Marion withdrew the balance of her account at the Ashmore branch on 15 October 1990 and 'spoke of starting a new life'. It's understood 1990 was a typo and should have read 1997.

24 October: Sally marries Chris Leydon at The Southport School chapel. Marion does not attend.

2001

20 July: Sally gives birth to her first child, Ella.

2002

7 March: Marion's son, Owen, takes his own life after years battling addiction. Marion does not attend his funeral. He was 27 years old.

2003

3 March: The Salvation Army Family Tracing Service writes to Sally acknowledging her request for help.

1 July: Jack (John) Wilson, Marion's father, dies after a lengthy illness.

2004

Sally does an interview about her missing mum in *Woman's Day* magazine.

Unclaimed money remaining in Marion's bank account is reported as $14,889.70.

6 November: Johnny Warren dies from lung cancer.

2006

7 February: The Family Tracing Service writes to Sally to inform her they have given up searching for Marion and that all their searches have turned up negative.

2007

January: Sally contacts Rebecca Kotz at the Australian Federal Police Missing Persons Unit (ten years after Marion's disappearance). The AFP asks Sally to be the face of Missing Persons Week for August that year. They pull her from the campaign at the eleventh hour claiming the NSW Police Force says they can't use the case due to its sensitivity.

6 July: Marion is put on the NSW Missing Person's Register for the first time.

3 October: The investigation into Marion's disappearance is transferred to the NSW Police Unsolved Homicide Unit.

2009

Detective Senior Constable Gary Sheehan, Byron Bay Police, takes charge of the investigation into Marion's disappearance.

2010

27 May: Sally signs a lengthy police statement and provides documentation and photos, as the original police file has been lost. Sally has a DNA test done at Byron Bay Police Station.

2011

22 September: Marion is removed from the NSW Missing Person's Register.

2019

1 April: *The Lady Vanishes* launches.

5 May: NSW Police announces its Missing Persons Unit will be disbanded and relaunched.

17 July: A decision is made to place Marion, under the name Florabella, on the Missing Person's Database. It will be the first time Marion will appear on the National Missing Person's Register.

2020

16 August: The NSW Coroner announces an inquest into Marion's disappearance.

24 September: NSW Police identify a Queensland driver's licence in the name 'Fernand Nocolas REMAKEL', born 2 December 1947.

15 October: Homicide detective Sasha Pinazza goes to the State Library of New South Wales and links the number in the lonely hearts advertisement in *Le Courrier Australien* under the name M(onsieur) F Remakel to Ric Blum. This led to the discovery that he also held a Queensland driver's licence in the name Fernand Remakel.

2021

21 June: The inquest begins in Lidcombe, Sydney.

26 June: Reward for information into Marion's disappearance announced by NSW Police.

2022

14 February: The inquest resumes at Ballina local court.

17–18 February: The inquest continues at then Byron Bay local court.

18 February: The Coroner announces an extension to the inquest in Byron Bay.

27–29 April: Final days of the inquest in Byron Bay.

19 October: Inquest reopens with new evidence from former Byron Bay Colonial State Bank manager Joan Hazlett.

26 October: Inquest final submissions.

28 November: NSW Coroner announces that her findings which she was due to deliver on 30 November, have been postponed indefinitely pending new investigation.

2023

31 May: The inquest resumes in Lismore court.

1 June: Blum gives evidence in Lismore court.

2 June: Blum gives evidence via audio–visual link. Inquest ends.

2024

29 February: Coroner Teresa O'Sullivan hands down her findings.

ACKNOWLEDGEMENTS

Special thanks to Sally Leydon, Bruce McWilliam, Craig McPherson, Richard Keegan, Bradley Smith, Justine Munsie, Rico Jedrzejczyk, Richard Henson, Neil Warren, the *7News* Brisbane newsroom, the *Spotlight* team, the supersleuths – especially Joni, Kristina, Jenn and June, Mandy Jennings and Kellie Patrikeos – Laura Richards, Estelle Sanchez, Jerome Carujo and Alliance Française de Brisbane, Charlie Dally-Watkins, Aurélien Ritter, Véronique D'Ursel, Evelyn Reid, Ghislaine Dubois-Danlois, Monique Cornelius, Alexandra Peereboom, Janet Oldenburg, Ginette Gaffney-Bowan, Chris Reid, Douwe Miedema, Tom Rudell, Yannick Lambert, Peter Huyberechts, Sarah Cames, Greg Cary, Madonna King, Paula Doneman, Lisa Chant, the Brisbane German Club, Jerome Otte.

Also, TLV listeners across the globe and our families for their patience and support.